CLARITY

A Memoir

DIANA ESTILL

Clarity
by Diana Estill

This memoir is a work of creative nonfiction because it is based on the author's memory, which is fallible. Others may have different impressions of events portrayed. Dates and times may be incorrect. Conversations in this book are based on the author's recollections and not exact quotes. Some characters are composites. Names and identifying details of various individuals and locations have been changed to protect privacy.

Cover design and formatting provided by Streetlight Graphics.

TABLE OF CONTENTS

To endure is the first thing a child ought to learn, and that which he will have the most need to know.

— Jean Jacques Rousseau

To understand how I came to believe that up is down and left is right, I should tell my story from the beginning. It didn't happen all at once. It never does. Over time and with sufficient influence, a child can be convinced of almost anything. Adults, too, if the payoff is appealing enough.

My family ignored the obvious when fantasies were more palatable. No one considered the cost. Or maybe they did and failed to care. The time has come for me to disclose the truth and break my bond with ghosts.

SECTION I

HAUNTED BEDROOMS

ONE

MY EARLIEST MEMORY OF MY father occurred at age four, when he almost killed me for the second time. Thankfully, I don't recall the first. When I was two, he poured paint thinner in my Tommee Tippee cup, and I drank it. For that, I held no grudges. That sort of accident could happen to anyone whose dad needed a small container and grabbed the nearest one, then forgot he'd set poison on his kitchen counter.

The second time, though, my dad's affront was intentional. He hadn't aimed for me to croak. He simply wanted to expose me to the *fear* of death, I guess. By then, I'd forgotten that whole stomach pumping episode. Most likely he perceived his joke as educational. In a sense, it was.

On that Halloween night, Mom tied the white strips on the back of my Casper the Friendly Ghost costume and sent me into the darkness alone. In 1958, unaccompanied preschoolers were of no particular interest to police unless they appeared lost or injured, and I was neither. My mission to collect candy from the house kitty-corner to my residence seemed benign. A more Rockwellian setting would have been difficult to find.

Our two-bedroom bungalow, the color of weathered wood, stood like a sentry at a T intersection in Emerson, Texas, a town where cattle outnumbered residents—and sometimes drew greater scrutiny. Passing trains and wandering heifers comprised the bulk of Emerson's traffic. Out-of-towners motored through on holidays to visit extended family, but we seldom entertained guests from afar. All Dad's relatives lived within five miles of us. Mom's kin resided in Florida, which from a visiting standpoint might as well have been Australia.

Our single-story clapboard home, built in 1910, featured a screened-in front porch my father had added. Plum trees dotted our one-acre yard. On both sides and behind the back fence, livestock grazed in open pastures. Across the street lived my great-aunt Georgia, a sedentary seventy-something-year-old with waist-length pewter-gray hair and a penchant for *As the World Turns*. Hers was the only house I visited on that memorable Halloween.

I exited our porch through the screen door that remained accessible to everyone, including strangers. No one ever latched that door for any reason. Sometimes I wondered if a thief might make off with my red rocking horse stationed there, though the odds seemed pretty steep.

Mom waved me on my journey. I glanced back at her only once, which was useless. Casper's eyes and mine didn't align, so the mask obstructed my view. To remedy that problem, after I'd collected the Tootsie Rolls, Life Savers, and Dubble Bubble from Aunt Georgia, I shoved the plastic contraption onto my noggin and made a beeline for home. My mother, I imagined, had been monitoring my every step.

The stretch between Aunt Georgia's house and mine engulfed me in blackness. About a mile to my right, near the cotton gin, existed a mysterious place my parents called "Colored Town." Neither offered me a definition for that confusing term.

"Don't go down that way," Mom had instructed me.

I didn't ask why. Maybe child snatchers lived there, I surmised. I'd never walked that direction to find out. Right then, darkness prevented me from seeing my feet, much less a kidnapper. I hastened my steps, listening as rock cinders crunched beneath my scuffed sneakers.

The night air induced a shiver, though it couldn't have been colder than sixty degrees. What had felt like a quick jaunt now seemed like a half-mile hike. I longed for Casper's powers to levitate and fly. With relief, I glimpsed our roof's silhouette and, directly beneath it, the welcoming porch light. *Almost there.* I needed only to traverse a two-foot drainage ditch that tunneled under our caliche driveway to reach safe ground. Crossing the expanse, I sought my mother's profile, but she had disappeared.

I looked left and right in search of her, fearful of spying an abductor. Behind me, a menacing growl erupted, followed by sounds of shuffling footsteps. If friction between two objects sparks fire, my sneakers should have ignited. At a decibel level normally reserved for tornado sirens—which didn't yet exist—I screamed, "M-o-m!"

My feet churned through dead Johnsongrass and gravel, our lawn. As I sprinted, the wind caught Casper and burst the thin elastic cord looped around my neck. The mask took to the skies as if inhabited by its namesake. I honed in on the screen door, seeking somebody, anyone, who would save me from the pursuing beast.

The snarling grew louder.

"MOM!"

Aunt Georgia was hard of hearing, so I knew not to count

on her. Yet I was aghast when neither Mom nor Dad came to my rescue. Perhaps that was my punishment for being a difficult child. Internally, I vowed to behave in the future if only *somebody would help me*. Never again would I pull the dill plants from the garden, mistaking them for weeds, an infraction for which I'd been belt whipped. I wouldn't break the blossoms from the plum trees and fashion them into bouquets again either. I would even stop inspecting Mom's scarlet lipstick, if only she would save me.

Like a cartoon calamity, I expected the chase would end when I reached home. *Monsters can't exist in bright light. Can they?* Barely outpacing my assailant, I lunged for the screen door and yanked the metal handle. It didn't budge. I tugged again and again, but the latch had been secured.

I whirled to calculate my escape options. The ogre stood no more than five feet away. Shoulders hunched, he lurched like an ape, his eyes, nose, and lips all compressed into a hideous blob. Black hair matted the beast's forehead. Shrouded in a dark cape, the creature beckoned me toward him.

Deploying the only weapon at my disposal, I released a series of ear-piercing screams capable of reviving the vegetative. Between my bloody-murder shrieks, Mom appeared. Casually, as if she were stepping outdoors to stargaze, she unlatched and opened the screen door.

The animal trailing me might have continued growling. If so, I couldn't hear him over my mother's cackling fits. Seizing her skirt, I buried my face in her dress and wailed. Speech was impossible. I could barely breathe. My overtaxed heart felt like it might explode at any second.

Mom hee-hawed. "It's only *Daddy*," she cooed.

I raised my head from her Donna Reed inspired skirt folds. The disfigured primate persisted.

"Ayyy-eee-uh-huh-huh-huh-huh!" I didn't want to look at him. *That monster is not my daddy. No, no, no!*

The flat-faced ogre straightened his posture. He dropped his cloak, which at a second glance, looked like a familiar blanket. From his neck and face, my father peeled a black nylon stocking and guffawed.

While my parents slapped their knees and doubled over, I stifled the urge to find a new family. It would be the first of many similar compulsions. Dad attempted a hug, but I shied from him. Still laughing, Mom led me indoors. I didn't want to hold her hand, but I did anyway. I had nothing else to grasp.

By morning, I'd forgiven my parents for their cruel trick. Dad offered me an individual-serving-size bag of potato chips, my favorite childhood snack. We sat inside the family car, a sapphire-blue Renault, a French sedan that achieved its fame as one of the "fifty worst cars of all time." The vehicle rested in our driveway, where it performed best.

For unknown reasons, my mother and I exchanged seats. She sat in my normal spot, and I in the front passenger position. Such foreshadowing seems difficult to ignore now. Possibly Mom was savvy to Dad's ploy. But in my mind, the change of seat order—and the chips—indicated a peace offering. I still smarted from Dad's Halloween scare.

Grasping the snack, I prized the top despite the odds of a successful open. Someone always had to assist me with packages. Neither parent immediately offered.

Dad studied me. "Would you like me to give you even *more* potato chips?"

My attention whipsawed from the treasure in my lap to his proposition. I nodded, my head bouncing like a bobblehead doll's. He smirked, a red flag I mistook for parental approval.

"Would you like a *thousand* potato chips?"

The subject of Dad's spotlight, I basked in the temporary glow. I hadn't yet learned that light emits radiation. I wondered how many bags a thousand potato chips equaled. *A hundred?* "Yes!" I cried.

Dad's eyes flashed. "Okay. Hand me the bag."

Briefly, I reconsidered. Unless he was a magician, I couldn't see how he would increase the serving size. Also, I could think of no way in which returning a gift would be beneficial. Maybe he planned to open the bag and count the chips. That way, he would know how many more packages to buy. Extending one arm in slow motion, I relinquished the goods.

Mom peeked around the passenger seat to get a better view. I waited for Dad to say "Abracadabra!" Instead, he tossed my chip bag into the air and smashed it between his palms. The seal burst open, spraying chip fragments onto the dash, his lap, and the floorboard.

Dad brayed like a donkey and pitched the half-empty bag to me. "Here you go! Now you have a *thousand* potato chips."

Mom's laughter joined Dad's in a mocking duet.

Tears dotted my pink gingham smock. I stared at the sack and refused to touch it. I no longer wanted *any* potato chips.

As much as I would like to report that Dad showed remorse and Mom discouraged further teasing, neither happened. Dad proudly recounted "the potato chip story" at future family gatherings. And with each iteration, he concluded by jeering at me, "The *look* on your face!"

TWO

SOON AFTER DAD'S HALLOWEEN PRANK, I started suffering night terrors. Today those memories seem more like alien abductions than bad dreams. I believed I was awake when the frightful levitations occurred, though my parents insisted I was asleep. Either way, my anxiety was real.

I slept alone in my room, at the back of our house, in an iron-frame bed, where as soon as Mom switched off the lights and retired, my sleeping quarters came to life. I would lie there, watching in trepidation as my bed floated upward, my face advancing ever closer toward the ceiling. Right when my nose seemed destined to scrape the plaster, I would squeeze my eyes tight and crash back to earth, gasping. My stomach rocketed into my chest. The bedsprings bounced like a trampoline, and the linens pitched until my mattress quivered to a halt. Before I could recover, the levitation resumed.

On my bed's third plunge to the floor, I would scream and race to my parents' bedroom. Always, their door was locked. Pounding on the barrier, I begged for entry.

"Don't let her in," I overheard Dad tell Mom. "Tell her to go back to sleep."

Without fail, Mom would crack the door two inches and recite his orders. I would withdraw and cry for what felt like hours, begging the God I'd heard about in Sunday school to come down from Heaven or wherever He lived and extricate me from the madness.

Morning admonishments failed to convince me that my nightmares were imaginary. My bed and I were locked in a critical conflict with a nocturnal monster, I insisted. Nightly, I battled a fear of being suctioned through my ceiling. I couldn't escape the recurring ordeal because I had nowhere else to sleep.

During the week, my parents' bedroom remained off-limits to me. On Saturdays and Sundays, though, Dad allowed me inside and sometimes even on the bed. Reclined on the mattress, he would invite me to sit on his gelatinous middle while he studied me without indicating deception. Displaying his fingers one at a time, he taught me to count. I savored the emotional and physical closeness his private lessons offered. Correct answers met with praise, so I quickly excelled at preschool math.

Occasionally Mom sat on one corner of the mattress, observing my progress, though she never interfered with Dad's coaching. He was the instructor. I was the pupil. She merely audited the class. Similarly, I learned my ABCs straddling my dad's bare midriff.

Once, after a productive teaching session, Dad asked what I wanted for Christmas. Ever since I had witnessed him shoot a trespassing water moccasin with his shotgun, my eyes had been opened to the advantages of firearms.

Hoping to abolish the ghost in my room and put an end to my nightmares, I chirped, "I want a rifle," as if such a Santa request was common from a five-year-old. In Texas, it pretty much was.

Dad frowned. "Are you sure?"

I nodded. Yes, as sure as I knew my room was haunted.

On Christmas Day, underneath our lopsided fir tree adorned with cheap glass bulbs and haphazardly splayed aluminum tinsel, I found a toy gun. Carefully I examined the present, a firearm constructed of carved wood and painted black and cherry, handcrafted by my father. The fake trigger wouldn't pull. Still, I thought that gun the best gift I'd ever received because my daddy had made it for me. But that wasn't the only surprise my parents had in store.

By the time my mother announced her pregnancy, she had shoved me from the nest and into service. "Take this," Mom instructed, a few months before my brother's birth. She handed me my father's paycheck. "Give it to the bank teller."

I didn't understand why she would entrust me with such a grown-up task. Without hesitation, though, I accepted the envelope containing our next two weeks' livelihood. I'd accompanied my mother many times on the four-block trek to Main Street. The bank was a familiar destination. Because I often combed the neighborhood in search of a playmate, I wasn't scared to walk to town alone.

The journey from my house to the depository was a straight shot, one that routed me past the farm implement business where Joe, the homeless town drunk, slept. "Pretend you don't see him," Mom warned anytime she noticed him stir. "He might ask for money." Seeing as I never had any dough on me, I wasn't concerned. When he hollered and waved to me that afternoon, I approached him.

Reclined against a hay baler, Joe peered at me from under his tattered hat. His coveralls, striped with grass and grease stains, looked too large for his wasting body. I studied his ragged auburn beard and mustache. Exposing a toothless grin, he pointed to one cheek. "Would you give an old man a kiss?"

I knew I shouldn't, but Joe seemed lonely and harmless. I gave him a quick peck.

"Thank you, sweetheart." From his pocket, he withdrew a dime. "Here, this is for you."

I accepted the coin and promised on one pinky finger to visit again. My greater concern was finding somewhere to stash my ten-cent piece. My elastic-waist sunsuit tied at the shoulders and had no pockets. Gripping my envelope in one hand and illicit wages in the other, I continued on my way.

Inside First National Bank, the teller tray exceeded my reach. Extending my arm high, I waved my envelope like a flag. That prompted the woman behind the glass to meet me in the lobby. The lady scanned for an accompanying parent. Finding none, she squatted and asked how she could help. I presented the envelope and waited while she sashayed back to her teller station and fumbled with something I couldn't see. She returned with my deposit slip, which I accepted.

"You're such a smart little girl," she praised.

With my head low and eyes averted, I strode home, willing Joe to please, please, pretty please be asleep. I felt powerless to ignore his requests. Though I'd heard the word "alcoholic" attached to his name, I had no reference for understanding. All I knew was that Joe was a man, which designated his authority over me. In my confused mind, based on gender, his instructions superseded my mother's directives. If he'd asked me for my father's paycheck, I would have handed it over.

I tiptoed past Joe without notice. Not yet out of the proverbial thicket, I still had to dodge Mom's appraisal. The coin I carried might lead to an indictment. Slipping past the screen door, I rushed for my bedroom to hide the dime.

Mom detected me before I made it through the living room.

"Bring me that piece of paper," she said, glimpsing the deposit slip. "What's that in your other hand?" She'd spotted my money. "Where did you get that?"

My chin dropped. Running through a short list of plausible answers, I settled on, "From Joe."

I grimaced, knowing I would get a whipping when my father found out. Mom apprehended me for violations. Dad delivered the sentencing. But that day, she kept my transgression to herself. Pregnancy made her more sympathetic, I presumed.

The following week, when Mom sent me into town for staple goods, I selected an alternate route. My pint-sized frame struggled to carry a half-gallon milk carton, so I disliked taking the longer path. Allowing extra time for condensation to dissolve my grocery sack made my job harder.

At the grocer, my uncle Henry, who owned the market, sneaked a pack of gum into my shopping bag. He knew I liked Doublemint. He wouldn't have imagined his charity could cause me trouble.

Finding the gum, my mom accused me of petty theft. She counted her change and, because none was missing, concluded I'd stolen the gum. Though I pleaded innocence, Dad spanked me with his belt and sent me to bed right after supper.

It was a mystery to me how the gum had appeared in my grocery sack. I feared maybe the ghosts that haunted my room at night had followed me to the store.

Days later, Dad made a big show of confessing my alleged shoplifting to my uncle. "I'm sorry to tell you this, but Diana stole a pack of gum when she was here. Can I pay you for it?" he asked Henry.

"Heck no. She didn't steal nothing." Henry chuckled. "I put that gum in her bag." He gave me a wink.

I waited for an apology, but one never arrived.

To avoid hurting her feelings, I never asked my mother why she'd relied on a four-and-a-half-year-old to run adult errands. Perpetually bored and always available, I didn't mind helping out. When not branded a thief, I was pleased to be of service. The postmaster, bank teller, and Uncle Henry all applauded me for being such a responsible child. Their compliments made me feel six inches taller than my true height. But Mom said my excursions to the bank were our little secret. I never told anyone about that special privilege, not even Grandma.

On Sundays, we visited my paternal grandparents after church when Grandma cooked scrumptious meals of fried chicken, okra, mashed potatoes and gravy, and fresh green beans simmered in bacon fat. As a special treat, she would prepare a vat of banana pudding.

Setting her hubcap-sized blue willow bowl next to my plate, she would say, "I made this just for you."

I shared the dessert, though. Nobody could have choked down a gallon of pudding all by themselves. Yet at times, I felt gluttonous enough to try.

After lunch, which my grandparents called dinner, Grandpa would carry me outdoors to his equipment shed and deposit me on his yellow John Deere tractor seat. Inside the corrugated metal shed, I breathed in the aromas of lubricant oil, dank earth, and acrid fertilizers. From my perch high above Grandpa's shoulders, cotton trailers shrank to the size of play wagons. Pitchforks looked like serving utensils. Lightning, Grandpa's hyperactive mixed-breed terrier, appeared no larger than a wild rabbit. Bouncing on his hind legs, the dog begged to join me.

On occasion, Grandpa would chauffeur me through his cow pasture in his surplus army jeep. For kicks, he would circle his eighteen-hundred-pound bull and watch me go bug-eyed. If that pointy-horned beast had decided to, he could have gored us. Grandpa's rusted Willys MB with cutaway doors and an open roof offered little protection. But Grandpa said not to worry. I would always be safe with him.

THREE

M Y BROTHER ALAN ENTERED THE world the same way
I had, which is to say with short-lived celebrity. My
grandparents, aunt, and uncle visited during his first
week of life to capture proof of his existence. Church members
dropped by, bestowing baby gifts. Somebody was clueless enough
to deliver a two-foot teddy bear. Mom thought it negligent to
give an infant such a sizeable toy, so I accepted the present on my
brother's behalf.

Each night, when shadows threatened to swallow me, that
plush toy protected me from the paranormal—or I believed it did.
I would tuck the stuffed bear under my covers, pleading, "Watch
over me, Teddy." The first few nights, I peeked through squinted
eyes to be sure Teddy hadn't disappeared. Finding him faithfully
where I'd ensconced him, I returned to slumber and dreamed of
kittens and bunnies. Just like that, as abruptly as the poltergeist
visits had begun, my nightmares disappeared.

That toy bear wasn't the only addition to my bedroom that
summer. In July, two months after Alan's birth, my parents
banished him and his crib from their boudoir and cast both into my

chambers. After that, Mom and Dad left their bedroom door open at night. Despite his cries interrupting my baby-animal dreams, I found Alan's invasion beneficial. The boogeyman, should he ever return, would not go unheard. My infant brother's presence assured it. For extra security, though, I kept his teddy bear.

⸺ ⚬✕⚬ ⸺

On my fifth birthday, before he left for work, Dad gave me an equal number of George Washingtons. "Spend these anywhere you like," he said.

I wanted to deploy those dollars at Disneyland, a fantastical place a neighbor had told me about, but my feet wouldn't carry me that far. My options were limited to the local five-and-dime, dry goods, or auto parts store. I'd already viewed all the trinkets in the dime store, and I wasn't going to waste my birthday cash on sewing notions.

"Let's go to Western Auto," I said to Mom, recalling the auto shop's sizeable toy section.

"Alan's too young to take outdoors," she replied.

I studied my napping brother. After he'd been born, I'd thought Mom would resume her travels to town and maybe even let me push the stroller. Four months later, that still hadn't happened. I tried to hide my disappointment.

"A big kindergartner like you can decide what she wants by herself," Mom consoled.

I was surprised she'd lifted the only travel restriction ever imposed on me. Normally I wasn't allowed to cross Main Street by myself, with no traffic light there to assist me.

"Just look both ways before you go," Mom said.

At ten a.m. that Friday morning, I stood on the sidewalk for about three minutes, wondering how I would know it was safe to step off the curb. My head swiveled so much I felt dizzy. Finally,

25

when I was sure both lanes were clear, I breached Main Street's center stripe.

With confidence, I strutted into the Western Auto, where a bride doll caught my immediate attention. The three-foot, crystal-eyed newlywed fitted with a lace dress and veil screamed, "Buy me!" She didn't actually shout words, but I imagined her voice telling me to select her. Her eyelids blinked playfully when I tilted her body. I bent her soft vinyl arms to meet mine and asked the store clerk to tell me her price.

The cashier, a rotund man who might have been in his early sixties, asked to see my money. "Aren't you John and Mary Ann's little girl?" he asked, counting my ones.

I confirmed my heritage and explained my mission. Accepting the bills, the man lifted the doll and rang the register.

"A bride doll," Mom mused when I dragged the oversized box through our living room.

"No," I corrected, catching my breath. "She's my sister."

———◦✦◦———

On Sunday, Grandma presented me with a pair of red sparkly shoes like the ones Dorothy wore in *The Wizard of Oz*. Seated at her farmhouse table, I opened the gift, kicked off my sandals, and slipped my feet into the glittery flats. With a double click, I tapped my heels together. Laughter ensued. I clicked my heels again to reproduce the response. But already the conversation had shifted. No one noticed me.

"Your daddy wants to talk with Grandpa for a while before we leave," Mom said. "I'm going to set Alan on the bed in Grandma's room." She gestured for me to follow her down the hallway. "He'll be asleep. You watch and make sure he doesn't fall off the bed. Okay?"

I nodded as if I had any say in the matter.

"You can turn on the TV if you'll keep the volume low."

My grandparents' bedroom furnishings were sparse—a double bed, a vanity, a black-and-white television stationed atop a braided rag rug, a few framed prints, and a wall clock. From previous inspections, I knew the dresser drawers concealed Avon facial creams. Sometimes I poked a finger in the jars and sampled the products. Nothing comparable existed at my house. Beauty balms, I'd surmised, must be meant for wrinkled people. I had no need to explore them further.

In the dresser mirror, I examined my reflection and pinched my cheeks. Maybe I could force indentations that looked like Shirley Temple's. My grandparents spoke of the child actor's dimpled smile and adorable personality. That girl had set an impossible standard for me to attain.

I wondered what program might be on TV, then remembered Alan. Watching a baby sleep was as boring as waiting for Grandma's cuckoo clock to chime. I studied my brother, careful not to lean on the mattress and wake him. He appeared to have been switched to off mode, so I spun the TV volume knob to its lowest setting and clicked on the set.

Lassie barked at me. Adjusting the sound level, I double-checked my charge. Asleep on his back, his rosy lips slack, arms raised next to his head, Alan looked like he'd been shot dead.

Seated on Grandma's rug, I listened to what dangers Timmy had gotten himself into this time. *How would that cherished blond boy survive without his genius dog?* Lassie was smarter than anyone in Timmy's family. I needed a collie like that.

Kerplunk! "Waaaaaaaaaaaaa!"

Alan!

Before I could scoop my distraught brother from Grandma's floor, Mom and Dad bolted into the room. No time to pretend he hadn't fallen, which had been my first idea. I hadn't even reached his side of the bed before my alarmed parents had appeared. Lying on his back, his pencil arms flailing and tiny fists balled, Alan howled. He'd fallen from a height of two and a half feet. I worried that his head might have been dented, but I couldn't see him through all the commotion.

Mom cradled baby Alan in her arms, trying to soothe him. He wailed louder. Dad's glare stung my face like fire ants. From their bedroom doorway, Grandpa and Grandma assessed the situation.

"It's not her fault," Grandma defended me. "Don't be mad at her."

Dad's death rays pierced my negligent soul. I was an unfit daughter *and* sister. I had imperiled my baby brother to gain ten minutes with a fictional collie. "Weren't you told to watch him?" Dad bellowed.

Like a fish gulping air, I tried to respond, but nothing came out.

He unbuckled his belt. "Answer me!"

I nodded and tensed my pelvic muscles. Sometimes I peed when Dad struck me hard. Puddling Grandma's hardwoods would embarrass me and guarantee an extra thrashing.

"Johnny, you're not going to whip her," Grandpa thundered.

Mom and Grandma retreated to an adjacent room, leaving me trapped between two men at odds over my punishment.

"I'll whip my daughter whenever I want," Dad blustered.

Grandpa planted his five-foot-seven, two-hundred-twenty-pound frame between me and Dad. "Not in *my* house, you won't."

"Move," my father commanded his dad.

Grandpa struck a Superman pose, daring his son to take him on.

"Get over here," Dad said to me, executing a counterplay.

I approached him, terrified.

He seized my left arm and, using my limb like a handle, steered me through the house. He didn't stop until we reached the Renault, where he hefted open the rear passenger door and shoved me inside. "You *stay* in here until I tell you to get out."

It wasn't my first exile to the family vehicle. Anytime I misbehaved at my grandparents' house, whether for "meddling," as Grandma called it, or interrupting grown-up conversations, Dad sent me to the car for a time-out. Grandpa usually retrieved me within five minutes, which exasperated my father. This time, though, I didn't expect a commuted sentence.

September's determined sun streamed through the car's translucent windows. Nervously, I watched as Dad stomped indoors, where he and Grandpa must have continued their brawl. I imagined the two squaring off, their jaws clenched, neck veins pulsing.

I cracked my window a few inches to let in a faint breeze. Still nursing my shame, I hoped for an intervention. My negligence had sparked a disaster. What began as a good day had devolved into a compound tragedy. My brother, I feared, had been brain-damaged. I was cooking alive inside a parked solar oven, and my dad and grandpa were caught in a duel that might end in mortal injury. All on a day dedicated to honoring my birth.

With a bang, the back door slammed shut. Out spilled Grandpa and Dad, still bickering.

"No, you're not!" Grandpa shouted. He glowered at Dad and opened my car door. With one hand, he gestured for me to get out.

I sat as immobile as a wax figure, albeit a melting one.

Dad pointed an accusing finger at me. "Don't you move!"

I wasn't about to exit that car without his permission. Any move I made might provoke a fistfight, and I did not want to see my daddy clock my grandpa.

"It's okay. He's not going to hurt you. Come out," Grandpa insisted.

I gave Grandpa a sad-puppy look and shook my head. His patience exhausted, he reached in and pulled me free of the Renault. Firmly, he clutched me to his barrel chest as if I were a football. With a quick sidestep, he steered clear of Dad to protect me from interception.

Dad fixed his gaze on his father.

As if bracing for a shoulder tackle, Grandpa twisted his torso. "It's her birthday, and it's ninety degrees. You're *not* locking her in that car."

Outmatched, Dad withdrew to the sidelines. His shoulders drooped as he retreated indoors. Grandpa and I followed him at a safe distance.

That day, I learned my father wasn't the all-powerful and fearless master of the universe he pretended to be. Like the deceptive wizard in the fictional Oz, he was a fragile man who hid behind closed doors, threw tantrums, and cowered to authority. I would need more than a determined grandpa and a pair of sparkly slippers to protect me from him.

As for Alan, I awaited his first words for four years. When his language didn't arrive, I worried it was my fault. But fault is a loose concept. When he grunted and pointed instead of asking for what he wanted, I fetched items for him. I owed him that much, I figured.

Diana and her grandpa (1959)

As it turned out, I *was* responsible for my brother's delayed speech, though not because of his fall. His pediatrician said Alan would talk when his big sister quit speaking and retrieving things for him, which was exactly what happened.

FOUR

I F MOM HAD BEEN MORE open to cooking or had any friends, she might have protested the time spent with her in-laws. But she had nowhere else to go for a decent Sunday meal and no other adults to converse with.

To suggest Mom didn't get along with other women would be a false statement. From what I observed, she made few attempts to blend in. She likely felt my grandparents' scrutinizing eyes and silent disapproval, though they refrained from any vocal criticisms. Grandma, a third-generation Baptist, had never envisioned having a Catholic for a daughter-in-law. A citified gal from Florida who couldn't cook and knew nothing about farming wasn't the most welcomed newcomer in Emerson either.

If I were to give them titles, Grandma would be the Queen of Southern Cooking and Mom the Lucille Ball of Domestic Mishaps. My mother found no reason to expend her energies in the kitchen. The shortest path to nourishment was the one she most preferred.

"You want a butter and sugar sandwich?" she asked me one day. I had come indoors in search of a snack after an afternoon of playing with baby horned toads.

I scrunched my face as she slathered margarine on a single slice of Mrs Baird's bread. That was the only brand she ever purchased. Dad forbade her to buy Wonder Bread. "Yankees in *Indiana* bake it," he'd said. I didn't know who Yankees were, but I suspected they washed their hands and bathed without soap.

Mom dusted the butter substitute with sugar and folded the sandwich in half. She bit into the feigned delicacy. "It's good," she taunted.

Gritty margarine didn't appeal to me. Registering my disgust, she assembled a peanut butter version minus the sweetener. I disliked jelly as much as she loathed her oven.

When Dad wanted a snack, he would make what he called a "bread sandwich" consisting of three sandwich slices smashed together with nothing in between. His dietary habits suggested mankind *could* live exclusively on the staff of life. From every indication, Mom was content to test that theory.

Dinner, otherwise known as supper at our house, consisted of chipped beef and gravy poured from a jar or mystery meat shaken from a can. Heated in a saucepan, most entrées were served over bread. Though never officially credited, my mother may have invented the sloppy joe. Undeniably, she developed several adulterated versions. Grandma would have called it hog slop if she'd seen it.

Mom's and Grandma's cuisines differed as much as their beauty regimens. Grandma kept a standing Saturday appointment to get her hair "fixed." By *fixed*, she meant tinted the latest bruise color and coiled tighter than new bedsprings. Frankly, I thought her hair looked better broken. She never asked my opinion, though. Her beautician held all the sway.

Mom, on the other hand, preferred a natural look. She wore her hair in a disheveled assortment of pin curls fashioned from crisscrossed bobby pins. Her unpolished fingernails looked unkempt. Cosmetically, she depended on crimson lipstick and a mocha-colored eyebrow pencil for every occasion. Sometimes she repurposed a number two writing instrument for a brow liner. She would have sooner attended a tractor meet than expose her head to a beautician's brush.

On her way home from the salon, Grandma often swung by our house. Observing her fresh hairdos on Saturday mornings drew my attention to Mom's haggard look. Maybe if she prettied up more, she would feel better, I considered.

"Why don't you ever go the beauty shop?" I asked her one day.

She looked at me as if I'd inquired why she never barbecued a brisket. "Because I don't *want* to."

"Why not?"

Mom waved me off. "You don't understand how women talk."

Maybe Emerson ladies had a private language my mother wasn't privy to. I'd heard they had formed a church auxiliary, the WMU, a female secret society of sorts, I presumed. No way to be sure. Mom wasn't active in that either. "They talk about other people," she clarified. "And I don't want them talking about *me*."

I wondered how she knew what happened inside a business she'd never entered, so I decided to ask Grandma. Sometimes, on her way home from the beauty parlor, she retrieved me for a brief outing. Mostly, we visited the grocer or dry goods store while Grandpa played a few rounds at Emerson's substitute for a golf course, the Domino Hall.

"Why, my lands." Grandma chuckled when I relayed Mom's beauty parlor fears. "Nobody's going to talk about her. Why would they want to do that?" I hated it when adults asked *me* questions that I relied on *them* to answer.

Brandishing a Nehi grape soda and a pack of Pixy Stix candies, I returned home and told Mom she was safe at the salon.

Her eyebrows crept closer to her hairline. "You told your grandmother what I said?"

"Uh-huh." I emptied half a grape Pixy Stix into my mouth and grinned. "She said nobody wants to talk about you."

Mom cocked her head and gave me a harsh look.

Aware this might not have been my most gallant act, I erased my purple-tinged smile. "I thought you'd be happy."

She was not.

I didn't bring up the subject again. Then one afternoon, out of the blue, Mom announced she'd scheduled a salon appointment for the following Friday. Her sudden reversal suggested she'd overcome her fear of beauty parlors and hen gossip. I loved my mom and wanted her to look as pretty as other women in our church, as attractive as I knew she could be if she dedicated a little extra effort.

To help Mom prepare for her first salon appointment, I suggested she play beauty shop with me. I knew what went on in a stylist's chair because Grandma had set me in one a time or two. "Let me fix your hair," I begged.

Mom obliged but warned, "Don't brush too hard."

I smoothed her thick brunette bangs back, pondering hairdos. "How come your hair's brown and mine's blond?" I asked.

"Yours'll turn brown one day too. Mine used to be blond."

I studied my honey-colored braids in the mirror. *My hair will never be the color of yours.*

"Ouch!" Mom cut her eyes at me.

"I'm barely brushing," I insisted. I stroked her hair more gently with the soft-bristle brush.

"Owwwww!"

34

In the mirror reflection, I caught her accusing frown.

"I'm tender-headed," she yelped.

Any beauty school fantasies I ever had died that day.

On Friday, Mom came home from the salon with her shellacked locks spiraled into a cone above her crown and looking like a futuristic movie star.

"Your hair!" I cried, wondering how she had withstood the rigors of such a complex style. Maybe anesthetics were involved.

She fingered her towering hairdo. "It's called a beehive."

"It looks great on you, Mary Ann," Grandma admired. She'd babysat me and Alan while Mom had undergone immersion therapy. But Grandma's car hadn't cleared our driveway before Mom withdrew to her bedroom in tears.

I followed her, curious about what I'd missed. Grandma hadn't said anything mean to Mom. She never did. "What's wrong?"

Seated before her vanity mirror, Mom shook her head. "That woman ratted my hair so hard my eyes crossed. I'll never get all the tangles out of this mess." She pulled free a couple of hairpins and loosened the beehive one tendril at a time. In less than three minutes, she destroyed all evidence of improvement.

FIVE

I RODE BEHIND MOM IN THE Renault's back seat, clinging to my door handle for dear life. Dad motored the family through Dallas, his sedan sputtering between gear changes. Alternately he stomped the gas and brake pedals, punishing the car for its pitiful performance.

"You son-of-a—" he chastised the choking motor. "You're going to run right or else!"

"Johnny! Be careful. You'll *kill* us!" Mom cried.

Dear Lord, please bring this car to a stop before I die.

With both feet pressed against the floorboard, I squeezed my eyes tight and prepared for a collision. Dad whipped the car from lane to lane, daring the French insurgent to defy him. Tires squealed. Horns honked. Scenery spun past my window. I gripped the door handle to prevent being tossed about like a crash dummy.

"Johnny, stop!" Mom screeched.

Dad paid her appeals no mind. If anything, her protests further enraged him. At high speed, he steered through traffic. The Renault lurched and decelerated several more times before Mom next spoke.

"Take us home, now," she demanded, "while we're still in one piece."

Dad pounded a palm against the steering wheel. "You piece of junk!"

By way of answered prayers or automotive intelligence, the Renault self-corrected. My body relaxed, but my imagination raced forward. Never would I disobey my dad, I resolved. When he raged, even his car feared him.

———— ⬦ ————

Dad drove home from work in a Volkswagen Beetle, the Renault's impromptu replacement. The buttercup-yellow, round-roofed car with an engine on the wrong end smelled of fresh adhesives, synthetic leather, and an odor nobody could quite pinpoint. I sat on the cream-colored seat, inspecting the auto and wondering how blistering that cushion might feel in direct sunlight. Maybe the new car would be more dependable than the Renault and I wouldn't have to fear my father's hotheaded driving.

Dad sniffed the air. "Do you smell something funny?"

We were about to leave home to show the new car to my grandparents. Mom checked Alan's diaper for evidence. She shrugged and continued balancing his baby carrier in her lap. Child car seats weren't yet mandatory. Ditto for seat belts.

Dad started the VW's engine. I reached for my window roller, but before I could turn the crank, the part broke loose in my hand. Over one shoulder, he gave me the stink eye.

"I was just rolling down the window," I squeaked.

"Exactly how hard did you pull on that knob?"

"I didn't pull it hard at all."

I couldn't figure out what had happened. My skinny five-year-old arms weren't *that* strong. Dad must have driven the vehicle off the showroom floor without checking for defects. If anyone had touched that window roller, it would have fallen off. It didn't matter. Excessive force was the only cause Dad could conceive of for the breakage. The Volkswagen had been built by a team of German experts. His daughter, though, was a product of two flawed Americans.

Dad exited the VW, opened Mom's door, and demanded everyone exit. On my way out, I timidly passed him the window roller. Custody of the broken auto part would distract him from his belt, I hoped. He was wearing that burgundy-and-clear-plastic one that stung my legs like a scorpion when he thrashed me.

Squeezed into the back seat, Dad tugged at the door panel until it popped loose. From the open cavity, he retrieved a brown paper sack cloaking a rancid German sandwich. "Look. Some guy left his lunch in here."

My accidental breakage saved Dad a prolonged search for that awful stench. The orphaned sandwich sidetracked him from whipping me too. The thank-you that I thought I'd earned never came, though. He wasn't inclined to verbalize his appreciation.

After a brief roller repair, we headed out to my grandparents' house.

"Keep your windows down," Dad said.

He hadn't needed to tell me that. My window roller might as well have been a rattlesnake.

My grandparents met us outside their house before we'd even exited the vehicle. While the family remained seated, Grandpa circled the auto's perimeter. Disapprovingly, he eyed the VW. Grandma's mouth gaped, but she offered nothing.

Standing next to the driver's window, Grandpa asked Dad, "What is this *thing*? Looks like a clown car."

"It's a Volkswagen," Dad said, "the fastest-selling car in America!"

He must have fancied himself a trendsetter. I could hear it in his voice. Instead of owning a Ford Thunderbird like Grandpa, he had opted for an unmistakable car with a sunny color. I wondered if its paint tint might improve his disposition.

Grandpa shook his head. "Son, why do you keep buying foreign cars? You're going to kill my grandkids."

Dad scoffed. "Why do you say that? It's a Beetle—safer than a Cadillac."

"It's a beetle, all right." Grandpa shoved his hands in his pockets, looking miffed. "And it'll squash like a *bug*."

We left soon after that. In a few short minutes, Dad had accomplished all he'd intended. He'd let Grandpa know he would do as he pleased with his family and his car.

SIX

I N THE SUMMER OF 1960, Mom delivered my *second* brother. With no space in my bedroom for another crib, the new arrival had to sleep in my parents' room. Our family having exceeded our home's capacity, the following summer, we moved into a newly built house in Renner, a growing suburb twenty-two miles south of Emerson.

Renner had streetlights and curbs and gutters and paid firemen instead of volunteers who might not be around when lightning struck. The growing community of four thousand, none of whom we knew, spanned a major freeway route to Dallas. We moved in August, right after Kerry—who was supposed to have been *Karen*—turned one.

"The school's going to be at the end of the street." Dad indicated a vacant field near our house. "You can walk there." Blackbirds dotted the freshly mowed grass where Dad had just

John, Mary Ann, Diana, Alan, and Kerry (1960)

pointed. No dirt had been overturned. The school year would begin in three weeks. I suspicioned this was another deceptive forecast.

I spent the next week testing the new furniture that had materialized, much like our house, from an invisible mist. An Early American sofa, two end tables, and a six-chair maple dining set filled our great room. In the galley kitchen, the copper-toned refrigerator, stovetop, oven, and cabinet fixtures shone like newly minted pennies. Behind a set of folding doors, an automatic washing machine awaited its inaugural use. Mom would never again have to run her laundry through a wringer washer connected to a sink faucet.

The spare bedroom that Dad converted to a den showcased a Danish modern sofa and two chairs. To further confuse styles and influences, my parents' mocha-colored bedroom set, with its lacquer finish and clean lines, better reflected Japanese culture than Texas traditions. Roaming between rooms in our house, I could experience the flavors of New England, Scandinavia, *and* the South Pacific in under two minutes. Our eclectic furnishings would have offended anyone with good taste, but Dad claimed the décor matched his unassuming values.

"We don't put on airs," he said with pride.

To me, our four-bedroom, two-bath brick home with an attached *two*-car garage seemed more like a governor's mansion than a middle-class dwelling. We had landed deep in high cotton. Though I couldn't identify the source of our newfound wealth, I suspected my grandparents. I'd overheard Grandpa say he'd recently signed an oil lease in Oklahoma. Possibly he had shared the royalties with his son and daughter. My aunt Janis and her family had acquired a new home too.

Our abrupt financial ascent didn't appear to stem from Dad's career progression. He still worked as a technician at Dallas Radio, like he always had. And Mom had been a stay-at-home parent ever since I'd turned three.

The Renner house was twice the size of our former one. All that extra space made me feel giddy, but my bedroom hadn't changed much. Same twin bed, same crib, same brother. Alan still slept in my room. Kerry's bassinet had not yet been ejected from the master bedroom, a critical detail I'd overlooked while celebrating my expansive closet.

Down the hallway, in what had been assigned as Alan's and Kerry's future bedroom, sat a pair of detached bunkbeds. One day, my brothers would share the largest of four bedrooms, the one farthest from Mom and Dad's sleeping quarters. As the only girl and eldest child, eventually, I would have a private room. But thanks to poor family planning, or no planning at all, that wouldn't occur for four more years.

<hr />

Dad said, before school started, I needed to learn to tie my shoes. I didn't see the connection, but I could imagine the advantages. If I were more self-sufficient, I wouldn't have to sit on my bed with my feet dangling while I waited for Mom to lace my sneakers. She rushed through the process, often overlooking my bunched socks.

Right there on the four-foot-square linoleum pad that we dubbed our entranceway, my father showed me how to perform the ritual I would conduct for the rest of my life. I got the hang of it quickly. All I needed was to find my missing school. The education building was *not* at the end of our street, where Dad had said it would be.

"It's going to take three years to build," he admitted when

I pushed for an explanation. "I'll walk you to the house where you'll be going until then."

House? That made no sense. *I'm going to start first grade in someone else's home?* He had promised me the new school would have a modern gym, an inviting playground, and a cavernous auditorium. *This has to be another trick.* Unfortunately, he was serious—this time.

Dad escorted me three blocks west to what once had been our community's model homes. I would advance from one prototype house to the next, he said, until year three, when the new elementary school would be finished. Until then, my playground would be an alley and a driveway suitable for jump rope and not much else. The subpar situation was worse than repeating kindergarten—which I'd done after Dad's strong-arm tactics had failed to intimidate Emerson's school superintendent.

I had been denied entry to first grade twenty days shy of my sixth birthday. And now, almost seven, I had to accept a phony school building. All that new furniture and extra space at home had gone to my head. I had anticipated an equally upgraded schoolhouse. From the looks of it, I was destined for scholastic disappointment.

On the first day of school, I received a series of rules and instructions from my teacher, Mrs. Adams. Students were permitted to use the driveway and alley for jump rope and ball play. However, the mature oak trees in the front and back yards were off-limits for climbing.

I forgot that dictate by the second week of school.

Scaling a tree trunk, I heard hoots and hollers erupt beneath me.

"She's wearing her pajamas!" cried a boy I didn't know.

A refrain of laughter alerted my teacher to my predicament. In my groggy morning haze, I had overlooked my bloomer bottoms before leaving home. The ruffled flannel sleepwear hiding my panties peeked from beneath my skirt folds. If not for those fugitive pj's, I would have suffered even worse humiliation.

When I returned home that afternoon, while Mom tended to Alan in my bedroom, I flung my bloomers to my closet floor.

She scrunched her face. "What's that all about?"

Reprovingly, I relayed my pajama blunder.

She cupped one hand over her mouth and tried to hide her amusement.

"When is he going to move out of my room?" I huffed, implicating Alan for my mistake.

Mom hadn't noticed my wardrobe mishap because she hadn't inspected me closely before school. She'd been up all night, stumbling in and out of my room, switching on and off the overhead light to see why Alan kept crying. Probably, he desired a less painful way to sprout teeth. I would have gifted him *my* molars for a night of uninterrupted sleep.

Mom refused to accept ownership for my slipup. Eyeing the empty crib in my room, she stifled her laughter.

I was tired of asking and never receiving a valid date. *How old does a baby need to be to sleep alone?* Alan had occupied my bedroom for twenty-eight months. Hoisting him from his walker, I carried him to his future bedroom—where he belonged. Mom followed us.

With a grand gesture, I set Alan on one of the vacant bunk beds. "Look, he's big enough *now*." I presented my brother like a game-show prize. If he didn't leave my room soon, I feared I might end up at school in my bathrobe and slippers. "He can sleep in here by himself. I slept by myself when I was his age," I reminded Mom. Unsure if that was true, I'd made a lucky guess.

Mom nodded. "I guess we can try it tonight."

I was more than ready to give up my poltergeist protection. The only nightmares I suffered anymore involved arriving at school naked on Picture Day.

The persuasive argument I gave Mom appeared successful. That night, Alan moved to his new bedroom. Unannounced, Kerry appeared in mine. I'd expected him to sleep in my parents' room until he moved in with Alan. But Dad said he and Mom needed a private room worse than I did.

The simple fix to my sleep deprivation would have been to assign my brothers' room to me. Then Alan and Kerry could have shared the room next door to Mom and Dad. I supposed no one thought of that.

<hr>

One Monday morning in early October, after I'd dressed and checked for runaway pj's, I slung my red plaid satchel over one shoulder and strutted to school. As I moseyed down the sidewalk, I observed no other kids. *Did Mom misread the clock?* If I were late, I would suffer a demerit. The thought of it made my knees wobbly. Disappointing my teacher might cause Dad to punish me for oversleeping.

At school, the grounds were silent, indicating classes had already started. I twisted the doorknob to enter, but it didn't turn. Someone had locked me out. I pounded the partition with my fists. No one answered. *Is this how teachers punish students for being late?* My emotions shifted from fear and hurt to rage. *How dare they? I don't deserve this!*

By the time the latch clinked and the doorknob turned, I verged on hysteria. I waited, my palms sweaty and throat knotted, to glimpse a familiar face. Surely, Mrs. Adams would be sympathetic. I would fault my absentminded mother for my tardiness, explain she didn't wake me on time. My teacher had seen my pajamas that day I'd worn them to school. She must have gathered Mom wasn't terribly attentive.

From behind the partially open door, my teacher appeared. "Diana?" She sounded as if she'd been expecting a floral delivery. "What are you doing here?"

"I-I-I'm sorry I'm late," I stammered.

She bent to my level and patted my shoulder. "Do you remember that ticket I gave you last Friday?"

I nodded, recalling the red paper voucher.

"Today's *Fair Day*." She smiled as if she'd given me a free puppy.

I recollected how my wide-eyed classmates had fingered their scarlet coupons on Friday, turning their mouths into big O shapes. I'd been excited to show Mom the prize I'd been awarded for no apparent reason.

A boy who sat next to me said the fair sold pink clouds of cotton that tasted sweeter than sugar cookies. "They got circus animals there too," he'd said, "and a real *snake* house!"

I couldn't wait to see what all the excitement was about. But when I'd presented my ticket to Mom, she'd tossed it in the trash and muttered, "Fair Day. Hmph."

Mrs. Adams's reminder felt like a double injury. "Oh, yeah," I said as if the whole mix-up had been my mistake, as if I should have been the one to remind Mom of Fair Day. I didn't know what else to say.

My abrupt return home startled my mother. Spooning cereal paste into Kerry's infant mouth, she flinched when I opened the front door. "What are you doing here?" she asked.

It seemed I wasn't expected anywhere. "You sent me to school on *Fair Day*," I groused.

"I *did*?" She set down the baby spoon and sniggered.

"It's not funny." I stomped down the hall toward my room.

"That walk didn't hurt you any," she called after me.

From my closet, I retrieved a troll doll and stroked its feathery hair. Though my mother's mistake was unintentional, in my mind, her flub exposed a significant danger. She was as unreliable as Dad. That newfound knowledge scared me more than spooks and flying mattresses.

Later that evening, while I continued moping over missing the fair, Alan sat in the hallway, waving an empty bottle.

Dad eyed him critically. "It's time," he said to Mom. "You've had your chance. I'm taking over."

"But he's not ready," Mom protested.

Dad cut his eyes at her. "He's two. Yes, he is."

I monitored their exchange from the safety of our living room sofa, a vantage point that offered full view of the rebel in question. Alan's bottle nipple squeaked with each pull. He'd drained the last of his juice.

Dad plucked the offending container from his chubby fingers. "I'll get you some water." From the kitchen, he returned with a bottle of clear liquid and presented the drink to his waiting son.

Alan took one draw and threw the plasticware against a wall. "Ehhh!" he cried.

Dad let out a sneaky laugh and retrieved the bottle. Again, he offered the refreshment to Alan. Wise to the deception, this time, Alan shook his head and made a bitter face. As if shooing bees, he fanned the air with both hands.

"*What* did you give him?" Mom narrowed her eyes at Dad.

He gasped for breath between laughs.

"I mean it, Johnny. Tell me what you gave him."

Dad unscrewed the bottlecap and held the contents to Mom's nose.

She scowled. "You filled his bottle with *vinegar?*"

Observing this, I recalled my paint thinner accident—or what I knew of it. According to Mom, I'd found the cup and chugged a swig before she'd noticed. She'd been quick to say I'd suffered no prolonged health effects, permanent medical anxieties aside. To save my life, my stomach contents had been vacuumed through my esophagus. I hoped Alan's innards wouldn't have to be emptied that way. Mom didn't look overly alarmed.

As it turned out, Alan suffered no residual harm. He never again desired a bottle or likely trusted Dad. I thought, compared to my Halloween scare, he'd gotten off pretty easy.

Completed on schedule, the new schoolhouse located two blocks from my home was everything Dad said it would be. The playground included monkey bars and merry-go-rounds and acres of fields where students could gallop like wild ponies. In modern classrooms that smelled of fresh paint, I entered third grade with an equal number of brothers—and no hope of ever gaining a private bedroom.

Kerry moved in with Alan. And Joel, Mom's latest reproductive surprise, was booted

Alan, Kerry, Joel, and Diana (1964)

to the rickety crib in my room. Secretly, I contemplated ways to murder The Stork.

By age nine, I had shared my room with babies for four years. Invariably, one had had colic or been teething or running a fever—always in the middle of the night. Their crying sometimes lasted for days before an underlying cause could be found and remedied.

My parents reserved doctor visits for broken bones and suture-demanding gashes. Only after multiple rounds of Vicks VapoRub, baby aspirin, and wet washcloths failed to silence infant wailing would Dad authorize a physician's visit. "We don't go running to the doctor every time something hurts," he said.

After Mom received Dad's blessing to visit a pediatrician, she had to summon a taxi. As normal as that might sound to a New Yorker, in Texas, that was unheard of. Beyond airports and hotels, taxis were rare sightings. Though Dad harped about Mom's dependence on car services, she showed no urgency in learning to drive. She'd grown accustomed to being chauffeured from one destination to the next, and that was the way she preferred to travel.

As the child of a non-driving mother, I lacked transportation to scholastic events. I had failed to consider that minor hitch when I joined the little league cheerleader squad that performed at fifth- and sixth-grade football games. It hadn't occurred to me that Dad couldn't deliver me to the football field at four p.m. No bus service existed from the elementary school to the city's only stadium. Because I had been brazen enough to enlist without seeking permission first, Mom said I could find my way to and from the ballgames. She didn't know the other cheerleaders' moms and had no time to fraternize. Securing rides for me was out of the question.

"We aren't millionaires," she said when I asked why a taxi couldn't transfer me to pep-squad practice.

To attend after-school events, I petitioned my friends' parents for rides. Dog-tired of co-parenting my brothers, I refused to let transportation issues sideline me. "Can you take me to the stadium?" I asked any girl whose uniform matched mine. "My mom can't bring me tonight." It wasn't a lie, I rationalized. My mom couldn't haul me anywhere on any night.

Most parents didn't mind delivering an extra child to the ballfield. Getting home proved a bit trickier, though. Our school district sprawled. The other cheerleaders didn't live in my neighborhood. During dinner hours, their parents weren't always keen on driving out of the way to drop me off.

On the way to the stadium one afternoon, my friend Lauren's mom announced her husband would be retrieving Lauren after halftime. Their family had formal dinner plans. I would need to find another way home.

I didn't start soliciting rides until the performance ended. One by one, I asked other cheerleaders to check with their parents about giving me a lift. I'd been taught it was disrespectful to directly address grown-ups. Always I relied on an intermediary. But that night, no one accepted my timeworn pitch.

Before I fully digested my dilemma, the stands emptied. I sat on the vacant bleachers, shivering in the brisk November air. My stomach ached. I envisioned my family dining without me, thinking I would arrive at any minute. Mulling over my mistakes, I prayed for a psychic rescue. *Mom. M-o-m! MOM! Send somebody to get me!* My mental distress calls were too weak to be heard, I guessed.

Overhead, the ballfield lights switched from radiant white to black. I squinted and tried to adjust my eyes. Moonlight glinted off the bleachers. I could see well enough to exit the stadium. *But then what?* Though I knew the path by heart, my home was too far away for me to journey afoot after sundown. I had no money to call home from a pay phone, and the adjacent neighborhood looked dangerous in a Little Red Riding Hood way.

Winds gusted. I buttoned my coat collar, ducked my head low, and ratcheted up my emergency signals. While I waited for ESP to kick in, I entertained disturbing thoughts. Whoever had switched off those field lights might have closed the gates. Possibly I was locked in. *Will I have to sleep in the stands?* It's sad to admit, but even *that* dire prospect didn't move me to action.

I sat there motionless, like I'd been told to do when lost. "Be still and wait for someone to find you," Dad had always said. So far, that hadn't worked well.

The football field lights fired bright once again. My surroundings illuminated as if it were midday. *I'm not alone! Someone sees me!*

From inside a rectangular office high above the bleachers, a man descended upon me like an angel. "Little girl, are you lost?" His eyebrows knitted.

I shook my head. I wasn't lost. I knew exactly where I was—in deep trouble. "I couldn't find a ride home," I muttered.

"Come with me." The stadium attendant motioned for me to follow him. Inside the press box, he lifted a phone receiver. "Do you know your home number?"

My father had drilled that information into my head a zillion times since I'd started school, and now I understood why. As I recited the digits, the guy I'd mistaken for Gabriel dialed.

Within minutes, Dad arrived. I waited in his car while he spoke to the gravely troubled groundskeeper. Braced for a whipping, I sobbed. Maybe if I looked remorseful enough, Dad would feel sorry for me. I knew he wouldn't lay into me in front of the man who'd called him. If he did, that guy would likely call the police, given his current mood. No, my father would wait to strike me where outsiders couldn't intervene.

Dad returned to the car. "How'd you end up here by yourself?"

"Nobody could take me home," I croaked.

He gave me a sidelong look. "How do you *normally* get home?"

I assumed he knew the answer and was testing me. "My friends' mothers usually take me home, but the lady who brought me this time said she couldn't." I stared at the navy-and-white pom-poms in my lap. "I asked everybody. I promise I did." Tears dampened my crepe paper streamers.

Dad grew quiet. I could feel the welts before he'd even administered them. The silence petrified me. He was a teakettle, quietly simmering before his whistle blew. The longer he heated, the more violent his release would be.

At home, his attention spun from me to my mother. He stormed from the garage and into the kitchen. "Have you lost your mind?" he asked the instant he saw Mom.

She was standing at the sink, washing dishes, while my three brothers played in the adjacent living room. "I can't drive, and you know it," she fired back.

Dad stood blocking the kitchen doorway, his hands on his hips. "So you expected her to get back on her *own*?"

I joined my brothers in their circle of toys, hoping to escape further notice. Mom was taking the heat for me, so I needed to keep the three boys entertained and out of her way. She bowed her head and blubbered something I couldn't hear.

"Don't you *ever* send her anywhere again unless you know who she's with and how she's getting home," Dad blustered, his face colored.

I regretted spurring a squabble. Mom had enough to deal with already. She didn't need me heaping extra responsibilities on her. To my already tangled emotions, I added a hangman's rope of guilt. I wanted to apologize to her, but I didn't know how to. I had no examples to follow.

The next week, Mom told me to quit the cheerleader squad and Girl Scouts. With no back talk, I did as she asked.

SEVEN

GRANDPA AND GRANDMA'S BACK DOOR slammed shut behind Mom and Dad. The two were headed for Grandpa's pasture, where Mom couldn't endanger other drivers.

"Don't hit no cows," Grandpa teased as they left.

I waved goodbye to my mother, possibly for the last time. Dad had said he feared she might be more accident-prone behind the wheel than at home. Recalling she'd once bruised two ribs by tripping over my brothers' die-cast cars and suffered third-degree burns from flipping a pot roast, I felt anxious.

It had been about a month since my stadium incident. Dad was determined to prevent anything like that from happening again. Standing there in Grandma's kitchen, I couldn't decide who was most at risk.

Together, my grandparents, siblings, and I waited to learn how Mom—and Dad too—had fared during her first driving lesson. It was sort of like a *Survivor* episode without any cameras following the contestants. I crossed my fingers behind my back and willed them to return uninjured.

Roughly twenty minutes passed before Mom staggered into Grandma's kitchen looking like she'd seen the Grim Reaper. Her face parchment-colored, she stood before the family wide-eyed and wordless.

My father strode in behind her. "Come on, kids." He gestured with one arm. "Time to go."

I thought maybe Mom had plowed through Grandpa's livestock barn, and we needed to skedaddle before he found out. But she hadn't struck anything besides Dad's weakest nerve. She admitted she'd missed a few gears and never found them.

"You'd do *anything* to get out of driving," Dad fumed while motoring home. "You're going to ruin the *transmission*."

To motivate Mom, which necessitated heroic efforts, Dad bought her a 1965 Rambler station wagon. The American Motors vehicle with an automatic transmission and power steering arrived like most big purchases at our house, without any advanced notice. Compared to the Volkswagen Beetle Mom couldn't command, the station wagon looked like a military tank—which might have been its main selling feature.

"No more excuses," Dad said. "You're going to learn to drive, or else."

"How am I going to drive this big ol' thing? It's longer than a *bus*," Mom argued. "I'm too short for this car. I can't see over the hood."

Exasperated, Dad resorted to what he always did when anyone defied his authority—trickery. Time wasn't on his side. The longer he waited, the less likely Mom was to pursue her driver's license.

One morning after Dad had directed his obstinate wife through a few spins around the neighborhood, he left us kids with a babysitter and delivered Mom to the Department of Public Safety. I don't know where she thought they were headed that day, but it wasn't to the licensing bureau. She didn't register what was going on until Dad parked and hissed, "We're not leaving here until you've taken that test."

Mom and Dad returned home regarding each other as strangers. They weren't screamers. When angry, they stewed, pouted, schemed, manipulated, and deserted each other, but they never yelled. Neither of their voices projected well, so they relied on other means to convey their hostilities.

Dad handed Cheryl, our babysitter, a few bills while Mom sulked in her bedroom. When Cheryl left, he lumbered into the den where my brothers and I were watching television.

From the sofa, I looked up at Dad. "What happened?"

He stood with his fists balled inside his dungaree pockets, staring out a window at nothing specific. "She failed her driver's test." He said it the way he might recite a weather forecast. "Stormy, with a chance of hissy fits later this evening" was what I heard.

"Does that mean she can't *ever* drive?" I asked.

Dad studied me as if trying to ascertain my IQ. Maybe I had dingbat in *my* DNA. "It means she's going to take the test again. And again. And again, until she passes."

I'm fairly sure he meant passes *the test* and not passes into the next realm. I'm reasonably sure, not entirely but mostly.

In Dad's eyes, Mom's disqualification for a driver's license was nothing short of insubordination. And *nobody* defied him and got away with it. After she failed the exam, my mother's mandatory driving instruction degenerated into a scorch-the-earth war of wills. To her advantage, Mom held the reigning title for passive aggression. On her second attempt to conquer the driver's test, she obliterated the agency's STOP sign. Dad claimed the collision had been intentional. With detectable glee, she denied his allegation.

Their exchange instigated a proliferation of compulsory tool searches and burned dinners that lasted for months until Mom consented to another attempt.

On her third try, my mother earned a driver's permission slip that might as well have been a surrender flag. Against her will, she became a legal driver—but not necessarily a safe one.

At thirty-one, Mom's freedom to go anywhere at any time removed the security of defined limits. Like a hesitant child, she ventured farther and farther from home, first motoring me and my brothers to Jerry's Dairy Way, where we bought ZERO candy bars and Dr Peppers, and later to the outskirts of Dallas.

One day, on our way home from the convenience store, Mom complained, "It's too *dern* hot in here." Before I could respond, she leaned across the car console to adjust the air vents.

Out of nowhere, a utility pole appeared. Dust clouds billowed. Two-foot-tall Johnsongrass brushed my passenger door. The Rambler barreled full speed toward a row of power lines.

"Mom!" I shrieked.

She jerked the steering wheel left, sending the car careening back to pavement. Tires squealed. A foreboding dark object swished past my window. Half an hour later, my body still felt electrified. It took a little longer, though, for Mom to recover.

If she'd plowed head-on into that unyielding target, she might have killed us all. Nobody had been wearing a seat belt. At least one brother had a glass soda bottle pressed to his lips. Tattletale that I was, I thought it best to inform my father of what had happened.

Dad gave me a stern look when I relayed Mom's near miss. He hurried from my room to the garage, to check the car for dents. He must have scolded Mom later because, the next morning, I caught her standing over the kitchen sink with a butter knife, scraping charred toast.

———◦✕◦——

After Mom's off-road mishap, she was in no rush to get back in the driver's seat. Nonetheless, Vacation Bible School and the chance to catch a break from four children rekindled her spirits. She drove me and my brothers to church and back for five consecutive days without crossing a centerline or hopping a curb.

A few weeks later, Mom motored us kids into town where retail possibilities lined the inlaid-brick streets. Renner's historic district offered tantalizing shops ready to welcome newcomers like us. For the first time since she'd married, my mother could spend money without Dad around to supervise. Past attempts, no matter how modest, had met with failure.

She'd contracted the milkman, once, without Dad's permission. But when he'd received the first bill, he'd made her cancel those morning dairy deliveries. I was none too happy. Dad's shortsightedness left me moistening my cereal with watered-down milk residue.

On her next attempt to exert financial authority, Mom had enlisted the Hostess man to furnish us doughnuts. That agreement, too, had met a swift death. Dad kept Mom on a short leash when it came to expenditures. Though he permitted her to stow the family checkbook in her purse, she enjoyed no active ownership.

For as long as Dad was the sole driver, Mom had no say over their joint funds. Every purchase she made—down to the most infinitesimal item—was micromanaged by him. He would march down supermarket aisles as Mom trailed him like a child, lifting products from shelves and asking, "This? How about this one? Can we get two of these?" Frequently, he denied her wishes, substituting generic brands for Mom's original requests. A penny saved at the supermarket was a penny he could spend on plywood or nails or hacksaw blades.

When Mom learned to drive, those days were over. She could grocery shop without Dad commandeering the process. *Maybe now I can get that Herbal Essences shampoo I've been wanting.* I'd been trying to sneak a bottle past Dad for months. "Nothing wrong with Breck," he'd said, snatching the coveted green liquid from my clasp. Right off, I saw the benefits of my mother's expanded purchasing power. She, unfortunately, did not.

***

"Window-shopping" Mom called it. To me, it was just loitering near a storefront and fantasizing ownership of some showcased treasure my mother couldn't afford. Big, fat waste of time. It required no action other than wishful thinking. I could do that anywhere. Making an actual purchase seemed to kill Mom's retail buzz, which was exactly what window-shopping did to mine. Longing for something she had no aim to acquire felt like an expressway to despair. I didn't think my mother needed any new routes.

Stationed in front of Harrington's Furniture Store with my mother and brothers, I wondered how long she would ogle the window display—this time.

Mom stood transfixed, staring at a ceramic tree adorned with colorful birds. "Isn't that pretty?"

I studied the cardinal, blue jay, purple finch, cedar waxwing, bluebird, and robin as I had on prior occasions. The three-foot, ornamental feature truly was exquisite, but I didn't reply. Mom wasn't searching for my opinion as much as she was talking to herself.

She sighed. "I wish I could buy it."

With one hand, I shielded my eyes from the sun's reflective glare. "Why don't you?"

She gave me an astonished look. "It's *fif-teen* dollars."

"So?" It had been fifteen dollars every time she'd viewed the price tag. The moment had come for her to pay up or move along.

If my grandmother had been there, she would have said I was acting "too big for my britches." At eleven, already I believed my logic superior to my mother's. Annoyed from standing in the heat for no good reason, I spoke to her like a grown-up. I wouldn't have talked like that in front of my father, but we wouldn't have been there at all if Dad were involved. He didn't window-shop, most assuredly not for home accessories.

Clutching her brown vinyl purse, Mom snapped, "I can't spend that kind of money on *decorations*."

Kerry and Alan tugged my arms, impatient the way five- and six-year-old boys are when idle.

"Don't you have your checkbook?" I asked. I thought all currency was merely paper exchanged for possessions. I didn't realize that every tendered check required cash in the buyer's bank account. Or a daringness for jail.

"Of course I do." She shifted two-year-old Joel to one hip.

"Then buy it or stop making us *look* at it." I turned my head to hide my eye roll.

Mom should have reprimanded me. Instead, she strode to the store's entrance, swung the door wide with her free hand, and paraded her entourage inside. She proceeded to the cashier counter. Before I had time to applaud her courage, she bought that decorative tree the same way Dad acquired most of his belongings, which is to say on impulse and without any remorse.

All she'd needed to claim her financial power was the provocation of her mouthy daughter.

Her bold action renewed my faith that she could be my role model. I'd been waiting to see a spark, a verve to emulate. Her purchase assured me that a fully functioning human *existed* inside my mother's body. She wasn't merely a puppet controlled by my dad. The bird tree confirmed her autonomy.

At home, Dad critically eyed the new arrival without commentary. Situated next to our home's picture window, the fragile birds glinted in the natural light. For hours, I marveled at the winged specimens and imagined them real.

Soon after Mom bought the bird tree, Joel moved into Alan and Kerry's bedroom, and I gained a room to myself. Looking back, I see that as a critical turning point. The social divide between my siblings and I became more pronounced after that. They formed a united trio while I faced adolescence alone.

My brothers' playthings no longer interested me. I abhorred sounds emitted by popguns, plastic whistles, and toy drums, so to counter the clamor filtering from "The Boys" room, Grandpa gave me an antique radio.

At night I listened to KLIF, a Dallas pop station that introduced me to rock and roll artists my dad said played the same three guitar chords over and over. He ridiculed lyrics proclaiming love, "yeah, yeah, yeah." To avert his criticisms, I shut my bedroom door and lowered my radio volume.

"Don't close that door," Dad admonished the first time I tuned him out.

I thought I'd been doing us both a favor. My choice of music irked him. He listened to Hank Snow and thought the Grand Ole Opry top-tier entertainment.

"What does that stodgy Ed Sullivan know anyhow?" Dad huffed when I gushed about the Beatles. "You ought to listen to artists that'll still be around in five years. And that won't be those guys."

Anytime Dad caught my radio tuned to current hits, he would wander into my not-so-private space and say, "You listening to those English freaks again? Pfft. Bunch of no-talents."

I wasn't sure what Mom thought about the Beatles. She didn't appear to have an opinion one way or the other. But once, when I came home from school, she gave me a thick, folded red poster.

"Here." She offered me the cardboard gift. "I bought this for you today."

Opening the accordioned banner, I found all four Beatles' portraits.

———— ⋈ ————

One Saturday morning, as I dreamed about Paul McCartney, I heard jingling.

Next to me, Dad's body compressed my full-size mattress. He'd slid under my covers and now lay propped on one elbow. In one hand, he held a baby rattle suspended in midair. "Time to wake up!"

I scowled at him. "Stop it."

"Oo-oo-wee!" He set down the noisemaker. "You've got *dragon* breath."

"Leave me alone!" I might as well have asked him to play "Reveille." Demanding anything of Dad assured that he would do the opposite.

Over the next several Saturday mornings, my father advanced

through a series of pranks bordering on torture. He tickled my nose with feathers, stuffed my troll doll's hair up my nostrils, and squirted my eyelids with a water pistol. A few times, when he caught me mouth-breathing, he dropped an Atomic Fireball on my tongue. I slept in fear of waking to the Heimlich maneuver. But always I coughed up the red-hot candy before its burning flames reached my tonsils.

Bewilderingly, the father who aggravated me on Saturday mornings turned lovey-dovey at night. After everyone was in bed, Dad would creep through the darkness and into my room. Easing under my covers, he would snuggle up to me in the spoon position. Not since he'd taught me my ABCs had he shown me so much affection. Folded around my midriff, his right arm felt warm and comforting. The limb he'd once used to strike me soothed me like a blanket.

Cocooned in his embrace, I listened to his rhythmic breathing. No longer was I the bad child in need of thrashings or the lazy ingrate avoiding morning chores or the depository for his self-loathing anger. Like fairy dust, adolescence had changed me from a waif to an enchanted princess. Any day, I expected my tiara to arrive.

During our late-night interludes, I welcomed my father's attention. In my head, I likened our clandestine meetings to daddy-daughter dates. Except ours took place in private, after-hours, and in my bed. Though his conflicting behaviors puzzled me, Dad's cuddling felt protective—maybe even repentant. His embrace relieved an ache I didn't acknowledge, an unmet desire hidden beneath a mantle of protective barriers.

"Nighty night," Dad cooed when we snuggled. He would linger for another ten minutes before retiring to his bedroom. Probably, Mom hadn't missed him. By nine p.m., most nights, she had clicked off her children's lights, retreated to the master bedroom, and crashed like a downed missile. She might have said good night to us first, though my brothers and I never asked her to read us a book or tell us a bedtime story. Such maternal inclinations weren't in her repertoire. When her internal clock switched off, she was done for the day. Period.

If, after Mom went to bed, her sleep was disrupted, she pouted the next morning, throwing barbs like, "If *someone* hadn't woke me up at *eleven* o'clock, I *might* be in a better mood." I can't say that she was wholly self-absorbed or inattentive. She was merely inflexible.

My mother fed, clothed, and for the most part, monitored her children. She didn't lock us in closets or beat us with a shovel or send us to school soiled and barefoot—in pajamas, yes, but never without shoes. She didn't pass out drunk or accidentally torch our house with a forgotten cigarette, and to her credit, she never shot anyone. For those qualities and more, I remained grateful. Still, I approached her the way I would a porcupine.

Mom wasn't a hugger. I couldn't recall her touch, yet as an infant I must have experienced it. My mother shied from physical contact and delivered no attaboy pats or praiseful squeezes. Seldom did I extend my arms to her because hers didn't reach back.

Perhaps my father's late-night visits were his way of giving me what I couldn't get from my mother. I figured nothing was wrong with that. Every child deserved to be hugged.

In the quiet moments before sleep, my guilty conscience countered, *You're a thief. You're stealing what belongs to your mother and brothers.* I shushed that irritating voice. Mentally, I justified being Dad's favorite, an irresistibly selfish role, but a whisper warned, *Beware.*

EIGHT

I F ASKED, MY FATHER MIGHT have described himself as an amalgam of Clark Gable, Cary Grant, Don Juan, and maybe Dracula. I couldn't guess what inspired his inflated self-image. He was vertically challenged (five foot four), portly, and prematurely balding. But when photographed at family events, he would smile seductively and make devil eyes at the camera. His antics suggested he'd been born a ladies' man, an irreversible plight in which he was hopelessly ensnared.

Everyone, including his four children, was invited to join him in the gutter where he kept a permanent residence. Routinely, he regaled his family with jokes and anecdotes fraught with inappropriate remarks. The countless lewd stories he told seemingly did not affect my mother. Either she didn't understand his innuendos, or she pretended not to. Her silence made me feel I should offer a comeback to my father's suggestive commentaries. The best I ever managed was a begrudged sigh.

Neither my dad's sexual fixations nor his temper prevented him from becoming a church deacon. No one outside our home was aware of his lecherous alter ego. But one night, during a Bible study at Steve and Pansy White's house, Dad must have slipped and broken character.

The following Sunday, after church service ended, Steve flagged down Dad as our station wagon backed from the parking lot. Seated directly behind the driver's seat, I sulked. I could think of nothing but the doughnuts Dad had promised to pick up on our way home. He shifted the Rambler into Park and lowered his window, guaranteeing no choices would be left when we arrived at Willy May's Bakery.

Before Steve spoke, he grabbed my father's necktie and yanked hard. Dad's head swerved through the open window. His face glowed scarlet as he gasped for air.

Stunned, my mom, brothers, and I froze.

"If you ever say another word to my wife, I'll *kill* you," Steve snarled. With that, he let go of the formal accessory he'd used to almost strangle his fellow deacon and strode off.

Dad sped away, one hand loosening his shirt collar as he drove. No one spoke for several minutes.

I recalled Steve's wife, Pansy, a petite gal built like Jane Mansfield. It was reasonable to assume Dad had said something inappropriate to her. Nonetheless, witnessing someone threaten my father's life enraged me. I wanted to tell Steve he'd better back off because I knew where he lived.

"I don't know what's gotten into him," Dad said when he recovered his composure.

Steve had purposely waited to attack when Dad was trapped inside his vehicle. The more I dwelled on it, the more I wished I had pushed open my car door and yanked Steve backward by his shirt collar. I fantasized about pummeling him until he lost consciousness.

My father's infatuation with women's breasts made me wonder why he had chosen a flat-chested wife. At home, he had few opportunities to ogle his favorite part of the female anatomy. He improvised by remarking on movie stars', church members', strangers', and later, even my friends' bust sizes. "She sure can fill out a sweater," he would quip, or "Looks like she's hiding a few cantaloupes under there," or "Uh-oh, looks like she left her headlights on."

For the less fortunate, he would wisecrack, "She couldn't fill out a twenty-eight, triple-A bra," or "Looks like all the sand ran to the bottom of her hourglass." Most of the time, his remarks fell short of his victims' ears. My mother and I, though, heard all his unsolicited opinions. Mercifully, we were unable to divine his thoughts.

Sometimes he would provoke Mom by taunting, "You know, Nancy had big breasts." He could bend almost any conversation in that direction, but Mom never bit that hook.

She stayed silent on the topic until, one day, I dared to ask, "Who on God's green earth is Nancy?"

Mom cut her eyes at me. "She was his fiancée before we met."

At no time was my father's preoccupation with boobs more pronounced than when he watched beauty pageants. Listening to him, I thought he was vital to the Miss America contest. He assumed the position of a remote judge with veto power. From his easy chair, he critiqued the contestants, one by one, while the rest of our family watched the spectacle with waning interest.

I paid more attention to Dad's reaction to Miss America candidates than I did to who won the crown. The room's energy vibrated to a climax during the swimsuit competition, when my father all but panted. Mom ignored him and his heavy breathing.

Studying the hopeful competitors, I prayed God would bless

me with a bustline. It seemed my mother's lack of one had relegated her to the sidelines. *Maybe*, I consoled myself, *a gal could inherit her breast size from her father.* Mom's profile gave me no promise. I didn't want my future husband fantasizing about other women's figures the way my dad did. And I was naïve enough to believe an ounce of cleavage equaled a pound of prevention.

My mother's physique could best be described as malnourished, though to my knowledge, she suffered no eating disorders. Possibly she was as unenthused with sloppy joes as I was. Even after birthing four children, her body looked like a twelve-year-old's. By the time I'd turned eleven, she and I could share each other's wardrobe—though she showed no enthusiasm for mine.

Despite her gaunt appearance, Dad expected her to emulate Elizabeth Taylor. Ever hopeful, he bought her a black negligée with a satin ribbon woven through its coquettish neckline. Snooping through Mom's lingerie drawer, I admired the elaborate negligée. I'd learned of the nightie's existence by overhearing conversations about it.

Night after night, Dad plied Mom, "Why won't you wear it?"

"Because I might have to get up," she whined.

Their voices spiraled until he would surrender, grumble, and fall asleep.

One night, Mom must have caved and worn the negligée to bed—a move Dad mistook for foreplay. I didn't yet understand the meaning of that word or the gown, but I knew disputes always followed Mom's utterances of the word "no." On this particular night, I heard her shout, "Stop it!"

A brief silence fell, then Mom cried out, "Now look what you've done. You've ripped my gown!"

The thought of Dad destroying my mother's beautiful negligée made me melancholy. That frilly gown with the satin ribbon and ruffled hem would never be mine to fondle again. I lay as still as a corpse, imagining the crime scene.

In the adjacent room, I could hear Mom sobbing. Softly I blubbered too. *Why would he ruin the gown he's been begging her to wear for weeks?* Maybe he was punishing her for nonperformance, the way he had his Renault. I wondered if he planned to trade her in for a better make and model, one with larger breasts and fewer boundaries. With both hands, I pulled my covers tight around my neck. If Dad was mad enough to rip Mom from her bedclothes, I feared what he might do to me.

<hr />

Obsession with breasts, I soon learned, wasn't unique to Dad. Boys in my fifth-grade class gravitated to the early bloomers. All girls, it seemed, were divided into two types: those who wore brassieres and those who didn't. By pinching backs and popping bra straps, the young bucks decided who to chase and who to ignore. I offered them nothing to grab. Like some cheesy magic trick, with one quick brush of a hand, my popularity with the opposite sex vanished overnight.

I appealed to my mother for help, though I should have known better. "I want a bra," I said to her one day after school. My request was apropos of nothing we had discussed.

She looked at me like I'd asked for a garter belt. "Why?"

"Because all the other girls in my class have them." I hoisted the Sears catalog from an adjacent end table and flipped to the junior girls' section. "I get teased."

"Do they make bras in your size?" she asked without a hint of snark.

I pointed to an image of a headless model. The unidentified torso showcased a possibility, a white band of soft, pliable cotton described as a "training bra." The accompanying description suggested my breasts needed guidance to grow uniformly. Like morning glories attached to a trellis, my boobs needed proper support to achieve a desirable shape.

It sounded like hooey to me. All I cared about was the bra's back strap—the more prominent, the better. Mom appeared to mull over my request. If she made a decision, she withheld it.

That evening, Dad took his seat at one end of our dining table, and Mom claimed hers opposite him.

Between bites of Salisbury steak and rehydrated peas, she blurted, "Diana wants to get her first bra." She said it without pretext, all but asking for permission to buy my puberty.

Until then, I hadn't considered my hormonal growth elective. *Why's she even talking to him about this?* Dad had no expertise as a ladies' underwear consultant. Somehow this oh-so-private matter had become a casual table topic. Heat emanated from my neck and face.

Dad looked up from his TV dinner and regarded me for several seconds. I stared into my instant potatoes.

"Mary Ann," he replied, straight-faced, "you don't buy a doghouse if you don't own a dog."

My father and schoolmates had assigned me to the same category—boobless.

I was too angry to feel demoralized. Dad could be snide all he wanted. I wasn't done with the subject. It was Friday night, and he'd mentioned a morning trip to Sears. While he studied power tools, I would divert Mom's attention to the girls' underwear section. If I begged loudly enough, I might guilt her into a purchase. "Puh-leeze, Mom. I really *need* a bra. I'm the *only* girl in my class who doesn't have one," I would say within earshot of a salesclerk. I'd had plenty of training on how to use shame to my advantage.

But on Saturday, on the way to Sears, a carload of teenage boys derailed my mission. Stopped at a traffic light, the guys in the vehicle next to us lowered their windows. As the light turned green, one kid pulled down his pants and waggled his bare buttocks at us. The car raced ahead, its occupants chortling at our alarmed expressions. I couldn't see my mother's face, but her jaw must have dropped.

"Johnny! Johnny!" Mom cried. "Get their license plate!" She meant "get the license plate *number*." In a dither, she couldn't find her words.

"Why?" Dad asked.

I giggled, having never before seen a grown man's rump.

Rifling through her purse to find a pen and paper, Mom shook like she'd been stricken with palsy. "You can't let them get away with that. They might *rape* somebody."

Any scantily clad man was a potential rapist by Mom's definition. News reports of college boys streaking through a crowded stadium five states away sent her racing to secure our front door. Dad smirked and accelerated, toying with Mom. At the next traffic signal, we regained sight of the mooning bandits.

"There it is," Dad said, pointing to the license plate. "Now what do you want me to do with it?"

Mom scribbled the number on a lozenge wrapper. Pinching the paper between one thumb and forefinger, she gave Dad a sour look.

Inside Sears, my mother practically tackled the first store clerk she saw. "Where's the nearest pay phone?" she demanded.

The lady behind the candy counter probably thought a purse

snatcher was on the loose. The gal dropped a scooper full of cashews and pointed to an aisle.

Dad gave Mom a bemused look. "You're not really going to report that guy, are you?"

Six steps ahead of him, she said, "You better believe I am."

Intrigued, I followed Mom to a pay phone where she deposited a dime and dialed the Dallas Police Department. "No. I don't have their location," she said into the receiver. "But they passed us on Preston Road, with their pants down! Near Sears."

I imagined the ruckus on the other end of that line. Mom likely didn't care whether police apprehended the *mooner*. She'd reported the atrocity and defended her dignity. Her nerves, though, wouldn't settle for hours. She ended the call and marched off, both arms pressing her purse to her abdomen. I didn't dare ask her for anything as risqué as a training bra.

NINE

As if I hadn't suffered enough embarrassment already, when I entered fifth grade, in 1965, Dad instructed Mom to register me for the free school lunch program. Every kid in my class knew who paid for lunches and who didn't. I couldn't understand why I was on the charity list. The prior summer, our household had been the first in the neighborhood to acquire a color television.

Dad had brought the new TV home with its retail price scrawled in white shoe polish across the picture tube: $610. My daily lunch subsidy equaled thirty-five cents, which meant my free lunches would pay for our entertainment upgrade in roughly six years. The contradictions were impossible to overlook, even as an eleven-year-old.

It didn't take long for word of our high-tech TV to spread through the community. My friends reported to their parents, "Breaking news: Diana's family is watching *Get Smart*, *Bonanza*, and *Batman* in *color*."

Soon, neighbors we barely knew were visiting us during prime time. Miss Myers, who thought nothing of arriving in her white-eyelet shorty pajamas, was among several uninvited guests. Mom was unnerved by all the company—and exceptionally so by Miss Myers.

The neighborhood siren and recent divorcee drove a convertible Chevy and kept her bouffant hair bleached platinum. At times, her makeup outweighed her clothing. Once, when I had visited her nine-year-old daughter, Linda, Miss Myers strutted past me in a pair of white bikini panties and a push-up bra. I'd never before seen anything like that.

My mother favored conical-shaped bras and high-rise undies, which I witnessed exclusively on laundry day. She lounged indoors in a ratty pink-and-white floral-print housedress that billowed at the waist and covered her knobby knees. The skimpiest garment she owned was a seldom-used maillot swimsuit with a modesty panel.

I wished my mother could be more like Linda's.

Miss Myers might not have been fit to teach Sunday school, but she would have made a great reality TV star. Considerably fashion-forward, the thirtysomething-year-old had a figure to envy and a wardrobe to match. Mom suspected she was a stripper. "The Sexpot," as my mother nicknamed her, rarely left home during daylight hours other than to get her roots dyed. Her closets overflowed with spiked high heels and scintillating eveningwear. I loved visiting her house because she let Linda and me play dress-up in her best shoes and ball gowns.

Miss Myers, who exuded sexuality and self-confidence, was everything my mother wasn't. Minus her annoying habits and saucy language, I wanted to be exactly like her.

That summer, when Miss Myers began sunbathing topless behind her six-foot-tall cedar fence, I alerted my friends. It was the most scandalous and interesting gossip I could share. Like wildfire, the news leapt from child to child, household to household. My parents were the last to hear of Miss Myers's latest impropriety.

"She's out there, sunbathing on her picnic table, naked," I announced one night during supper.

"How do you know that?" Dad's eyebrows tented.

"We can see her from the top of our swing set," I said.

Alan and Kerry giggled and nodded. My brothers and I had whispered and laughed at Miss Myers's partial nudity. If we could spot *her*, I reasoned, she could see *us*. No one had asked me to be the Decency Police, of course, but I'd volunteered.

Mom shook her head in disgust. "Then *stop* climbing on top of the swing set."

Not too long after that, Dad replaced our shingled roof. Rather than hire a roofer, he provided the labor. Parts of the job he assigned to me.

While I was hammering roofing nails into asphalt, I accidentally struck my left thumb. "Owwwww!" I cried, pain radiating through my hand and wrist.

Dad glanced at me and sniggered. "Hit the wrong nail?"

His remark infuriated me. I was up on that hot roof to assist him, not to be made fun of. When I caught him staring off into Miss Myers's backyard, I sneered. If he was hoping for a peep show, he wouldn't get one. Her picnic table displayed no breasts that day. I'd already checked.

———— ◦✧◦ ————

Within a few months, our TV novelty wore off and neighbors returned to their old viewing habits. Dad had tired of keeping his britches on indoors, anyway. He preferred hanging out in front of the tube in his boxers. Though I expected life to return to normal—or our distorted version of it—Miss Myers continued showing up unannounced.

DIANA ESTILL

One evening, the bombshell arrived half-dressed in one of her shorty pajama getups. "Can I borrow a hammer?" She fingered her puffy bangs.

Still dressed in his work attire, Dad practically tripped over his scuffed oxfords to grant her request. I heard him stumbling through the garage, searching for what he normally would have ordered me to find. He owned four hammers—a claw hammer, a ball-peen hammer, a tack hammer, and a rubber hammer. Seldom could he locate a single one without my help. Born legally blind in one eye, he became sightless in the garage.

Miss Myers waited inside our living room, simpering, while Dad picked through his tools. Sporting a pair of pedal pushers and a button-up blouse, Mom turned a cold shoulder to her. The two women gave each other a disapproving once-over, casting insults with their eyes.

"Home-wrecker!"

"Hag."

"Man-teaser!"

"Sex repellent."

From the garage, my father appeared with his best hammer—the one with the black rubber handle and heftiest weight. Mom sniffed and gave him a what-the-hell look.

The next day, Mom told me to tell Linda to inform her mother that, unless she was fully dressed, she was unwelcome at our house. It was a circuitous way to convey her displeasure, but Mom avoided direct confrontations. When she was upset with my schoolteachers, she made me deliver handwritten messages—a distressing exercise. My teachers had better things to do with their time than draft replies to my reclusive mom. That was what parent-teacher night was for, they curtly reminded me.

To Mrs. Rogers, the school superintendent's wife, Mom had

written, "Please quit keeping Diana after school. I worry when she arrives home late."

Mrs. Rogers had detained me every school day for two weeks before Mom had questioned my delinquency. My third-grade teacher had kept me after school to rewrite poems. She didn't explain what was wrong with my original, though I'm sure I was no Robert Frost.

"Write it again," she would command, scratching a red mark through my paper each time I offered her a new draft.

Mom's note to Mrs. Rogers only annoyed her. She kept me after class for several more days. Eventually, though, I managed to so insult her literary tastes that she released me from poetry prison. By then, Mom had moved on to indirectly addressing other frustrations, such as Miss Myers's continued disregard for family-friendly apparel.

Three weeks after the neighborhood sex kitten borrowed Dad's hammer, I returned home from school to someone wailing. Mom lay in her bed, bawling like a sick calf.

"What happened?" I braced for news of a car accident or deceased relative.

With one hand, she covered her face and mumbled, "That *Myers* woman."

I set down my schoolbooks. "What about her?" *Did the harlot run off with Dad?* She flirted with my father every time she saw him, and he egged her on. I'd been anticipating a catfight between the two women.

"She cursed me out." Mom buried her head in her pillow.

I recalled the roundabout message she'd sent Miss Myers through me and Linda. "Why'd she do *that*?"

Mom lifted her face and sucked in a breath. "She brought the hammer back. Then she said, 'It's not my problem, you know, if your husband likes my legs.'"

I didn't wait to hear the rest of the story. Before I'd even noticed my feet had left home, I stood on Miss Myers's front porch. With conviction, I knocked on her front door.

The vixen answered my angry knock, her lacy underwear exposed through a sheer robe. Before she could say any nasty words, I blurted something along the lines of, "If you ever cuss at my mother again, I'll come over here and use that hammer on your *head*!" Hoping I'd scared some sense into her, I clomped away before she could respond.

She must have thought I was as peculiar as my mother.

That next summer, in 1966, I begged to accessorize the neon-print dresses Mom had sewn for me by adding go-go boots, the latest in fashion footwear. Several of my fifth-grade classmates wore those stylish white boots with a back zipper. Owning a pair might secure my sixth-grade *cool* status, I decided. I didn't want to be classified again as an *undesirable*. I'd graduated to a bra, but for all I knew, boots could be the next reputation essential.

"I want a pair of those," I said to Mom, pointing to a *Hullabaloo* dancer's feet on the TV screen.

She glanced up from her ironing board. Through pop-bottle-thick lenses, Mom examined what I craved more than a Barbie doll figure. "You can't have those. We're Baptist."

"What's that got to do with it?"

"Those are *dancing* boots."

Our minister condemned dancing as one of the "devil's many temptations." Mom had taken his denunciation to the furthest extreme. Her rigid moral code, I feared, would prevent me from ever being *hip*. She returned to scorching Dad's dress shirt while I simmered.

My mother had suffered polio as a child, which caused her to lack normal balance. For her, kitten heels were a fall threat. Boots portended a wheelchair. Hence, I had Mom's equilibrium *and* my assigned religion to blame for being *square*.

When it came to ladies' fashion, Dad was the more astute parent. His expertise, though, was confined to ladies' lingerie— the kind my mother wouldn't wear.

On my parents' thirteenth wedding anniversary, Dad gave Mom a box of chocolates and a small package I hoped contained a diamond necklace. For once, he'd remembered the date and even bought a gift-wrapped present that looked too little to hold a negligée.

"You probably want to open that later," he advised Mom.

She set the gift-wrapped box in her bedroom and unsealed it after I was in bed. Our open-door household, however, hid few secrets. From my bedroom, that night, I overheard my parents' lively exchange.

"You bought me bikini underwear?" Mom asked, her voice sharp.

Yes! Maybe she'll buy me some too.

"What's wrong with that?" Dad sounded hurt.

"You've lost your mind. Who do you think I am? Brigitte Bardot?"

That name doesn't ring a bell. Sounds French and oo-la-la!

"Nobody's going to see you in them," Dad persisted.

Yup, you're right about that!

"They sure *won't*," Mom said.

I heard a dresser drawer open and slam. From the sound of it, she'd banished the provocative panties and any thought of ever wearing them. Dad's reign extended only so far. Nobody breached Mom's lingerie drawer. Except me. Dying to see how I would look in bikini panties, I set a mental reminder to locate that underwear.

Almost twelve, my body lagged my mind's maturity. I was too

busy devouring the written word to detect my physical changes. In fifth grade, I'd won a library award for reading fifty books. With school closed for summer, I had no access to literature. The city library did not yet exist. Mom didn't read books, and Dad's only literary interest was *National Geographic* magazine. All the elongated breast pictures in those issues kept me from perusing his periodicals.

Out of boredom, I had delved into our home edition of Funk & Wagnalls. Though the encyclopedias held my interest, I considered them poor substitutes for *The Black Stallion*.

The same tedium that drove me to read reference books compelled me to find those bikini undies. I waited to snoop until Dad was at work and Mom was grocery shopping. She'd asked me to go with her and The Boys to the A&P store. But I had said I would rather finish the "L" volume I was working through than stare at canned goods. I was geeky and bookish enough to make that sound convincing.

I listened to the Rambler back from our driveway before making a beeline for Mom's dresser. Rummaging through her granny panties, I found the lurid treasure. The double-layered nylon glided through my fingers as smoothly as cream rinse. Admiring the briefs, I noted the underwear looked exactly like the ones I'd seen Miss Myers model.

Shamelessly, I ditched my denim shorts, stripped off my little-girl cotton undies, and shimmied into forbidden territory. Standing on my parents' mattress, opposite their dresser mirror, I studied my image. Underneath the loose clothing I'd worn all summer, I had sprouted hips. Like green shoots heralding a daffodil's debut, that underwear announced my puberty. The sensual briefs fit me perfectly.

TEN

MOM AND DAD QUARRELED ALL morning. I poked my head past my bedroom doorframe and looked both ways before scurrying to my brothers' room. Maybe there'd be safety in numbers.

I found Mom sniveling on a twin bed. The three boys played on the floor next to her. Oblivious to her despair, they mimicked murdering each other with cap guns that hardly ever worked. Unsure what to do, I slid into bed with Mom and hugged her. She didn't acknowledge me. Though I couldn't name the source of her sadness, I suspected my mother's pain stemmed from Dad's mercurial moods. Her primary defense was withdrawal, which didn't always work.

When Dad sparred with Mom, typically, he would flip his kill switch and nap for hours. While he slept, Mom would cry herself dry. Then they'd revive, pretend nothing had happened, and go about the rest of their day. That was the optimal resolution.

At times, though, rage generated in my father an astonishing urge to destroy beloved items. Previously, he'd taken scissors to Mom's lingerie, smashed her wedding china, and discarded the family dog. During a mental meltdown, he'd simply driven off with our border collie one afternoon and returned without it. We never saw the pooch again. Consequently, when Dad threw a tantrum, his family sought cover.

Hunkered down in my brothers' room, I didn't know where Dad lurked inside the house or what he might do next.

Dozing off, I heard my father's footsteps.

Steadily he advanced, calling, "Oh, Mary A-n-n," his voice threatening.

I gulped. If I'd had any place to run, I would have pumped my legs to get there.

Dad stood in the doorway, blocking the only exit. Clasping my mother's bird tree in one claw, he lifted the ceramic fixture to his highest reach. The delicate fowl hovered precariously above the linoleum floor.

Mom bolted to a seated posture. I mirrored her and held my breath. Time slowed the way it does during a car crash.

Dad opened his fist. The tree dropped like a payload of dirt, exploding into multicolored shards.

"You *monster*!" Mom shrieked.

My brothers stared in confusion at the broken glass surrounding them. Possibly they thought the slip had been an accident, but I was old enough to register the hatred and negligence involved. I detested the meanness that consumed my father, loathed the way he bullied my mother and traumatized his children. He seemed possessed by satanic forces.

Yet, like other children dependent on their parents for protection, I rejected thoughts of endangerment. It was easier to believe in an imaginary, safe world than to accept a contradictory reality. I clung to the hope that one day the demons inside my father would disappear. Then the family-sitcom dad controlled by evil spirits would be freed.

Shortly after my father destroyed the bird tree, I met Glenn, a thirteen-year-old hipster who lived four doors from me. Obsessed with Monopoly, he was searching for a board game and dance partner near his age. Almost twelve, I was looking for a cute boy to flirt with. His tight pants, surfer shirts, and Beatle boots immediately impressed me. In his dining room, the freckle-faced, chestnut-haired Glenn taught me how to dance the twist, swim, and Freddie.

When we tired of shuffling our feet to Chubby Checker music, Glenn and I battled over Park Place and New York Avenue and Reading Railroad cards like young tycoons. I soon became a regular tenant at his house, though I never invited him to mine. The only games played at my dining table were emotional ones, and dancing was strictly forbidden. Escaping to Glenn's house provided the balance I needed.

One summer afternoon, Glenn's mom, Dorothy, asked if he and I might like to attend a matinee—*The Trouble with Angels*, starring Hayley Mills. Probably, she wanted to get us out of her hair. We eagerly abandoned our real estate holdings for a trip to the movies.

Before we left, I called home from Glenn's phone to ask permission to attend the show.

"As long as you're home before supper and Dorothy's paying," Mom said, "I suppose you can go."

I had assumed Dorothy planned to watch the show with us, but I was wrong. She drove to the theater entrance, let Glenn and me out, and told us to have a good time. Maybe she went shopping for a few hours. She didn't explain.

Inside the theater, I sat on a burgundy velvet seat next to Glenn, aching to hold his hand. Nonchalantly, when the lights dimmed, I inched my forearm onto the chair rest between us and waited for him to make the next move. He ignored my veiled offer.

What felt like fifteen minutes passed. My forearm fell asleep, forcing me to resituate. Glenn didn't notice that either. His eyes were transfixed on Hayley. Everything about her was adorable, from her wheat-blond hair to her pouty lips and perfect teeth.

The movie was entertaining, but Hayley's looks annoyed me. I couldn't copycat her idolized image any better than I'd imitated Shirley Temple's smile years earlier. Already, my hair had darkened to an ash color. My eyebrows looked like a seagull's silhouette. My Irish-green eyes would never be as captivating as Hayley's crystal-blue peepers. My teeth were so unhealthy that, at my first dental appointment, I had lost a molar to abscess. The longer I stared at Hayley Mills, the more I disliked myself. Halfway through the feature, I was ready to leave.

Glenn's mom was waiting for us at the exit when the movie ended. "Was it great?" she asked.

"Yeah!" Glenn answered for both of us, his hands stuffed deep inside his pockets.

At home that evening, Dad asked me, "What'd you do today?" Our family sat gathered around the dining table, where such inquisitions were standard.

Before I could answer Mom chimed, "She went to the movies with Glenn."

Dad extracted a bread slice from a loaf package, bypassing pieces near the opening. "Was his mother with them?"

Mom's eyes answered for her.

"She dropped us off and picked us up after the show," I interjected.

Solemnly, my mother shook her head. "I didn't know that."

Dad pointed his fork at me. "You're too young to be going on *dates*."

Later that night, beneath my covers, Dad nuzzled up close. "So, what happened at the movies with Glenn? Did you hold hands?"

I pulled my top sheet to my chin. "No."

"Did he kiss you?"

"No."

"Did you want him to?" He moved his face closer to my nape. I could feel his warm breath when he spoke.

"No!"

"Okay. I just wondered. You don't need to get all mad." He pulled free of my bed linens and left my room.

I stopped visiting Glenn after that. Our courtship held no promise. From what I'd seen on TV, dates involved hand-holding and shared sodas and secret conversations. Glenn had offered me none of that. He only wanted a dance and board game partner, and that wasn't enough to justify the scrutiny he'd sparked. Besides, I'd already lost him to Hayley.

<hr/>

To the many ambush theatrics Dad deployed around this time, he added a particularly distressing one after I "broke up" with Glenn. One day, when I wasn't looking, he sneaked up and bear-hugged me from behind. I'd been standing in the hallway, searching for something in the storage closet. Executing a two-stage move, Dad twirled me in his arms.

"What are you doing?" I screeched. "Let me go!"

He gave a fiendish laugh and dipped me backward as if putting the final flourish on a ballroom dance routine. Holding me in a simulated lover's embrace, Dad passionately kissed me.

His slobbery lips ground against mine. I thought I tasted blood. I fought to free myself from his python grip. But the harder I resisted, the tighter he squeezed. I couldn't move, couldn't breathe. Succumbing to defeat, I went limp. Finally, he released me.

Mom shook her head. She sauntered past us as though we were two kids scuffling.

"Yuck!" I yelled, wiping my mouth on my arm to remove his cooties.

The kissing stunt became Dad's signature move, one he confined to places that afforded him a passive audience. He never initiated the so-called joke anywhere he might be called out for it. This number he reserved for family. Holiday gatherings, in particular, were his favorite times to humiliate me in front of kin.

I took responsibility for my father's smack attacks. For two years, I'd been letting him snuggle with me in bed. I hadn't asked him to cool it or leave my room. *What did you expect? Why did you let it get this out of hand?* I didn't know how to make him stop.

In actuality, I had no authority over my room, my bed, or my body. My father owned me, and his Lover Boy Move was my reminder. I'd done nothing to deserve his violating behaviors. He was wholly responsible, though it would be years before I accepted that fact.

The first, second, and maybe tenth time my grandfather witnessed one of Dad's smooch assaults, he bellowed, "Now, Johnny, you know it's not right to kiss your *daughter* like that! That's how you kiss your *wife*!"

It had no effect. Dad was made of Teflon. Accusations and reprimands hurled at him never stuck. He merely giggled as if he'd been caught sneaking a cookie before supper and went right on doing as he pleased. To my grandfather, Dad delivered a wily "he-he-he-he-he." His laugh implied he had hoodwinked us all.

At a younger age, Grandpa might have shoulder-tackled Dad for forcefully kissing me. But the three-hundred-pound fifty-six-year-old had lost his agility and spunk. He must have slipped some in the memory department, too, because my father didn't kiss my mom in public—ever. I couldn't recall when I'd last seen him give her so much as a peck. What transpired between me and Dad didn't occur in his marriage.

ELEVEN

MY FATHER ANNOUNCED HE PLANNED to build our next house all by himself. He had, by that point, constructed a brick patio, a recessed sandbox, and a cement splash pool without assistance. The patio rippled like a boardwalk. Stray cats used the open sandbox. And because Dad had omitted a pump and filter, the kiddie pool had become a tadpole pond. Naturally, when I learned he'd purchased ten acres and a manual cement mixer, I predicted trouble. Like that couple in the TV series *Green Acres*, our family would be moving from the suburbs to the country with or without my approval.

"You were going to change schools next year, anyway," Dad said to me. "What's the big deal?"

The big deal was that I had anticipated entering junior high in my current school system, alongside students I had known since first grade. The tract Dad had purchased sat in an alternate school district, one lifted from the pages of a Laura Ingalls Wilder novel. Classrooms in that rural town featured walls of crank-style windows that half opened. The school buildings lacked air conditioning, which sounded like hell on earth. In our area, triple-digit temperatures often hung around through mid-September.

To make matters worse, my new school's dress code required me to wear church attire in class. No shorts, culottes, pedal pushers, jeans, slacks, or T-shirts were permitted. I noted no mention of swimwear.

At first, I had threatened to run away if Dad made me move to the boonies. That had only amused him.

"Can I get a pony? I'll go if you'll buy me a pony," I bartered.

"You don't have a choice." Dad laughed. "I can move you anywhere, anytime I want. You're my daughter."

As chipper as a quokka, he drove me, Mom, and my brothers to see the property he'd purchased. "Here we are, kids!" Dad parked the car next to a stretch of featureless land. "Y'all hop out."

We did as instructed but couldn't set foot on the acreage. A four-by-five-foot drainage ditch separated the tract from the white rock road where we stood.

"The house'll be back there." He indicated nothing I could anchor. "Opposite that big tree," Dad pinpointed.

The live oak he'd identified was a good fifty yards from where I stood. Later, I learned that tree was a boundary post. Our new home would stand on the wrong side of that monument, forcing my school switcheroo.

"Will the house be finished in time for school?" I asked, hoping it wouldn't be. Maybe I could squeeze another half year or so with my friends.

Dad gave me an indignant look. "Of course. It doesn't take that long to build a house if you know what you're doing. I've had the blueprints for years." He tapped an index finger to his forehead.

My brothers scuffed their shoes against loose rocks and lobbed stones into the ravine next to us, making splashes in the stagnant water.

"How will we get to the house?" I asked.

"Easy. We're going to build a bridge," Dad said as if talking to an experienced road crew.

I looked to Mom for confirmation. Smiling at her imagined dreamhouse, she offered no qualms.

My brothers, ages three, six, and seven, were too young to enlist in Dad's ambitious endeavor. I couldn't conceive how I would learn bridge construction skills in less than a month. But I didn't need to. Like the house, Dad claimed he had the project psychically engineered.

"It's not that big a deal. I'll walk you through it," he reassured.

Within a week, he'd built the wooden forms, installed rebar, and relocated his concrete mixer to the jobsite. He didn't call a cement company and schedule a delivery date like most people would have done. Instead, he relied on nonmotorized equipment that had to be churned like an ice cream freezer to convert cement and rock and water into semipermanent structures.

Nothing made of cement lasts forever. With time, concrete cracks and deteriorates under stress—much like human emotions.

On Bridge Day, our family arrived at the construction site under overcast skies. Ahead of any rain, we needed to complete the car-length culvert.

"Wear some shoes you don't mind ruining," Dad had instructed in advance.

My mother had arrived in culottes, a short-sleeve cotton blouse, and a pair of soiled white nurse shoes, the kind she preferred for stability and comfort. She didn't look one bit like a day laborer. My attire, denim cutoffs, a sleeveless T-shirt, and some worn-out sneakers, appeared equally ill-suited for the job.

I didn't own any rubber galoshes, the proper footwear for cement work. I'd been provided no goggles, hat, or sunscreen.

Dad declared those protections unnecessary. Hats would fall off. Goggles would obstruct vision. Sunscreen was pointless, he said, stressing, "It's overcast."

According to Dad's calculations, we were on schedule and in the clear. Spinning the orange mixer barrel by its handle, he churned the slurry and poured the blend from a wheelbarrow into wooden forms. Afterward, Mom and I leveled the gray slop with a hoe and trowel. It would have been useless to argue with him. Like the Pied Piper's victims, we foolishly followed Dad to our potential peril.

The Boys waited, roadside, while Mom and I obeyed Dad's rapid-fire orders. Against the clock and skies, we toiled in high gear. My arms ached from repeated troweling motions. I'd been at it for three hours when Dad warned me, "You can't stop. Concrete sets up fast."

Already, temperatures had plunged. Warm air gave way to cool gusts, warning us of approaching thunderstorms.

Mom brushed a lock of hair from her eyes and pointed to the clouds. "We need to get going soon."

Dad spun the mixer and pretended not to hear her.

Precipitation fell, first as a drizzle, then steady drumming.

"Hurry up and level that spot there," Dad barked at Mom.

She combed the hoe through the section he'd indicated.

Lightning split the sky.

"Johnny, we need to go," Mom insisted.

Already, my brothers had sought shelter in the station wagon. I sloshed through the ravine, troweling the bridge between glances at ominous clouds.

Dad approached with a wheelbarrow of fresh concrete. Lowering the handles, he glowered at Mom. "Look, there *is* no stopping. We're going to be here 'til this is finished. You *got* that?"

Lightning struck, again, this time closer. The thunderclap shook the ground so hard my heart quivered. I startled and checked Mom. She bawled and pushed, bawled and pulled, bawled and pushed her hoe through the muck.

Skin peeked through my rain-soaked shirt, but I would not cry. No, no, no. I would not act like my mother. Sobbing never engendered Dad's pity. My father's jaw clenched, and his forehead creased. His body language confirmed it would take more than inclement weather to defeat him.

"Ow!" Mom cried. She'd slipped and tumbled into the liquid concrete and struck her hoe blade. Below a four-inch gash, a rivulet of red snaked from her left shin.

Dad threw dagger eyes at her. "What's the matter with you?" His scowl suggested he would sooner let her bleed out than declare a work stoppage. Cranking the mixer faster, he ignored Mom's wound.

She smoothed her hands over her injured leg, flicked concrete from the gash, and resumed hoeing.

"She's *hurt*!" I yelled at Dad, modulating past the thunder. If she wouldn't speak up for herself, I would be her mouthpiece. We'd done our best and had nothing more to give. If mutiny was the only option, then I was all in.

Pausing the mixer, Dad stared silently at me for several seconds. I feared he might rip me a new orifice. Never before had I shouted at him. I'd blurted my concern for Mom before I'd assessed the consequences. Still, I wasn't afraid. If a beating was necessary to stop this insanity, I was ready to suffer one.

At last, Dad spoke. "Y'all get in the car. I'll finish."

I didn't wait to be told twice. Mom and I made a hasty exit, leaving him to finish the job alone—or suffer electrocution, whichever occurred first. Mentally, I withdrew my request for a pony. When I joined my brothers in the station wagon, I vowed to never work on another project with Dad. But he had many more do-it-yourself plans for me and Mom, none of which required my consent.

Mom's passive aggression must have glommed onto me because I took guilty pleasure in watching Dad's plans go awry. I would be lying if I said I didn't snicker when, two months later, the bridge split down its center and collapsed.

The bridge failure wasn't the only fiasco my jack-of-all-trades father suffered. He should have known better, but he entrusted me to grout a shower surround.

"I asked the guy at the lumberyard"—Dad handed me a notebook-sized sponge—"and he said it was so easy, a kid could do it. So here you go."

Outdoors, it was about a hundred and ten degrees that July afternoon. Inside the windowless bathroom, it must have been closer to a hundred and twenty. Dad applied thinset to the shower walls before carefully positioning the twelve-by-twelve-inch tiles. The mosaic situated, he instructed me to smear grout over the walls, wait ten minutes, and sponge the surface clean. The result, he said, would leave rows of midnight-blue tiles separated by white gridlines. With no further discussion, he made a hasty exit to work on another project.

Using a float, I slathered the walls in double time. The job nearly finished, I wiped my brow and studied my handiwork. Underneath the chalk-colored goo, the blue tones had disappeared. It was time to sponge away the surface grout and expose the high-gloss squares.

I raked at one wall, near the point where I'd begun, but the putty had adhered to the tile the way paint sticks to glass. I scrubbed harder. Nothing dissolved or rinsed clean. My stomach knotted. *Did I let the grout dry too long?* Absent a watch, I had expected Dad to return when it was time to sponge the tiles. After all, I wasn't a sundial.

Heavy footsteps told me Dad was on his way to check my progress. I caught him staring at me from the bathroom doorway. "You're just now wiping those tiles?"

"It hasn't been ten minutes since I finished," I replied, pretending to know how much time had elapsed. From the looks of it, my internal stopwatch had malfunctioned.

"I didn't say ten minutes after you *finished*. I said ten minutes after you *started*." Dad shut his eyes and sucked in a breath. "You were supposed to do part of one wall, then sponge it, and then do the next section." He studied me as if I might have inhaled a few too many fumes. I didn't think grout contained any toxins, but the way he looked at me rang alarm bells.

I was no longer sure what he'd said. Maybe I hadn't thoroughly listened, or Dad had meant to explain but hadn't. Either way, I'd failed my duty to decipher his directions or intuit his thoughts.

He departed and returned with a wire brush. "Here,"— Dad handed me a wooden block with three-inch steel bristles— "you're going to need this."

Indeed I did because he didn't correct other people's mistakes. According to him, he never made errors. I'd screwed up, so I would have to fix my mess.

Every Saturday afternoon for seven months, I kept a standing date with that shower surround. In about equal time, we completed the house—six months *after* school started. In the interim, we camped indoors like we were vacationing in park shelters. That worked okay until winter arrived and subfreezing temperatures set in.

Bunked like campers and separated by dislocated furnishings, our family suffered through the first half of winter with nothing but two space heaters to discourage frostbite. We slept in an unfinished expanse above the garage, where Mom and Dad shared one glowing square of electrified heat and their four children crowded around the other. The unfinished main floor underwent completion on weekends.

The game room where we resided had three walls of windows offering a panoramic view of barren farmland. The single-pane glass didn't buffer the cold much. In December, when temperatures plummeted to seventeen degrees, I slept under a wool blanket in a flannel gown and two pairs of knee socks.

Between shivering and scratching, I entertained resentful thoughts. *What were they thinking? This isn't a family adventure. It's insanity.*

Anxiously, I awaited the heated school bus that transferred me and Alan and Kerry to school. Our house was the first stop on the bus route, so I claimed the bench seat nearest the heater. Alan and Kerry fell in behind me, kicking their feet forward to find warmer air. They never sat next to me despite ample room. My menacing glares discouraged their company.

I wasn't comfortable anywhere. At school, boys teased about my curly hair, bushy eyebrows, and scrawny figure. A gal named Reba made a habit of walking behind me between classes and shoving my textbooks from my side grip.

Once, my books had landed, facedown, in a muddy rut.

"Shove her hard and knock her down!" Dad said when I showed him my ruined textbook. "If you let people get away with stuff like that, they'll keep doing it." He studied me reprovingly. "If you don't stand up for yourself, nobody will."

I blotted a damp rag against the smudged pages, attempting to salvage my book.

"Your hair sure is getting *dark*," Mom observed for no apparent reason. She seemed stricken by a sudden urge to make me feel worse.

Frizzy brunette waves had replaced the straight blond mane that had once been my best feature. From a downy yellow duck, I'd turned into a drab mallard. I wanted to time travel back to fifth grade, to that year when I'd played Monopoly and danced the twist with Glenn and felt likable. Until I'd changed schools, I'd never been bullied or shunned. When they weren't taunting me, students in my seventh-grade class rarely spoke to me. Even worse, I didn't blame them.

<hr />

Every family member's winter garments hung from a rope clothesline strung twenty feet across the game room. A vacant section in the middle of that sagging curtain permitted passage from the makeshift den to the unisex bedroom. No interior walls or bathrooms existed on the second floor where we resided.

Mom and Dad seemed to fare better than I did in the communal arrangement. Sharing quarters with their children didn't appear to faze them. Maybe they adapted better than I did to discomforts. I turned thirteen inside what amounted to an overcrowded storage facility where nighttime urinary urges necessitated a flashlight-guided descent to an unfinished first floor. One of the two toilets downstairs was operable.

My living arrangements negated any elation I felt about becoming a teen. My situation seemed insufferable. I'd been relocated from a comfortable suburban home with central air and heat to one that offered neither. My childhood friends lived miles away and no longer waited for me every evening under a corner streetlight. Now we had no streetlights—or community.

Hiding between three chests of drawers and two double-stacked dressers to change clothing distressed me—as did a restroom with a four-inch-diameter hole where the doorknob should have been. I stuffed a washcloth in that void when I remembered to carry one with me. An overturned five-gallon bucket wedged behind the bathroom door served as my intruder alarm. Yet always I felt invisible eyes staring at me through shadowy crevices.

The television no longer had its own room either. When anyone switched on the set, the whole family was forced to listen. My father crowned himself the king of content, which might not have been so bad if he'd had normal viewing habits.

Adult programs weren't yet available, but Dad discovered a poor man's substitute. After nine p.m., the local public television station broadcasted British programs. The foreign shows weren't as censored as American ones, which all but guaranteed an occasional flash of breast or exposed derrière if he watched diligently enough.

To Dad's dismay, UHF—Ultra High Frequency—stations in our area lacked the transmission power to produce a good picture. After nine, when the British programs aired, UHF stations switched to reduced power. When Dad jumped from *Mission Impossible* to English lasses—or something that rhymed—the image scrambled.

"What on earth are you doing?" Mom asked the first time she noticed him peering at a bisected, muddled pictured. Dad told her he was watching a British flick. She twisted her neck and stared at the scrolling horizontal bars. "Oh, yeah? What's the title?" After that, she was wise to his deception.

In January, when we moved downstairs to our assigned bedrooms, the TV didn't come with us. The interior wasn't fully completed. My bedroom closet, like my brothers', remained unfinished. Open-faced studs greeted me when I entered to find my dresses.

"There's a rod in there to hang your clothes on," Dad said when I whined about the appearance. "It doesn't have to be pretty to work."

That first night in my new room, after everyone retired to their chambers, I shut my door and relished the silence. My door hardware had no lock, but after six months of sleeping in the same room with five family members, I was grateful for a partition.

Before I fell asleep, Dad opened what I couldn't secure. "Listen," he groused. "You're not allowed to close doors in this house."

"Why not?"

"You'll learn soon enough." He chortled as if he knew something I didn't. "The heat can't circulate when you shut the doors."

I didn't follow his reasoning. No heat source in our house projected beyond six feet.

While I'd been freezing upstairs in that game room, I had believed the situation temporary. But Dad had built our home without central air or heat—and the only gas connection powered the kitchen range. "We'll almost never have to buy propane," he'd bragged.

An attic fan in the main hallway and several box fans in bedroom windows cooled the otherwise well-appointed dwelling during summers. In the wintertime, ceiling-mounted bathroom heaters, portable space heaters, and a kitchen oven furnished our heat.

To warm our feet on frigid mornings, Mom baked our shoes inside her range. Empty stovetop burners flamed in the chilly kitchen while the broiler door yawned wide to exhale its fiery breath. Before school, my brothers and I took turns squatting next to the open broiler door. Seated on the floor, our arms extended and palms thrust forward, we thawed our fingers.

In a dining room corner, Dad built a fireplace that never hosted a single spark. The dark cavity centered on a wall of manila-colored brick stood like a memorial to his eccentrics.

"Why can't we use the fireplace?" I asked him.

"Wood's too expensive," he replied as if waiting for prices to lower. "And I'm not about to chop down what few trees we have."

"Why don't you buy wood and have it delivered?" I argued.

He gave me a condescending look. "I'm not shelling out money for something other people get for free." Folding his arms, he signaled his decision was final.

I returned his stupid expression. "Let's get some *free* firewood, then."

"You know where there is any?"

The argument ended with me admitting I did not.

That floor-to-ceiling brick fireplace had been built for one purpose, to appease Mom. She didn't care if the hearth ever housed a flame. She had a real, honest-to-goodness brick chimney, one Dad had designed and built to please her. Pride of ownership was enough to warm her spirits. My brothers and I, though, would have preferred real heat to a cold firebox.

TWELVE

S PRINGTIME BROUGHT RELIEF FROM COLD temperatures but not from Dad. We were farmers now, he said, and that meant rising early. In the city, I'd been used to leisurely waking on Saturdays to participate in craft ideas Mom had turned up. I don't know where she had found them. She showed us how to make tornadoes in jars of colored water. Sometimes she let us crystalize marbles in her oven or bake toy worms, called Creepy Crawlers, in goo-infused metal molds. Dad's weekend farm assignments, though, had ruined all that.

Like a drill sergeant, one Saturday morning, he marched into my bedroom. "Time to get up. It's seven thirty." With a flourish, Dad yanked my bed linens from my inert body.

Instinctively I tugged my nightgown from my waistline to my thighs to hide my panties.

"Got planting to do," he said before he disappeared.

He strutted into my brothers' bedroom, where he repeated his call to rise three more times.

I was in no rush to learn what awaited us that morning. He never ran out of weekend projects to keep his children busy. And unlike Mom's, his ideas were never fun. Dad's inventiveness was limited only by the materials at hand. When he'd needed to plow three acres, he'd hitched me and Alan to a makeshift harness crafted from leather belts. Steering a giant spade behind us, he'd driven us like a pair of mules.

I listened as, one by one, my brothers startled awake and groaned. Seven-year-old Kerry must have ignored Dad's rise-and-shine directive. I heard a bed overturn, followed by Kerry's indignant protest. "You're crazy!"

Indictments like that only goaded Dad.

"Thank you," Dad would reply when I called him weird. "I'd never want to be accused of being normal." We couldn't damage his outsized ego with generic insults. Criticisms emboldened him. Outbursts like Kerry's only increased his resolve.

With my pillow under one arm and my bedspread trailing behind me, I dashed across the hallway. I had to claim the bathroom before a sibling beat me to it. Half asleep, I locked the door and tossed my bedding into the tub. It would take Dad a good fifteen minutes to realize I was asleep in there. Before long, he would pick the lock with a nail he kept on the door ledge. That was how he ensured no one ever homesteaded the family restroom. Either we exited within the designated time limit, or he forcefully removed us.

Dad wasn't so much safeguarding the primary restroom as he was fortifying his own. The master bathroom was off-limits to his kids because, well, just because. He never explained why. Like a bulldog, he instinctively marked and defended his territory.

Darting between rooms, my brothers and I could elude Dad for minutes in a game of Whac-A-Mole. He wasn't omnipresent. That human frailty gave us an advantage. We scattered in different directions faster than cockroaches. Once he corralled us, though, we surrendered.

Outdoors, Dad would peer over our shoulders and bark

instructions like a prison guard. "Cut the eye off first, and plant that slice facing up," he instructed about potatoes. "Space 'em two inches apart," he advised for spring onions. Cautioning me, he said, "Don't let those cucumber seeds get too close to the cantaloupes." Ignoring his warning, I invented the *cantacumber*, a melon so inedible it made me gag.

Our garden included lettuce, cabbage, onions, carrots, and other produce nobody but Dad would eat. My brothers and I preferred corn and potatoes—the kind found in chips. Mom had no interest in breaking up with Green Giant, and she loathed the smell of boiled cabbage. Despite Dad's sincere requests, she refused to cook odiferous greens. She did, however, agree to boil peas.

I considered Mom's premier attempt to cook fresh vegetables a breakthrough on par with her driving. She seasoned a pot of purple hull peas with salt and pepper and simmered them in water for about an hour. *What more was there to do?* Betty Crocker had failed to lend her sage advice, assuming Mom had sought it. She didn't consult books with oxymoronic titles like *Joy of Cooking*.

Mom presented her china bowl full of lavender-colored legumes to Dad as if she were serving the president. In my mind, her gesture meant we were on our way to more nutritious meals. *There might even be leftovers!*

Unaccustomed to leftovers, we usually had left-outers, as in, "Hey, pass that bowl this way before I get left out." I'm not suggesting any of us were malnourished. We were blessed to have three hygienic, if not savory, meals a day. Not once, to my knowledge, did any family member suffer food poisoning.

Judiciously, Dad tasted Mom's prized dish. "These aren't cooked right."

Mom made a bitter face. She searched my eyes for a second opinion.

I chewed the crunchy, flavorless nuggets and shrugged. "They're a little hard."

With his fork, Dad rolled the half-done peas around his plate. "How long did you cook these?"

Mom pushed back her chair and crossed her legs. I couldn't see it, but I knew she'd turned her suspended foot into a shield. When she felt defensive, she crossed her legs and extended one sole vertically like a stop sign.

"I don't know," she snapped. "'Til they looked *done*."

Dad set down his fork. "Mary Ann, don't you know you have to cook fresh peas longer than canned ones?"

Like an airline passenger stuck in turbulence, I searched for the nearest exit.

"Why don't you just go eat at you mama's house if you don't like my cooking?" Mom huffed.

She'd made a valid point. Grandma heavily seasoned her black-eyed peas with ham hocks. Where Mom's dish had gone south, I didn't know. But if I'd been in her predicament, I would have called Grandma to find out.

"Why don't you learn how to cook?" Dad asked her. "It's not that hard."

I calculated which direction to lean if dishes started flying. Once, in a similar dispute, Dad had hurled a serving bowl of hot corn at Mom. A shard had grazed my leg. I'd bled but not enough to stop their bickering. Any second, I feared those purple hull peas might soar past me at eye level.

"I've had it with you criticizing me," Mom said. "I'm *leaving*." She pushed her dining chair farther back and stood. "Come on, kids."

Dutifully, my brothers followed her. The lone dissenter, I stayed put.

Mom's driving scared me, even when she wasn't fuming mad. I had no wish to be involved in an accident—or petty arguments. She would gripe about how Dad had "done her wrong" until nightfall, I suspected. Leaving with her meant choosing sides and surrendering brain cells. Dad was a bully and Mom a petulant child. I couldn't muster much sympathy for either one.

Dad studied me. "Just so you know, you'll be taking home ec as soon as it's offered."

I nodded, pretending to understand. What I needed was a mediation class. I excused myself from the table and stepped outdoors.

Mom stood in the driveway, shoving her purse into the Rambler.

"Where're you going?" I asked, still calculating my options.

"Does it matter?" She froze and stared at me.

It took me a minute to grasp that wasn't a rhetorical question. The Boys spilled into the back seat, jostling each other, ready to join Mom's mystery tour. I was the only child demanding details.

"Yeah, it kind of does," I replied. "I want to know where you're headed before I decide to go." *Backroads or freeway? Department store or fabric shop?* Weighing the possibilities, I pondered whether to hop aboard.

Mom shot dagger eyes at me. "Fine, then. Stay here. I don't care." With bravado, she shut the car door and cranked the station wagon's engine. From the vacant driveway, I watched the Rambler speed away, a cloud of white rock dust trailing its bumper.

After I'd finished my lunch in solitude, I peeked in at Dad. True to form, he'd ruptured and retired. He lay prone on his mattress, eyes closed, ankles crossed like a corpse.

From the fridge, I grabbed some raw bacon. Fishing for crawdads seemed like as good a way as any to escape chaos.

Crayfish weren't the most intelligent creatures. I could apprehend them without a fight. I only needed to drop a bacon-threaded string into their underground hideouts and tug. Once they latched on, they wouldn't let go. If my bait was appealing enough, I could catch, release, and recapture them again and again. And that was what I did.

❦

After four hours of mock desertion, Mom returned home. Dad was still asleep—or pretending to be. I wondered if he might be conscious and lying there, eyes closed, wishing he'd never taught her how to drive. If he had any remorse, he kept it to himself.

It was after six p.m. when Mom entered the house, ignoring the clock and her stove. My stomach rumbled. Alan, Kerry, and Joel sauntered past me without stopping to inspect the fridge. *Is no one else famished?* I pulled Kerry aside to ask where he'd been. He admitted the group had spent the afternoon at a burger joint. Annoyed, I made a peanut butter sandwich, grabbed a recycled *Reader's Digest* Grandma had given me, and withdrew to my room.

As I settled in with "Laughter: The Best Medicine," Mom caught an itch to start a late-night load of laundry. By eight thirty, she'd tired of the ruse and gone to bed. Grateful the feuding had ended without breakage or injury, I nestled under my sheets. One by one, the household lights switched off.

Someone padded through the hallway. One of my brothers taking a last-minute leak, I guessed, or Dad returning from upstairs. He'd probably been up there, squinting at scrolling static lines again.

As if lifted by a ghost, my top sheet floated upward. Behind me, Dad squeezed in under my covers and snuggled close—boxer shorts, no shirt, bare feet. I detected the aromas of hair tonic and yeast bread. One arm looped around my waist, he asked, "Comfy?"

This was not the father I encountered on Saturday mornings or in the fields or at the dinner table. This was an altered and portentous version of the dad I feared. This dad was needy and desperate and vulnerable and even less predictable than his twin. New Dad made me momentarily forget the original one still existed.

I didn't understand his question. Was I comfortable with these bedtime visits, or did I feel snug? Inside me, a void persisted, a deep fissure carved from unshed tears. I longed to feel nurtured and safe. For touch, I thirsted enough to drink poison. I squeaked out an unconvincing, "Yes."

Over the whirring attic fan, I heard my mother ambling toward us. Though I'd done nothing wrong, my stomach tightened and my ears hummed. I felt dirty and ashamed. We'd been caught.

Dad held his position, his back to my open door. Twisting my body, I scooted free of his grasp. But I had no way out, no way to pretend I hadn't been nestled in bed with the man who should have been cuddling my mother.

Mom leaned against my doorframe with her arms folded. In the attic fan's crosscurrents, her smock billowed. "What are you doing in here?" she asked Dad.

Finally. She knows.

He rolled to face her, still firmly rooted to my mattress. "I'm tucking Diana in."

I stiffened. I was thirteen, not three. The only boogeyman in my room anymore was *him*. When I'd been a scared toddler, he had pushed me away. His timing appeared considerably off.

Mom didn't buy his excuse any more than I did. "I notice you don't tuck in your *sons*."

Now that she'd brought Dad's neglect into focus, I couldn't unsee it. I'd never heard him bid my brothers good night. Mom's disquieting observation confirmed my suspicions. My father paid more attention to me than he did to his sons or wife. Guilt washed through me. I hadn't meant to steal anyone's affections. *Will Mom believe me if I tell her that?*

Dad proffered no further defense. Propped on one elbow, he stared at Mom, daring her to say another word. Though I'd never witnessed him strike her or her hit him, I didn't exclude the possibility. Briefly, I considered locking myself in the bathroom for good measure. The two held their entrenched positions, Mom glued to my doorway and Dad affixed to my bed. After several minutes, she withdrew to the master bedroom in silence.

Come back here! Take him with you! You can have him! I didn't know who was the worst traitor. She'd left me to fend for myself. *If she can't control Dad, how does she expect me to?*

Staring at a wood-paneled wall, I said, "I'm tired."

Dad took the hint. But he would be back, if not that night then another. Mom's dismissal had all but assured it.

THIRTEEN

AFTER MOM CAUGHT DAD IN bed with me, she never mentioned the infraction or asked me about that night. I didn't want to address the topic any more than she did. It was creepy. Nothing had really happened, I convinced myself. But it seemed Mom didn't look at me quite the same after that.

Dad was his old self by the next morning when we visited the Hostess Outlet Store in Garfield. He motored the family twenty miles to load up on snack cakes and stale bread. To save money, he'd renounced Mrs Baird's slices and converted to day-old Wonder Bread. If he'd disavowed Dr Pepper, I would have been less astonished.

We visited the outlet store about twice a month. In between, when supplies shrank, Dad hid the few remaining snack cake packages on top of the fridge, reserving them for himself. I didn't know why he chose that location. My brothers and I were short, not stupid. When we discovered his stash, which we almost always did, we played finders keepers.

If the kitchen was amply stocked with baked goods, Mom included desserts in our sack lunches. Every once in a while, she forgot to add a sandwich to my bag. I didn't consider my missing entrée intentional, though she laughed about the omission when I mentioned it. Mom was absentminded, I figured, not malicious.

Regardless of how hardy our lunches were, every afternoon, my brothers and I stepped from the school bus famished. This day, in particular, was no exception.

Before school, I'd noted the last package of cupcakes stationed atop the fridge. The single cellophane sleeve held two miniature cakes. Alan, Kerry, and I had spied the package and its deficient quantity. I'd imagined they would forget about the snack by the time we returned home, then the cupcakes would be mine. I would grab the package when no one was looking and sneak to my closet to devour the chocolate prize.

Home from school, I exited the bus first. My brothers spilled out behind me. I broke into a trot and beat them to the kitchen by several seconds. In no time, they shoved through the doorway, clamoring to steal what I'd already nabbed. Each proclaimed himself the rightful owner.

"You can't have them! I saw them first! That's not fair!" they shouted in turns.

I held the package high above my head, beyond their reach, instigating a food war. The equitable solution would have been to cut each cupcake in half and share them, but I wasn't that self-actualized.

Mom bounded into the room. "What's going on in here?" she asked.

I confessed we'd been battling over cupcakes, which I'm not proud to admit now. At that moment, though, I was unashamed. My brothers and I were used to competing for scarce resources. I believed we were simply doing what we'd always done—dividing into winners and losers.

"Give me those cupcakes," Mom demanded.

I handed over the dessert.

She opened the package and emptied a cupcake into one hand. "Is this what you want?" She presented the snack in one palm as if displaying it for a TV commercial. The only missing element was the chocolate icing's radiant twinkle and a *ding*.

I saw where she was going. She wanted me to beg for my portion like a trained seal. *Fine, then.* "Yes!" I exclaimed. If I had to drop to my knees, stretch my neck, and spin circles, I would. I was that ravenous. Everything else in the house required preparation time. Even TV dinners took twenty-five minutes to heat—the microwave had not yet become a standard appliance. Half a cupcake was better than no cupcake at all, I decided.

Mom charged me. Before I registered her intent, she smashed the cupcake into my face and spun it like a dial. Cake bits invaded my nostrils. I coughed and viciously exhaled crumbs onto the floor.

My brothers didn't even laugh.

I glared at Mom.

Doubled over, she clutched her middle, pointed a mocking finger at me, and cackled. "Wasn't that the best pie-face joke ever?" her antics suggested. But she hadn't surprised me with a plate of whipped cream, and the audience wasn't amused. The joke had been no better than Dad's Lover Boy move.

My brothers glumly stared at their feet. They would have to split the last cupcake three ways, now that four-year-old Joel had wandered into the kitchen. He studied the near-empty package in Mom's hands.

In the bathroom, I rinsed my face. "Nobody's getting this," I heard Mom say as I cleaned cake bits from my nostrils. I didn't know what she planned to do with that last cupcake, but I had a strong opinion about where she could stuff it.

My brothers were nowhere in sight when I returned to the kitchen. Probably, they'd gone to their shared room to plot revenge. Mom sat at the dining table with a coffee cup perched next to her. Dark crumbs flecked her saucer.

———◆◇◆———

Any self-esteem I had ever possessed slowly dissipated. I could barely stand to look at myself anymore. In the mirror above the bathroom sink, I studied my reflection—with the door open, of course. I wasn't allowed to secure the restroom unless I was using the toilet.

"Don't be primping," Dad said one evening when he caught me staring in the bathroom mirror. "That's not what that room's for."

I loathed my features, pocked complexion, and curly bangs. The curtain that hid my unibrow behaved like a malfunctioning roller shade. With a strip of cellophane tape, I anchored the wet fringe to my forehead. From the hallway, Dad scrutinized me. "Vanity, vanity. All is vanity," he heckled, misquoting the Bible.

Vanity? I scowled at him.

"Natural beauty can't be faked," he said, firing a second shot.

Maybe not, but the band spring concert was the next day, and I wanted to look half-decent for the event. If I couldn't be the prettiest girl on stage, I hoped to avoid being the ugliest—a formidable challenge.

The next morning, when I searched the bathroom countertop for my foundation, eyeliner, mascara, and lipstick, all were missing. "Da-a-a-a-d!" I hollered. A familiar snigger told me I'd correctly guessed the bandit. Tearfully, I approached him. "Please. This isn't funny. I have to catch the bus in fifteen minutes. Give me back my makeup."

He blocked the hall with his half naked body. "You don't need it."

I suspected he'd hidden my "war paint," as he called it, in his bedroom. "Yes, I do!" I gestured wildly. Without my makeup, I couldn't be seen. Boys called me "dogface," as it was. Attending class with my face stripped bare would invite worse disparagement.

"You look fine. Go to school and quit whining."

Why is he doing this to me? In my mind, this was the most degrading trick Dad had ever played on me.

Mortified, I boarded the school bus and kept my head low.

During band, my first class, I forced back tears and braced for second period. The jeering, I knew, wouldn't come from my fellow musicians—half of whom were in junior high, like me. Our school was so small that seventh- and eighth-grade students were combined with the high school band.

The band kids were used to seeing each other with sweaty hair and runny mascara and soaked armpits. They traipsed through dew-covered fields at dawn and broiled beneath wool uniforms in August. That was why most band girls carried their makeup to school. Though it was late May, long after marching season had ended, many still kept cosmetics in their lockers and purses. An ingrained habit I'd never adopted.

A clarinet player loaned me her foundation and a wand of mascara. I quit moping after that, despite my newly acquired orange tint. I preferred a carroty color to a ghostly complexion.

The next day, Dad took pity on me and returned my cosmetics, but I didn't trust him. On a whim, he might repeat the infraction. I refused to be susceptible to such torment again. Within a week, I'd saved enough lunch money to purchase a secret makeup stash. After that, I never left home without my backup beauty supplies.

Diana, 8th grade (1968)

FOURTEEN

SUMMER BROUGHT A REPRIEVE FROM school teasing, but I still suffered indignities at home. The lime-green polka-dot two-piece I'd talked my mother into buying might as well have been hers. The high-rise bottoms climbed within an inch of my navel and wrapped me like a second skin. The top, though, was designed for a gal with breasts. I still had nothing that qualified, just a couple of rosy disks that made me claw my chest when no one was looking. I tied the halter top strings tight behind my neck and pretended I was equipped.

Midway, below my collarbone, the suit gapped open when my shoulders slumped. Almost fourteen, I slouched often. When I caught my suit's malfunction, I press the bubbled fabric to my breastbone to reverse its curve. Rarely was overexposure a problem. I had nowhere besides home to wear a swimsuit. Community pools didn't exist in rural areas like ours. To reach the nearest shore entailed a five-hour drive. I wore the bikini when I mowed.

One June morning, right before I sauntered outdoors to cut grass, Mom snapped open the newspaper. "Want to hear your horoscope?" It wasn't a question so much as an alert for me to listen.

"No." I emptied cereal into my breakfast bowl. I didn't need astrology to forecast my future. I didn't believe in that hogwash. Neither did Dad, which was why my mother never read horoscopes aloud when he was home. But he wasn't there that morning to save my ears.

"Okay, here's yours. Veer-go," she said.

"That's Virrrrr-go," I corrected.

"Yeah, okay." Mom scrolled the newsprint with one index finger as she read. "Unexpected travel plans come your way. The full moon on the third brings love and harmonious relationships. Be cautious with money until after the fifteenth—"

"Nonsense," I spouted.

"You don't believe it?" Mom looked mystified.

"Nope. Only place I'm going is back to school this fall. Don't have a boyfriend. And I got no money." I emptied the last of the skim milk into my bowl.

Mom set down the newspaper and sipped her coffee. "Your father's taking us to San Antonio. To the *World's Fair*."

"First I heard it."

"See. That's what your horoscope said! '*Unexpected* travel plans come your way!'"

———✦———

The year was 1968, a time when protests and labor strikes and looting dominated the nightly news. I registered almost none of that. Dr. Martin Luther King had been assassinated in Memphis, followed by the fatal shooting of Senator Robert Kennedy. While I understood the tragic nature of murder, I didn't comprehend the social upheaval. Race relations hadn't been a topic in my household or classroom. Insulated in a predominately white community in Texas, I'd learned zilch about civil rights. Yet I felt the stress of unnamed threats the way one senses an approaching hurricane. In the distance, somewhere beyond view, a powerful storm brewed.

My father studied the nightly newscasts and offered few commentaries. "We're going to have another civil war if this doesn't stop," he uttered.

I stared at the screen, attempting to interpret his remark. Like a telescope image of the Milky Way, film footage of protests piqued my curiosity but provided no construct. My juvenile thoughts centered on Hemisfair '68, the world expedition that commenced two days after Dr. King's assassination.

In San Antonio, Hemisfair offered people of every nationality a diversion from the political unrest and racial tensions dominating lives and headlines. Demonstrations became regular occurrences outside the fairgrounds, all of them peaceful. The event, which drew seventy thousand visitors a day, was a place to be seen and heard.

Our six-member family attended the fair that July to experience its novelty. Inside the ninety-two-acre fairgrounds, an array of fountains, canals, and art performances excited my senses. It was unlike any event I'd ever attended. Girls wearing hot pants and couples linking arms undulated amid dancing troupes, flower parades, and marching bands. Mothers steered overladen strollers through crowded walkways. A mini-monorail and skylift carried passengers above congested streets. Beneath the elevated transports, boats and train-trams crisscrossed.

Indoor exhibits flashed futuristic images. I experienced a space-age culture shock. *How will our family ever embrace all these modern advancements?* Months earlier, my dad had purchased a 1950 Allis Chalmers tractor with a hand-crank engine. Our family didn't belong at Hemisfair. We belonged in a museum.

I stared up at the Tower of the Americas, the seven-hundred-fifty-foot attraction at the park's epicenter. The structure's crown resembled a flying saucer I'd seen in a science fiction movie. "Can we go up there?" I begged. I wanted to view the fairgrounds from the observation tower.

Dad studied the queue. "No way. I'm not standing in that long line."

He hadn't strategized for our trip. His last-minute decision had made it impossible to secure a hotel room near the fairgrounds. That was what he told me anyway. Probably the room rates had been hiked higher than a cat's back, as he often complained, and he'd been unwilling to pay the prices. Our family camped in Blanco State Park, on the banks of a river, forty miles north of the event.

The second evening, after our family returned from the fair, we refreshed in the shallow pools beneath Falls Dam, where emerald-colored waters cascaded over a limestone embankment.

I sat flanking my father on the spillway. In the springs below us, my brothers tooted souvenir plastic horns. Between tuba sounds, they playfully splashed each other. Mom glanced up and smiled at me and Dad. It was a picture-perfect moment no one caught on camera, though I can still see it vividly in my mind. As the sun slid lower on the horizon, pink hues danced across the waters. In that instant, we might have been any ordinary family set against the pastoral backdrop. Momentarily, I forgot we weren't.

To my right, Dad sat with his arms hugging his knees. I mirrored his posture and stared straight ahead. Shadowing him, I felt safe. A hawk can't easily attack a sparrow at close range, I remembered. Raptors rely on distance and surprise to outmaneuver their prey.

Dad leaned close. "Those are some pretty bad mosquito bites."

I swiveled to meet his eyes. He continued staring down into my gaping swim top. With both hands, I slapped my suit bra flat. I'd forgotten about the troublesome fit. No telling how long he'd been taking advantage of his sideways view. Outraged, I scooted farther from him, but he persisted.

"Looks like those mosquitos got you pretty good!"

My lips welded shut. Something seized my throat every time I wanted to scream *How dare you!* at him. His remarks made me feel *I* owed *him* an apology for being a late bloomer. That warm glow I'd experienced earlier had ignited a scorching fire inside me. Dad didn't deserve my company. I left him sitting there, alone, where he belonged. Awkwardly, I crept along the rock ledge and descended to the pond.

"You finally decided to join us," Mom said with false surprise.

I didn't explain my decision to relocate. I didn't want to ruin our vacation.

———✦———

Home from San Antonio, I listened to the blaring sounds of drug-culture music emanating from the previously vacant shanty a quarter-mile away. Eight renegades my dad called "hippies" had discovered the empty farmhouse and taken advantage of its absentee owner. Through our open windows, Blue Öyster Cult and Grateful Dead music hijacked the normal nightly serenade of croaking frogs and whirring crickets.

Dad greeted our new neighbors by standing in the darkness and shouting, "Knock it off!" at a volume any tomcat could have muffled. No one but our dog paid him any mind. The more sleep he lost, the more earnestly he vowed revenge. "I'm putting an end to this," he declared, one night when "Light My Fire" had set his nerves ablaze.

The next afternoon, spying on the hippies through binoculars, Dad watched the group pile into a van and leave. From prior observation, he knew they often disappeared for hours. "Come on, boys," he said to my brothers. From his chest of drawers, he retrieved a loaded 22-caliber pistol. "Get your rifles," he ordered Alan and Kerry.

Though the rickety farmhouse was a short walk away, Dad

drove his posse to the hippies' driveway. Standing under an electric pole, he said to my brothers, "See if you can shoot that, right there." He indicated a glass insulator.

Nine-year-old Alan fired the first bullet, but it struck a wire.

"No, not *that*." Dad pointed with his pistol. "The *insulator*."

The boys shot their guns. After each round, Dad evaluated their marksmanship. If they had hit the recloser on that ten-thousand-volt line, they would have eliminated power service to *our* house.

In areas like ours, it was legal to discharge weapons—but not to kill utilities. To circumvent any federal charges, Dad never fired his pistol. One of his accomplices, he presumed, would hit the intended target, and he was right. The crew returned home, celebrating their daringness and marksmanship. But Mom and I didn't catch on to their victory right away.

The hippies returned that night to total darkness. They must have relied on candles and flashlights to get through the evening. Alerting the electric company of their outage would have caused more harm than good. Penalties for unlawful utility connections could have forced them into alternate free housing, the kind with metal bars.

By the next afternoon, the squatters had moved on. We never saw them again. Dad bragged about how cleverly he'd defeated the obnoxious scoundrels, which was how Mom and I learned about the power pole shoot-out.

If I'd known where the chatterbox who hogged our party line lived, I might have asked Dad and The Boys to visit her phone service pole. Multiple residents shared our common telephone line, which worked marginally better than having no phone service at all. The substandard system required me to check for a dial tone before dialing out. If I heard someone talking, I had to wait my turn. Another teen girl routinely monopolized the line, preventing me from using it.

Party Line Pig refused to release the phone wires to me, even after I clicked the cradle button multiple times. I schemed ways to force my nemesis to end her calls. I'd learned from Dad how to use what was handy to get what I wanted. At my disposal was a cattle dog, a tabby cat, and thirty free-range chickens. The dog rarely barked. The cat only purred. But the hens squawked like crazy when I upset them. I set a mental reminder to enlist one when I next needed to dial out.

After Mom and Dad drove to town one Saturday morning, I lifted the phone and heard familiar chatter. Party Line Pig, again. With my parents gone, I could finally talk to my friends in private, but a nameless girl stood in my way. I couldn't wait for her to hang up. It was time to bring in the poultry.

From outdoors, I caught a chicken—which was easy because they were all pets—and carried it inside. With one hand, I removed the receiver and set it on a table. Cradling the Rhode Island hen, I lifted and lowered her about six inches. The chicken's neck contracted and extended like an accordion. *Bwahhhhhwk, bwahk, bwahk, bwahk*, the confused bird complained.

"Do you hear chickens?" Phone Pig asked her crony.

The counterparty confirmed she heard a chicken squawking.

"Hang up, and I'll call you right back," the swine advised.

Nope. That's not happening. The instant that bag of wind disconnected, I intercepted the dial tone.

When my friend Connie answered, I said, "Hold on while I put this chicken back outside." Remarks like that made perfect sense to her.

I'd been talking to my former neighbor for several minutes

when I asked, "What's Miss Myers up to now?" I couldn't wait to hear what I'd missed out on.

Kerry darted into the room. "I want to call Tim and see if he can ride his bike down here."

"You can wait your turn," I snarled. My brother's thirty-second call wasn't worth the associated risk. When I surrendered that phone line, it would be lost to me for hours. The way I saw it, he could come back later with his own chicken.

"You've been on there long enough," Kerry fumed. "Get off."

He must have forgotten I was his big sister and didn't take orders from him. Annoyed, I pulled the phone cord into my parents' bedroom and shut the door in his face. Barricading the door with my back, I continued speaking with Connie and fending him off.

Kerry heaved against the partition, propelling me forward no more than an inch. Furious, he kicked the hollow-core door several times. I heard a crack.

"Hold on," I said to Connie once more. "I think Kerry just busted Mom and Dad's door." I peeked out and checked for damage. Sure enough, a foot-shaped hole marred the thin veneer. "You're in big trouble," I told Kerry, but immediately I regretted not releasing the phone to him. Dad would go berserk when he saw the damage, and one or both of us would suffer brutal punishment.

Kerry slinked away. He didn't call anyone after I relinquished the phone to him.

About an hour later, Kerry and I heard the dog barking and tires crunching white rock. We met each other in the hallway, ready to assign blame for the accident. Evidence of our scuffle was impossible to miss. The master bedroom door opened inward, displaying its wound for all to see.

Dad noticed the broken door right away. He had a sixth sense that informed him of most misdemeanors. This one, though, constituted a felony. In our house, he was the only one permitted to destroy property. It was okay for him to throw fits but not his kids. "You tear up something in my house, I'm going to tear you up," he'd forewarned.

When Dad spied the damage, I blurted, "Kerry did it."

Kerry stood before Dad, trembling.

My father's eyes narrowed. Indicating the busted door, he asked, "Did you do this?"

Kerry averted his gaze and nodded.

"Come out here." Dad opened the patio door between his bedroom and the driveway.

I wondered what punishment would follow. Maybe he would make Kerry pull weeds until his fingers bled or dig postholes until he collapsed or carry forty-pound hay bales to the barn loft until he barfed. Any radical penalty seemed possible.

Through the sliding glass door, I watched Kerry follow Dad. The two halted next to the burn barrel, our substitute for trash service. From inside the fifty-gallon drum, Dad recovered a well-barbequed coat hanger. He pointed at Kerry, instructing him to freeze in place.

With dedicated effort, Dad fashioned the metal coat hanger into a single-wire strand. Clenching Kerry's left arm, he thrashed my brother's hips and legs with that metal rod again and again. The two spun counterclockwise in a battle of rage and fear. Frantically, Kerry tried to free himself from Dad's grip.

"Johnny, Johnny, stop it!" Mom screamed, bolting from the house. "You'll kill him!"

He paid no attention to her cries. Dad struck Kerry with that coat hanger until the boy wailed like an injured animal and crumpled at his feet. A million times I've wished for a do-over.

FIFTEEN

WHEN DAD WASN'T AIMING HIS wrath at me and my brothers, he targeted us with hoaxes. Holidays, in particular, roused his sinister urges.

My aunt Janis said her brother's compulsion to vex family during Christmas began when he was twelve. As his first victim, she'd accepted and proudly worn a scarlet beaded necklace he'd gifted her. Initially, she'd thought the necklace a token of brotherly love. A week later, though, when one of the beads cracked open, she'd caught a malodorous whiff of the truth. Her conniving brother had handcrafted the jewelry from sun-dried sheep manure and their mother's red nail polish.

Once, my dad had camouflaged a case of bottled Pepsi to fool my mother. She believed the gift-wrapped box concealed an electric organ she'd been pining for. Scrutinizing the package, she said to me, "I know he got me that organ. That's the only thing it could be."

My mother didn't yearn for many material possessions. In her imagination, the organ was an altruistic request. That Sears keyboard she'd been eyeing would foster family sing-alongs. It might even transform her children into a harmonious quartet.

Dad registered Mom's desire for an organ as the perfect setup for a Christmas con. But he'd underestimated my mother's capacity to hold a grudge.

After opening the twenty-four pack of cola, Mom snubbed her trickster for a week. When Dad tried to engage her, she would salute him with a Pepsi bottle, chug the beverage, and smirk. Her expression said, "You think you got one over on me, huh? I'll make you regret you ever tried." Tired of being the family underdog, she wasn't the most gracious loser. Dad's pranks were hilarious until she was the stooge.

I was seven when Santa Clause brought me a talking doll named Suzy Smart. The chatterbox spoke various sentences at the pull of a string. When activated, she would say, "Hi, I'm Suzy Smart. What's your name?" Though the doll dressed in a plaid skirt and white blouse hadn't been a joke gift, Dad turned her into one. Secreted inside our hallway closet, he listened for my footsteps. As I passed by, he mimicked my doll's singsong vocals. "Hi, I'm Diana *Dumbbell*. What's your name?"

He was no ventriloquist. Immediately, I identified his voice and hiding place. I opened the accordioned closet door, my new doll crooked in one elbow. Crouched in between two oversized suitcases, Dad sniggered like a five-year-old.

"That's not funny." I examined him the way I would a deceased pet. Before Dad had lampooned her name, I'd believed my doll affirmed my intelligence.

Dad gestured to Suzy Smart. "Diana Dumbbell." He wheeze-laughed.

"Diana Dumbbell? You're terrible." Mom pretended to scold Dad, but the congratulatory laugh she'd given him might as well have been a high five.

Throughout the next seven years, the trickery continued. On my fourteenth Christmas, Dad presented me with a cylinder-shaped object wrapped in foil paper. Mom watched as I tore through the gift-wrap. Inside was a copper tin the size of a toy drum. With trepidation, I pried open the lid, expecting an artificial snake to leap out at me.

"Potato chips?" I asked, thankful the tin hadn't been booby-trapped. I'd requested a fringed leather belt, bell-bottom jeans, and a Simon & Garfunkel album for Christmas. The canister contained two pounds of fried spuds and, unlike Cracker Jack, no prize.

Dad had restored himself in Mom's graces by giving her that electric keyboard she'd wanted. Maybe, I speculated, the family grinch was ready to make amends to me too.

Dad chuckled, his grin twisting into an evil smirk. "Hey, would you like me to give you *more* potato chips?"

I'd given him too much credit. He was incapable of reform.

"Remember when I gave you a thousand potato chips?" he brayed. "You sure fell for it! The *look* on your face!"

Every time he revived that memory, I wanted to sandwich his head between two cymbals. His gloating insinuated I'd been an easy mark. This time, I planned to have the final laugh. The same way Mom had paid him back for that Pepsi trick, I would swallow my disappointment with vengeance.

The next day, Dad said, "Give me some chips." He'd believed the "family size" claim on the label meant there would be plenty to share.

I'd anticipated his craving. Every Halloween when I'd been young enough to trick-or-treat, he'd stolen my favorite candies while I'd slept. I'd hidden my potato chips from him to prevent their disappearance. By midmorning, I had consumed all the chips. "They're gone," I said, willing my face not to crack.

"Impossible. You couldn't have eaten two *pounds* of potato chips in *one* day." He studied me as if I might be lying.

I peeled open the tin and displayed the empty innards. The *look* on his face.

——— ◆◇◆ ———

With each tilt of the Earth, Dad revised his hijinks. In the summertime, he ambushed the family with water pistols, garden hoses, and ice cubes. From outside, he would creep up to my open bedroom window and, through the screen, spray me with a water hose. It didn't matter if he doused the floors or ruined a magazine or destroyed my phonograph. It was all about the art of surprise. Instigating any startle response was worth the sacrifice.

Sometimes Dad sneaked up behind me and dropped an ice cube down my shirt. With one arm pinning me in a loose chokehold, he used his opposite hand to press the frosty lump against my back. I would spin free, then he would deposit a second frozen bullet down my neckline. We rarely had enough ice to chill our beverages because Dad wasted the cubes on pranks and seldom refilled the trays.

I learned to dodge my father the way I sidestepped spiders. Extending him a wide berth, I edged by him when I encountered him in our hallway. A favorite scare tactic of his involved thrusting one arm violently forward, his hand fisted and within striking distance. When I ducked his faked blow, he would nonchalantly open his fist and slick back his hair. It looked like a move from *The Three Stooges*.

Weekends and holidays were the most nerve-racking times to be home. Boredom compelled Dad to taunt his dependents. But for two contiguous weeks each summer, when our family motored cross-country, we enjoyed a brief reprieve. Our station wagon had no extra room for Dad's bully weapons. To fit everyone and all our luggage inside, two children had to lie in the cargo hold. Ice, no longer free, swiftly became a precious commodity saved for the travel cooler.

Each year the family set out for different destinations, from Seattle to Sarasota and Denver to Gettysburg, meandering through every governor's mansion and president's birthplace along the way. The lower the admission fee and more historic the site, the greater likelihood Dad would stop to sightsee.

"Kids, by the time y'all are grown," he told us, "you'll have seen all fifty states."

Seldom did we visit prime vacation spots, though. We toured obscure museums, Native American burial mounds, Civil War battlefields, and anywhere else Dad's interests led us. My favorite state was Florida, where we visited the Ringling Bros. Circus Museum when I was ten. The *museum*, not the "World's Greatest Show on Earth."

From the circus museum, Dad continued driving south through the Florida Keys. At a tourist trap, he positioned me in front of a cage full of monkeys and lifted his camera. My chest swelled with pride. Rarely did my father take a photo of me without my brothers in the frame. I gave him a toothy smile.

He clicked his camera. "That's gonna be a good one," he said as I beamed.

A week later, when Dad showed the photograph to my grandparents, they guffawed. Grandma gave me an apologetic hug.

"What are y'all laughing at?" I felt left out.

Dad handed me the photo, still sniggering. I had posed next to a boldly printed "Diana Monkey" sign.

I couldn't let my guard down around Dad, not even on vacation.

When traveling, we spent most nights in state and national

parks. Routinely, we rolled into campgrounds at dusk. "Kids, clear out all the rocks," Dad would instruct before we pitched our room-size tent. The inflatable swim mattress I slept on invariably snagged a sharp object overnight, and I would wake to a pancaked piece of vinyl beneath me and my aching back. "Next time, you'll look closer," Dad would reprimand.

My father's body never touched punishing terrain. He and Mom slept on folding army cots while my brothers and I made do with four-for-a-dollar pool floats. Replacements were found as needed, though Dad didn't go out of his way to locate them. "We'll stop in the next day or two if we pass a Woolworths," he would say. "Indians slept on the ground for hundreds of years."

Compared to our native ancestors, we were embarrassing imposters, he suggested. But in my mind, we were Lewis and Clark roughing it through the woods with an accident-prone, real-life Wile E. Coyote as our guide.

Unlike most vacationers, I prayed for bad weather. Dad would splurge for a motel room when we encountered storms. Never did we stay at a name-brand inn, though. He preferred dives of last resort. "They want twenty dollars for a room," he said when I asked why he'd bypassed a perfectly fine Howard Johnson with a swimming pool.

"There's one!" I would shout, spotting a Vacancy sign. While I bird-dogged, Dad would swing into parking lots and let Mom out to confirm availability. More times than not, a clerk had forgotten to switch off the neon light. Sometimes the unclaimed rooms weren't large enough for the six of us, though Mom never volunteered an accurate headcount. She would admit to four, then we would sneak in our two army cots for the verbally denied.

In 1969, on our way home from Yellowstone National Park, thunderstorms had convinced Dad to stop at a horseshoe-shaped motor court. Inside the cramped room, I overheard my parents arguing about binoculars.

"I don't know why you have to bring those inside," Mom huffed. "There's nothing to see out there but pavement."

I set my lumpy pillow on one army cot and glimpsed Dad. With his field glasses affixed to his eye sockets, he stood next to the windows.

Mom addressed him from the bathroom doorway, her arms folded. "What're you looking at anyway?"

Dad continued peering through his lenses. "Not sure."

She aimed an accusing finger at him. "You're not fooling me. You're looking in that other window over there."

"She must not know her curtains are open," Dad drawled, his eyes still pressed to the binoculars.

"You've got no business spying on people like that. Put those away right now." Mom sauntered across the room and parked next to Dad, her hands on her hips.

He set his field glasses on the window ledge and faced her. "It's not my fault she left her curtains open."

Later that night, from my cot, I witnessed Dad sneak to the window and ease back the drapes.

After about ten minutes, Mom called out, "Are you coming to bed? Or are you going to stare in other people's windows all night?"

By the next day, Mom had patched up her dispute with Dad. Once we were on the road, they had other issues to resolve—like finding the nearest restrooms and drive-in restaurants.

Stopped at a burger joint in Kansas, Dad said to Mom, "I'll have the usual."

"What do y'all want?" she asked, addressing me and my brothers.

"Mayonnaise on mine," I replied.

"No onions," chimed Alan.

Kerry said he wanted mustard, which was never an issue. Mustard was every restaurant's default spread. Before Joel could speak, Dad interrupted. "Hold it. Nobody's getting special orders. You'll eat your hamburger however it comes. You got that?"

"Why?" I challenged. "They'll make it any way you ask." I'd seen the commercials on TV. The chain had built its reputation on honoring customer requests.

Twisting in the driver's seat, Dad glared at me. "You'll eat it the way it's served, or you won't eat at *all*."

I studied my sneakers and sulked.

"People in China'ld be happy to eat a burger with *nothing* on it," he snapped.

Best as I could tell, we weren't in China. We were in Kansas, where condiments were free with fast-food purchases. Only he cared about a mayonnaise request. I didn't deserve to have what I wanted. I had to accept whatever I received. That was what I heard him saying.

Mom plodded to the order window with her shoulders drooped. While she placed our meal request, Dad exited the station wagon and proceeded to a pay phone. I watched him remove a slip of paper from his shorts pocket. Fuming over my burger restrictions, I shot murderous looks his way. Imagining mustard on anything other than a hot dog wrecked my disposition.

Mom lumbered to the car with our supper, a bag of hamburgers slathered with mustard *and* ketchup. To salvage my meal, when Dad looked away, I raked a forefinger across my bun and smeared the nastiness onto my wrapper. Alan plucked an onion from his burger like it was a dead fly.

"I called Jack," Dad said to Mom. "He said we could watch the moon landing there."

Busy dissecting my meal, I only half listened. *Do they not have mayonnaise in Kansas?*

Mom adjusted her cat-rim eyeglasses. "Have they got room for all of us?"

"I guess." Dad popped a french fry into his mouth.

After I quit pouting, I learned that a US spaceship would land on the moon that night—and that I would be sleeping with strangers.

I didn't know Jack, the man who'd once been my father's coworker. Married, with two children, he'd moved to Arkansas to become a forest ranger. Dad hadn't stayed in touch with his former friend, which made our layover seem all the more awkward. But we couldn't miss Neil Armstrong's and Buzz Aldrin's historic moon landing, Dad said. And the rack rate at Jack's house was beyond fair.

At nine p.m., our host and his wife, son, and daughter clustered with our family around their TV set. We listened to Walter Cronkite drone on for *eight* excruciating minutes as images of a simulated spacecraft wobbled onscreen. The mock lunar module looked like a prop from *Lost in Space*. Out of sync with NASA's audio feed, coverage of the moon voyage created little tension. Thrilled to the point of stupor, I fought to stay awake. The delayed-action footage produced a kill-me-now effect. The screen picture flickered as programming switched to live coverage. Applause erupted inside Jack's family room. But within seconds, the camera feed inverted.

We bent our necks to see the astronauts.

"Four hundred people are standing on their heads right now," an unidentified person jeered offscreen.

Instantly, the recording righted, and a black-and-white video so grainy and distorted it could have been a shadow puppet show appeared on the set.

A blob that vaguely resembled an astronaut's leg descended from *The Eagle*'s stairway. Walter Cronkite identified the murky shadow as a limb and foot belonging to Neil Armstrong. As the studio camera cut away to Walter, the newscaster removed his trademark eyewear. Overcome with emotion, he wiped away tears.

"That's one small step for man, one giant leap for mankind," Neil Armstrong said, but the scratchy audio feed sounded indecipherable.

Studio staff repeated Armstrong's remark to viewing audiences.

Studying that archived footage now reminds me of my first sonogram.

"You can see the head right here."

Hmm. I don't know. Could be my kidney.

"And there's an arm!"

Uh, are you sure?

"A-n-d it's a boy!"

I'll have to take your word for it.

The recording appears as lackluster today as it did then.

I wanted to be as awed as Walter Cronkite by that monumental achievement, as fascinated as my dad by the televised coverage, and as euphoric as NASA staff about the mission's success. Yet I felt nothing. Through dull eyes, I watched the greatest scientific feat in my lifetime. While astronauts walked on the moon, I wanted only to return home. Escaping gravity didn't interest me.

SIXTEEN

THE NIGHTLY NEWS HAD JUST ended, and every family member except Dad was in bed. He padded into my room and sat on my mattress. He didn't slide under my covers and cuddle anymore.

"I don't need to be tucked in," I'd advised him soon after Mom had confronted him.

He'd given me a hangdog look but had agreed to limit himself to bedside chats.

For several minutes, Dad used his whisper voice to make small talk. "I've got something to ask you," he said, out of the blue.

I was used to direct orders or general inquiries from him but never requests. My stomach lurched. *Is he divorcing Mom? Please don't ask me which parent I want to live with.*

Normally, I sided with Dad on marital matters the way third-world countries aligned with global powers. The choice was simple, if unfair. Dad was America, and Mom was an impoverished island in the hurricane belt.

Braced for his confession, I straightened to a seated position, adjusted my knee-length nighty, and waited.

Dad sat there in his boxer shorts despite the October chill. He tilted his head low as if readying himself for a proposal. "Will you show me your breasts?"

"What?" I thought I'd misheard him. *Did he just ask me to undress?*

"Will you show me...your breasts?" he repeated with no detectable guilt.

My pulse skipped to a foreign dimension. Warning sirens blared in my head. "Why?" I wondered if there could be a valid reason. I could think of none.

He must have anticipated my question. "Because I'm like a farmer who wants to see how his crops are growing. You're the crop."

I hadn't realized I'd been expected to yield a harvest. *What am I producing? Cantaloupes? Peaches? Kumquats?* My bust had grown modestly since the prior summer when I hadn't filled my swim top, but I was no calendar girl. Embarrassed and confused, I balked. "I don't want to." I held my breath, not knowing what to expect. I had never before refused his directives. *Is my body mine to defend? Or does it, like everything else in our house, belong to him?*

Dad's shoulders slumped. "Look, I won't touch you. I promise. I'm just curious to see if you're going to be bigger than your mother. I'll leave as soon as you show me."

Is this why he's been sneaking peeks down my shirts and swim tops for two years? I wondered what he planned to do if I didn't measure up. This obsession with my bustline, or lack of one, had to end. If I showed him what he'd been struggling to see, maybe he would finally leave me alone, I decided. Lowering my scooped neckline, I flashed him a plum. "There." I whipped my gown back into place.

As soon as I did it, I knew I'd made an awful mistake. He'd only been trying to arouse himself, and I'd been the stimulant. My room lights had been switched off. At most, he might have seen a shadowy molehill. Incensed, I wanted him to take his farm references and get out of my room. Regret knotted in my throat.

"Looks like you're coming along fine," Dad praised.

"You promised to leave."

With a nod, he exited, his footsteps lighter than normal.

Nauseous, I burrowed beneath my bedspread and berated myself. *Why did I do that? Where's my common sense? How does he make every sick idea he has sound normal?* Presumably, I would have to bear our dirty secret forever. I wouldn't dare tell anyone I'd willingly displayed a boob to my father.

With revulsion, I rewound and scrutinized the scene. Another daughter would have screamed for her mother and disclosed the violation, I imagined. For unknown reasons, I had not.

I needed a boyfriend. The stronger, bigger, and more aggressive, the better, I decided. Ronny met all those requirements. The skating rink where I met him converted to a sock hop on Saturday nights. To attend the dances, I lied by omission. I didn't ask permission to go *skating*. I asked for a ride to the skating rink. Neither parent cared to step inside the metal building, a character trait I counted on. Mom drove me to the entrance at eight p.m., and Dad retrieved me from the same spot at eleven. I exited the rink by ten forty-five in case he decided to sleuth.

Dad never asked me questions about my skating. If his British TV programs weren't interrupted by an ambulance call, he regarded both our evenings a success.

At the sock hop, I gamboled and faked merriment with other girls equally short on sex appeal. Now and then, a boy would ask one of us to dance. One night, a guy had taken a risk on me.

Ronny Harrison strutted across the dance floor and addressed me like we were best friends. We'd never before met. Confident of himself and my response, he led me to the center of the polished hardwood rink. My knees trembled. Heat prickled my cheeks. It seemed impossible that a guy with a face like a rock star and an athlete's body would want anything to do with me. Anyone could see that I was freakishly thin, cursed with clown hair, and pocked with acne. I prayed this wasn't a mean joke.

Ronny's left arm caressed the curve of my back. Turning my face opposite his, I leaned into his embrace. For three whole minutes, I breathed in the scents of British Sterling cologne and burnt cedar.

Half a foot taller than me, Ronny looked like he could body slam my dad. His chest cushioned my brow as we slow danced. If *this* boy wanted me, I theorized, then I was worth having. The ridicule I had suffered at school was based on a lie, one I'd swallowed like a bigmouth bass. I was neither ugly nor undesirable. The guys who'd called me dogface were a bunch of dolts. Their charades only worked as long as I believed myself defective.

Almost seventeen, Ronny had what boys in my freshman class didn't—thick sideburns, a grown man's build, and a valid driver's license. I had stuck to him like a cocklebur.

The first time I left the skating rink to go smooch in Ronny's vintage Ford pickup, I was barely fifteen. The vehicle's snow-colored dome matched its whitewall tires, in stark contrast to the truck's royal-blue body. Everything about my boyfriend seemed stylish, from his bell-bottom trousers to his classic wheels—which he had borrowed from his dad, but I gave him credit for refusing his mom's Cadillac.

We'd been exploring each other's mouths for about fifteen minutes when I anxiously noted the time.

"I can take you home," Ronny said, intercepting my thoughts.

I collected my purse. "Maybe next week. My dad'll be here any minute." With that shuddering thought, I opened the passenger door.

Ronny escorted me to the skating rink entrance, where he kissed me one last time before disappearing inside. His return to the dance caught me off guard. I had expected him to leave. Reapplying my Pink Ice lipstick, I waited for Dad and sulked. Imagining Ronny flirting with other girls demoralized me. *He's probably dancing with someone prettier than me now.*

Two weeks later, Ronny began giving me rides home on Saturday nights. Mom didn't ask for details when I said Dad wouldn't need to fetch me. "I've got a way back," I said, sounding like an adult.

"Oh, okay," she replied, motoring in the dark, her chin four inches from the steering wheel like she was eighty-five instead of thirty-six.

All went as planned until, one night, Dad spied Ronny's truck in our driveway. I witnessed the porch light flick off, then on, while the pickup idled. Dad had accidentally killed the beacon before realizing I wasn't yet inside, I suspected.

It was only ten fifty-five. I still had five minutes until curfew. The next four I spent necking with Ronny. It was early December, and I was in no rush to exit the heated vehicle or my boyfriend's arms.

At straight-up eleven, when I stepped into the house, Dad lay in wait for me. "Who was that?" He followed me to my bedroom.

I waved him off with one hand. "Just a friend." My insides jumped like a bucket of grasshoppers. I peeled off my artificial suede jacket and hung it in my closet.

Dad plopped on my mattress corner. "How old is that boy?"

From my dresser, I grabbed a nightgown and glided past him. "Seventeen," I called from the hallway. I didn't know why I said that. Ronny would be sixteen for another two months. I shut the bathroom door to Dad's debriefing. My ploy didn't work. When I returned, he was sitting right where I'd left him.

I flicked out the overhead light, looped past Dad, and climbed into bed. With a little luck, I reasoned, I might avoid him asking me how long I'd known that guy or what his name was or where he lived. I didn't want to admit that I'd been making out with him. Dad didn't react well to situations beyond his control, and this flight had already left the runway. It was too late to request proper clearance.

"Did he kiss you?" Dad sounded more like a jealous lover than a concerned parent.

Mentally, I willed him to quit drilling me. With a punch, I fluffed my pillow. "Maybe."

"Ah-hem." He pretended to clear his throat. "I'm going to be watching him. And if you see that porch light turn on and off"—he nodded toward the front door—"that means it's time for you to get your tail in this house. You got that?"

I said I did. When he exited my room, my mouth gaped wide. He hadn't forbidden me to date.

———— ◦✕◦ ————

Ronny and I spent more days together than apart that next spring and summer. When we ran out of places to go, he annoyed Mom by pretending to be her fifth child. She wasn't overly enamored to find a 165-pound teenager with a goat's appetite rummaging through her fridge. To give her a break from daily food raids, Ronny and I spent many afternoons at the local lake. And that was how the fire started.

Dad retrieved a tub of ice cream from the freezer. "What'd you do today?" he asked me.

"We watched a hill burn," I replied, speaking of myself and Ronny.

"Grassfire?" he asked.

"Uh-huh. Ronny lit it."

Leaning into the fridge, I grabbed the last Shasta soda from behind an almost-empty carton of skim milk.

Dad claimed a Melmac bowl from the cabinets. He paused and gave me a confused look. "He lit a grassfire?"

"At the lake," I clarified. "Struck a match and threw it out the window. We left when we saw the fire truck coming."

The blaze had scorched about an acre between the roadway and muddy shoreline. Damages were minimal, limited mainly to insects. On that breezeless July afternoon, the flames had nowhere to travel. Buffered on three sides by concrete, the fire would have petered out on its own. Ronny and I passively watched the blaze until firemen arrived.

"Those guys needed something to do, anyway," Ronny had joked.

Dad stopped spooning ice cream into his dish and studied my face. "Why would he *do* that?"

I shrugged. *Boredom? Hopelessness? Sexual frustration?* Dad must have had better insights than I did.

SEVENTEEN

ANY LESSONS I RECEIVED ON dating and marriage I garnered from outside my home. Mom offered me no guidance in that department. She hadn't dated much before she met Dad at age nineteen. Their whirlwind romance, if I could call it that, had ended in matrimony six weeks later. She knew nothing about fending off boys' advances because she'd never honed that skill. Before she met Dad, she'd planned to become a nun.

Consensual sex being a taboo topic, we didn't discuss how to delay it until marriage. Mom was too fixated on rape. Any man might be a sexual assailant, given the right opportunity. That was the sum of what I learned from her about intercourse, so I turned to Grandma for what little advice I could glean. Grandma had secretly married my grandfather at age nineteen. I listened, one more time, as she told the story forty years later, in case I'd missed her point.

"His daddy was a drunkard, and Momma thought I'd be marrying an alcoholic," Grandma said. "So, we went to Oklahoma and got married. And on the way home, we stopped and bought a calf for five dollars."

What the calf or its price had to do with their hush-hush nuptials was never clear, but Grandma included bovine in her elope story every time she recited it.

She continued. "We didn't tell Momma and Daddy we were married for two days. When we did tell, Momma said, 'I don't believe it.' I told her it was the gospel truth, and she said, 'Well, if you're married, go over there and sit in his lap.'" Grandma lifted her chin and straightened her posture. "So, I walked across the room and sat in his lap. And Momma said, 'I guess you *are* married!'"

This anecdote was Grandma's way of underscoring the impropriety of sitting in a suitor's lap before marriage. It seemed she hadn't communicated that lesson to her son. With regularity, Dad grabbed me and pulled me onto his thighs. Different rules for different relationships, I guessed. Still, sitting on my father's lap at age sixteen made me uncomfortable—far more so than parking myself on Ronny's legs.

Ronny and I had been dating for fifteen months. Soon, I imagined, we would be engaged. He had never spoken the word "marriage" to me. But he'd mentioned sex often enough, which I'd interpreted as a sideways proposal.

"Why won't you do it with me?" he'd pleaded. "I could have any girl I want, but I picked you. Don't that matter?"

Yes, it mattered to me more than a senior prom or high school graduation. If I were Ronny's wife, I would be set. Never again would I be bullied at school or afraid of my father. I could stay out until one o'clock in the morning if I wanted, wear hot pants and halter tops, and dance until my feet blistered. I could sleep as naked as a newborn and get out of bed when I felt like it. I could skip church on Sunday mornings. I could lock my bedroom door and stop looking over my shoulder. In my viewfinder, Ronny looked like the Statue of Liberty.

To show how much I appreciated his charity, I let Ronny feel his way closer to his target. I planned to restrict further access until we married. Also, I intended to reject a calf as a wedding gift. Some goals were easier to achieve than others.

Neither my religious upbringing nor Grandma's advice squelched my wish to keep my boyfriend. I didn't think it strange to avow virginity one minute and strip off my daisy-print panties in Ronny's Plymouth Fury the next. I'd heard and seen enough to know that commitments and actions didn't always agree. It was the intent that counted. Dad had excused all manner of indignities with that defense.

To celebrate Ronny's eighteenth birthday, he took me for a spin in his new vehicle. Parked amongst a stand of live oaks, we tested each other's willpower. Mine proved the weaker.

On that fateful night in February, after I returned home deflowered, I constructed a force field around my bedroom. I was in no mood for a bedside chat. I hoped to close my eyes and wake to learn it all had been an illusion. The romantic interlude I'd anticipated had felt like a human sacrifice.

Dad crept into my room and assumed his position on my mattress.

Lord, just take me now.

"You awake?" he asked as if it would have mattered.

"I am now."

"What'd you and Ronny do tonight?"

"I'm sleepy. Can we talk about it tomorrow?"

"Set anything on fire?" Dad snort-laughed.

I wanted to reply, "*My genitals!*" Instead, I offered a lackluster, "No."

Dad's fire reference led to his standard inquiry, the question he'd been asking me for months. "Have you had sex with him yet?

You *do* know he could be arrested for that, now that he's eighteen, right?"

That alarming thought had not occurred to me. Legally, Ronny was an adult, and I was jailbait. I had never heard of statutory rape, and I wondered why Mom hadn't mentioned it. Aside from those health videos I'd viewed in fifth grade, ones where legions of male sperm raced toward a prize egg, I was equally ignorant about pregnancy.

If I told the truth and showed remorse, maybe Dad would pardon me and Ronny. I would beg his forgiveness and pledge to anchor my panties to my pelvis forevermore if he wouldn't turn in my boyfriend. "Yes, I have." I blinked back tears.

"You did?" Dad's tone sounded congratulatory. "What was *that* like?"

"I hated it and don't want to ever do it again," I blubbered.

He chuckled. "Oh, I imagine you will." His voice struck a more serious timbre. "Did you use protection?"

"What do you mean?"

"Did he use a rubber?"

I was unsure what a condom looked like. "No," I finally decided.

"Well, tell him to use one next time," Dad huffed. And with that, he left my room.

<hr />

It was early May when "next time" arrived. It took that long for me to forget my initial pain. "My dad said you should use a rubber," I told Ronny, who hadn't yet shucked his pants.

We were parked near an abandoned rock quarry. In the twilight, I registered his stunned expression.

"You told your *dad* we had sex?" Ronny's voice pitched high. He slumped against the back seat, slack-jawed.

"He asked." I shrugged.

"And you told him the *truth?*" Ronny's eyes bugged. "What did he *say?*"

"He said you *need to use a rubber.*" I studied him to see if he knew what that meant. Possibly, he'd attended the same health films I had.

Ronny scoffed. "Do *you* have one?"

Dad had proffered his overdue counsel, but he hadn't gifted me a box of prophylactics. I shook my head.

"Neither do I." Ronny waved aside my concerns. "Don't worry. I'm sterile. I take medicine that makes me that way."

A smarter girl might have registered the statistical improbability of an infertile eighteen-year-old. The likelihood of a randy young man honoring the truth instead of his libido shared similar odds. But I was used to believing the implausible.

Almost seventeen, I thought my future was stamped and sealed. Ronny and I would marry, despite our childless fate. We'd been doing the hanky-panky for about six months when he said, "I'll find a job, and you can finish school. We'll get us a place to live and tell your dad to stay out of our lives."

Already I'd quit telling my father every thought that entered my head. He still asked intrusive questions, though. I hadn't shared the worst with Ronny for fear he would go for Dad's throat.

"Did you enjoy sex this time?" Dad prodded during one of his routine interrogations. "I've always thought women look beautiful right after an orgasm." He spoke to me like I was his college buddy. "Don't worry. I won't tell your mother," he reassured.

Undoubtedly, he wouldn't tell Mom he knew I'd been having unprotected sex for six months. Or that he hadn't confronted Ronny, spoken with his parents, or done anything to safeguard my future. That wasn't a concern. It was a certainty.

Like handcuffs, secrets bound me to my father. We shared a prison cell. With no obvious way out, I succumbed to his psychological blackmail. Deeper and deeper his cross-examinations delved into the explicit, leaving me no safe way back to terra firma.

I waited for Ronny to find a good job and marry me. Already, we'd laid the plans. In thirteen months, I would be old enough to wed without parental consent.

EIGHTEEN

"OVERSEXED" WAS THE ADJECTIVE GRANDMA used when I asked about Dad's obsession with female anatomy. It was the politest way I could think to pose the festering question. She said Dad was oversexed the same way she spoke of his defective vision. Her diagnosis, I supposed, was meant to absolve Dad of his carnal violations, infringements she chose to overlook.

I loved my grandmother too much to shatter her impressions of Dad. In her mind, he was a dutiful son with exceptional integrity, a deacon in his church, and a hardworking veteran. Sure, the man had some quirky behaviors. But his peculiarities could be written off with words like "oversexed" and "practical joker" and "oddball."

Grandma needed a son with a positive image as badly as I craved an ordinary dad. At a psychic level, she and I understood each other. That was why, when she learned I was pregnant at sixteen, I let her draw her conclusions. Probably she thought it was all my fault for sitting in Ronny's lap.

Pregnancy jettisoned me into premature adulthood. I skipped

my final two years of high school, discarding my youth like a broken glass. All my life, I'd grown up too fast. Having a baby too soon continued a journey I'd begun at age four.

"You made your bed. Now you'll have to lie in it," my father said. He acted like I had cheated him of his last nickel instead of myself of a high school diploma. "Just to be clear," he added, "I raised my kids, and I expect you to raise yours. Don't go asking your mother to babysit."

I hadn't envisioned Mom as a nanny. When I'd confessed my pregnancy to her, she'd bawled and covered her eyes with one hand. "You're making me a grandmother at thirty-eight!" she'd yelped. But after a doctor had confirmed my condition, she'd settled down and accepted the facts. Her first grandbaby would arrive in seven months. She wasted no further time assigning blame.

Mom planned my wedding the way she might prepare for a hurricane, with haste and trepidation. She didn't have much experience as a wedding coordinator. Her own affair had been a no-frills event while my father was on a brief military leave. She had worn a white frock, matching Mary Jane flats, and a hat that could have doubled for an Easter bonnet. No veil. No bouquet. Just a simple pin-on corsage.

In my parents' sole wedding photo, Mom and Dad stood in a church doorway, gazing at each other like awkward teens. Dad's left arm rested limply across my mother's shoulders. Her left hand clutched a pair of white gloves, and her opposite one gripped my father's jacket hem. The expanse between them left enough room for six photobombers. Understandably, Mom's expression implied misgivings.

"How, exactly, did y'all meet?" I asked Mom.

We were upstairs in the game room she used as her sewing

area. She threaded ivory satin through her Singer machine while I served as a dress form.

Mom lifted her foot off the machine pedal and stared wistfully at an adjacent window. "I was working in downtown Dallas for an insurance agency, and I looked out the window and saw a couple of sailors standing on the corner," she said. "I pointed Johnny out and told my friend, 'That's the guy I'm going to marry, right there.'" She snickered, seemingly amused by her confession. "So, my boss, Chuck Jackson, came to see who I was talking about, and he recognized Johnny," she continued. "They'd gone to school together. He said he'd introduce me to him, and that was that." Her foot resumed pumping the sewing pedal.

For my wedding, Mom whipped together a zip-up-the-front smock from a Simplicity pattern. She finished the dress by stitching one sleeve with beige thread after she'd run out of lighter colors. An imperfect wedding dress for an imperfect bride. It would've been a lie for me to have worn pure white anyway.

"Just get her down the aisle before the head crowns," my father might have joked if I'd been someone else's daughter.

But Ronny showed up on time and under his own volition.

"You've brought shame to our family," Mom had chastised

John and Mary Ann (1953)

me. "How could you do this to your daddy?"

Her words had zero effect. I couldn't feel anything but elation over my early release from confinement. Wherever I was headed had to be a quantum leap from where I'd been.

Maybe I should have confessed to her what *my daddy* had been

147

doing in my room for the past six months, how he'd been grilling me for salacious details about my sex life. "How many times? Was it good for you? Where did you go to do it?"

Mom had enough worries without me dumping a double load of disappointment on her head. By withholding the truth, I thought I was protecting her.

Ronny and I were too young and naïve to be scared. No one except him and me expected our marriage to last. We kept our nuptials top secret from all but our immediate families. No pictures cataloged the confidential event. Others would have no dated images to consult when the baby arrived.

Ronny's father and mine must have flipped a coin to see who would take us in until we mastered self-sufficiency. To my dismay, Dad won the toss. Yet Ronny and I didn't have to consummate our marriage inside my childhood bedroom. His folks paid for a night in the honeymoon suite at the Green Onion motel, a one-story, twenty-room establishment that catered to truckers and factory clientele. That night, though, it offered dignity to two flat busted newlyweds.

The next morning, after we returned home from our brief honeymoon, Dad cornered me indoors. "You can earn your keep by helping with the housework, cooking, and dishes," he said as if I'd inquired. He stared disapprovingly at my thirteen-dollar wedding band purchased from Kmart. "But that husband of yours is going to have to find a job that pays," Dad demanded.

"Okay." I noted his scowl, inflated chest, and protruding chin, wondering what had come over him. Maybe he'd been arguing with Mom about expenses again.

My situation was the pin dangling next to an already distended balloon. Dad has been underemployed for two years, thanks to a major recession. I didn't want to increase his burdens. The only solution I could envision was to seek work. I wasn't showing yet. The local Dairy Queen might need help, I reasoned, because summer was over and the school year had begun.

When I asked about openings, the DQ manager hired me on the spot. I didn't even have to fill out an application.

"You can have the five 'til close shift," he said, which was perfect.

Too many people clamoring for one bathroom in the mornings upended my family. With me working evenings and Ronny barely working at all, we could stay in bed while my brothers readied for school—and make love after Dad left for work. The thought of him slithering through the hallway, listening for telltale sounds, turned me to ice.

Ronny worked randomly at his father's employer's warehouse. When a trucker arrived seeking cargo help, his dad would call him. Drivers paid freight handlers twenty-five dollars to unload a rig. Most truckers emptied their trailers to save time and money. But now and again, one was willing to wait on a handler to arrive. In our first week of marriage, Ronny earned fifty dollars. The second week, he earned nothing.

"That ain't gonna cut it," Dad said, pulling me aside.

He never discussed finances or employment with Ronny. I didn't find that unusual. Ronny stood five inches taller than Dad and, if he'd wanted, could have pinned him to the floor. Dad didn't know how to manage a son-in-law he couldn't intimidate— or anyone else for that matter. To buffer any flack, he sent his orders by messenger to his greater kingdom. It was my job to relay what Dad expected of my husband and to absorb the blowback.

Ronny recoiled when I told him what Dad had said. "Who made *him* God?"

Only a newbie would ask such a question. "He did."

The next Saturday, at eleven p.m., I returned home from Dairy Queen to a sink full of dirty dishes. Mom had a habit of filling her stainless steel sink with sudsy water and setting adrift her tableware. Normally, though, she didn't leave plates and glasses soaking overnight. Staring at the brackish water, I stifled a dry heave. Two months pregnant, my gag reflex had a hair trigger.

Dad met me in the kitchen. I smiled, grateful to see a familiar face after serving strangers all evening. He'd waited up for me, which was more than Ronny had done. "Those are for you." He gestured to the sink swamp.

My swollen ankles throbbed. For five hours, I'd been standing on concrete floors, filling and washing malt glasses. I stared at him in disbelief. "You're kidding, right?"

"No. I had your mother leave those for you. You need to do something around here." He stood in his boxer shorts, cupping his elbows. "Oh, and by the way, your *husband* ate all the Doritos, in case you wondered where they went." He spun on his heels and marched to his bedroom.

Dad had never before spoken to me with such disdain. When angry, he had raged or glowered or struck me with whatever was handy. Once, he had flogged me with my brothers' Hot Wheels racetrack. Right then, I would have preferred a beating to the reception he'd given me. His cool detachment left me dispirited.

I was pregnant and married and no longer of any use to my father. I'd shut him from my bedroom, usurped his authority, and severed his perceived ownership of my mind and body. He was nothing but my landlord now, and my rent was due. I needed to pay up or get out. That was what I made of his hostile greeting.

Standing at the sink, thrusting my hands into the cold dishwater, I felt as much a hostage as I ever had. My marriage had not extinguished the need to escape home. All I had gained was a cellmate.

A month of living with my parents was the motivation Ronny needed to find a full-time job. His employment at a roof truss factory allowed me to quit my soda jerk position. Right away, we moved to a hundred-year-old shotgun house that rented for sixty dollars a month. Now Ronny could fart without first seeking permission. And I didn't have to be anyone's maid—except maybe his. Finally, we had attained emotional and financial freedom from my dad.

Our rented dwelling was nothing to brag about. Still, I didn't mind the broken porch steps out back or the neighbors arguing next door or that, when the light was just right, I could see through our home's clapboard walls. Previously, I'd grown accustomed to a lack of forced heat and air.

We had four generous rooms to ourselves: a living room, a bedroom, a kitchen, and a bathroom. I couldn't have been happier if I'd won a sweepstake. Any day, I expected to open my front door to a cheerful balloon bouquet and a confetti-throwing agent holding an oversized fake check.

Our dilapidated bungalow might not have looked like much, but it was my fire escape. It had permitted me to flee peril. My eye twitch disappeared. I quit listening for ominous footsteps at night. Dad's behaviors couldn't affect my life anymore, I observed with relief. I was too jubilant to contemplate any other scenario.

Section II

Pictures and Lies

NINETEEN

Five years later.

I T SURPRISED NO ONE BUT my husband when I fled my abusive marriage, taking with me my four year-old son, Ronny Junior, a used car, and some clothing. My divorce had been forecasted from the day I'd said, "I do." My parents' split, though, came as shock to everyone—including me.

Mom and Dad had suffered each other's wounded spirits so long that I had imagined refereeing them until one died. It was unthinkable that my mother would consent to a divorce. Stray underwear in Dad's vehicle, on the other hand, hadn't been *that* surprising.

"I found these in your daddy's glovebox." Mom stretched wide a cheap pair of cotton panties large enough to conceal three shoulder hams. "How big must this woman be?"

We stood in my parents' front yard, next to the crime scene— Dad's ivory-colored Karmann Ghia with fifty-plus thousand miles on the odometer and alien germs in the passenger seat. Mom held the evidence in one hand. She'd insisted that I see proof of his betrayal.

Somewhere inside the house, Dad was holed up—probably asleep.

I marveled at the unsightly panties. "Size twenty?" I guessed.

Mom clumped the underwear into a tight ball. She bowed her head and briefly hid her eyes before meeting mine again. "Why would he have an affair with a *fat* woman?"

The obvious answer was *because he could*. I shrugged and didn't say it.

Mom had made it easy for him. We all had. She hadn't balked when he'd accepted a traveling job or quit attending church. He'd given up religion after he and Mom moved near East Texas State University, where they completed their college degrees—his in economics and hers in elementary education. While Dad traveled for his employer, Mom taught kindergarten. They sandwiched their relationship between weekends and holidays. It had worked that way for three years until Dad veered off course.

Motoring through Alabama on a job assignment, Dad had taken a quick detour, a departure that fed his addiction, a stop that would end his marriage. Like a nuclear bomb, the radioactive fallout extended well beyond the blast zone.

For twenty-seven years, my mother had surrendered to my father's mistreatment. He could have controlled her no better if she'd operated by joystick. She'd witnessed him abuse her children, destroy property, and thumb his nose at God. Valiantly, she'd marshaled onward. In the end, she'd needed only a pair of oversized panties to break her resolve.

I couldn't fault Mom for holding out so long. She'd been waiting for her fantasy husband to replace his insufferable imposter, just as I had. Maybe we weren't as different as I'd previously thought.

From the passenger seat of my Chevy Camaro, Dad relayed how he'd met the owner of that unsightly underwear. Shamelessly, he recited the events of that afternoon. He had responded to a citizens band—CB—radio invitation to rendezvous for sex. The woman inside those full-coverage drawers had directed him to her home for a good time, the kind advertised on men's restroom walls. From a radio base station in her dining room, she'd recruited him.

Movies like *Smokey and the Bandit* had inspired my father and half of America to catch CB fever in the 1970s. No longer solely for truckers, the citizens band radio was embraced by mainstream society. Dad had installed one of those square boxes with a handheld microphone in his vehicle to advise him of speed traps, he'd said. The unit had helped him locate loose women too.

"I went to her house, and she came outside," Dad continued, his eyes sparking at the memory. "She had kids at home," he went on, implying they'd used discretion.

The deed had occurred in the woman's driveway, Dad confessed, most likely within window view of her children. I could have lived forever without knowing the tryst had taken place in his Karmann Ghia. The logistics were too dreadful to imagine, but I didn't have to concoct the details. He volunteered them.

"She was willing to do anything," Dad said. "*Anything.*" His face lit up like a slot machine.

I curled my lips and blinked hard, fighting to hide my disgust. I wished I could go and clean my ears with disinfectant.

Dad gave me a wounded-puppy look. "What? You want me to be happy, don't you?"

"Sure," I lied. What I wanted was for him to become a eunuch. Nothing less would properly socialize him. I wanted the father I'd invented in my dreams to eject the one with no conscience seated next to me. I wanted my heart to heal and pain to cease. Most of all, I wanted to find the missing inner component that kept me from saying any of that to Dad.

———— ✦ ————

For obvious reasons, I didn't care to meet Anything or her three teen daughters, Candice, Chloe, and Caroline. My father wed his former mistress in December, the same month and year he divorced my mother. I didn't attend the wedding. Dad had had the good sense not to include me on the guest list—if there was one.

Despite multiple offers, I refused an introduction to my new family. I didn't want more kin. My existing ones were damaging enough. Over time, though, guilt seeped into my heart. I questioned my motives. *Is it right to disconnect from my parents? Under what circumstances is that okay? Am I protecting myself or punishing them?*

Mom and my brothers had moved three hundred miles south of me. She'd said she didn't plan to be there long. We spoke frequently by phone, but I had seen her only once since she'd relocated. For that, I felt ashamed. I blamed my absence on my hectic work and college schedule. The travel distance made visiting problematic.

Much less geography lay between me and my father. Dad lived across town, in Dallas, about a half-hour away. I'd been declining his invitations to meet Anything since Christmas. It was April, and I had run out of polite excuses. I would go once, I conceded.

On Easter Sunday, I made my first drive to Dad's new home and parked in the driveway. "Be polite," I instructed Ronny as we exited the car. "I don't plan to be here long. We're just visiting to check these people out."

A wildebeest of a woman, Anything smiled incessantly. Seated at her dining table, she disclosed her inglorious backstory. "We were living on welfare." She grinned at Dad. "Then John came along and saved us from getting evicted."

Ah, yes, my father the rescuer, friend to the needy and the poor. It wasn't an extramarital affair. It was philanthropy!

As much as I tried not to hate her, I couldn't shake the urge to condemn her actions. Desperate women often took drastic measures to avoid homelessness. That much I understood. Maybe I would've done the same if I'd lived her life, but I doubted it.

I wondered how many times Anything had been bailed out by paramours. Somebody must have been paying her bills before Dad rolled into town in his white Karmann Ghia. She wasn't fooling me with her Tiny Tim tale. I knew the real story.

I wanted to ask why she'd had a CB radio station inside her prior residence. Not that it mattered. She had destroyed my family, defective as it was, to save her own. That was how I saw it. I was too aligned with Dad to pin all the blame on him, though I accepted he'd been the one steering his car.

Ever since the divorce, my mother had functioned solely with the aid of pharmaceuticals. My youngest brother had dropped out of school. Even my grandparents had suffered losses because of Dad's foolish choices. They'd canceled their fiftieth wedding anniversary party because of Anything.

"We'd never be able to explain her to our friends," Grandma had said of Dad's new wife. "She doesn't look a thing like Mary Ann."

As much as he deserved it, it would have been masochistic to heap shame on Dad. He would have handed me that emotion to hold. Already I was buckling under enough feelings that weren't mine.

I stared at Anything, watched her spear the last ham morsel

on her plate and swallow. At least she could cook. That was the only upgrade evident in Dad's new living arrangements.

Does she know what was sacrificed to give her a better life? In a reversal of fortune, Anything had progressed to a four-bedroom brick home, and my mother had downgraded to a rented shanty. Dad's paycheck supported his new wife and her three daughters while my brothers did without their father and essentials.

Anything's daughters hadn't asked to be involved in their mother's escapades any more than I had. I tried to imagine the situation from their perspectives, but I couldn't. Mine was too glaring. Maybe they were thrilled their mother didn't have to get it on in her driveway anymore. I couldn't read their body language or speak their lingo. I was twenty-six with a nine-year-old son, and they were still children. The instant I felt sorry for Candice, Chloe, and Caroline, ages thirteen, fifteen, and sixteen, they squashed my sympathies.

Candice strutted over to where Dad sat in a recliner while I looked on from across the room. Without invitation, she planted herself in his lap. From his pocket protector, she confiscated a ballpoint pen and clicked it several times. "Can I have this?"

Dad gave her an affectionate squeeze and said yes. I would have thought he'd given her concert tickets from the way she leapt and bounced. Seizing the opportunity, Chloe took her turn straddling Dad's thighs. She hugged his neck, then checked my reaction.

I gave her the stink eye.

Unable to stomach their saccharin theatrics, I mumbled an excuse for leaving, collected Ronny, and headed for the door. Normally, Dad would have escorted me to my car, but he couldn't that day. Caroline and Chloe had him pinned to his ratty lounger. He gestured to me as I passed him, his arms extended wide and palms upturned. His look said, "Can I help it if I'm a chick magnet?"

———✧———

"Oh, my word," Grandma exclaimed. "Those girls. The way they sit in his *lap*." She shook her head. "I can hardly stand it."

In her living room, we commiserated about the looming holiday season. Or in this case, the *horror-day season*. Mom and Dad had been divorced for one year. Anything and her bunch would be attending their first-ever Christmas dinner with the extended family.

"Believe me, I know," I sympathized with Grandma. The first time I'd witnessed Dad's stepdaughters sprawl across his thighs, I'd cringed. I'd hoped to live the rest of my days without again enduring that scene.

"I wish he'd never left your momma. I'm plumb ashamed of him." Grandma shut her eyes in disgust before seeking my opinion. "What do you suppose he ever saw in her? She's not attractive. She's got all those kids." She waved a hand as if swatting away a notion. "I can't understand it."

I couldn't tell her the truth. Anything hadn't been Dad's first affair. He'd enlisted me in an earlier love triangle. Then he'd found Anything. Next, I suspected he'd entrap one of Anything's daughters. Dad hadn't changed. He'd simply let his disguise slip.

———✧———

Mom wept into her phone receiver, as she had each time we'd spoken since her divorce. She never asked about my life, college classes, or son. All she wanted to know was whether Dad was still living with "his whore" and if I'd seen him. I'd become her indentured spy because she had no one else to recruit.

When I confessed to Mom that Dad and his replacement wife would be visiting my grandparents on Christmas Day, she screeched, "What? I can't believe *she's* going to spend Christmas with you!"

I held the receiver two feet from my face and waited for the hysterics to stop. "Believe me, I don't want to see her face. It's not my choice. Grandma and Grandpa invited her. They don't want to spend Christmas without Dad. This is my future, I'm afraid."

"You should come here, then," Mom said. "*You* ought to be with *me*."

"Here" meant driving six hours to celebrate the holiday with a despondent parent and three brothers who resented me for a host of reasons, some of which I'd earned, some of which I hadn't. "I can't," I said, choking back the truth. I could have driven to her house for the holiday. I didn't want to.

"Why not?" she pressed.

"Because I'm going to Alaska." The thought spilled from my lips before I'd fully decided. My aunt Janis had offered me an airline ticket, but until that moment I hadn't seriously considered it. I had a cousin in Anchorage who couldn't come home for Christmas that year. When I'd whined to Janis about my circumstances, she'd suggested I spend Christmas in Anchorage. In midwinter, Alaska was only marginally better than Siberia, but I didn't yet know that.

It was Ronny's year to spend Christmas with his dad. Nothing could have discouraged me from visiting Anchorage except the weather forecasts, which I hadn't bothered to consult. It was my turn to run away from unpleasantries. Favoring one parent over the other seemed unfair. Deserting both felt like poetic justice.

"*Alaska?* Why would you go there?" Mom asked.

I couldn't articulate why. Subjecting myself to subfreezing

temperatures and days of depressing darkness sounded preferable to my other options.

———— ✦⋖⋗✦ ————

Alaska made me more appreciative of Texas and less averse to family chaos. No matter how challenging life was at home, I could find my vehicle each morning without a flashlight and shovel. The change of scenery worked miracles for my perspective.

By spring, Mom's mood had improved too. She met a suitor at a Parents Without Partners dance—and I stomached that news without queasiness. She no longer needed me to fill the vacancy Dad had left. She even quit expecting me to act hostile to him. We spoke about the weather when she called.

Though I'd re-established contact with my father, I kept him at an arm's length. I visited his home only once that summer. I can't precisely recall what led me to Dad's garage on that sizzling August afternoon. He'd said he had something to give me. Though I don't remember the item, I can't forget the outcome.

Earlier that day, my friend Susan had asked me to give her a ride home from DFW Airport. When I mentioned dropping by Dad's house, she agreed to a quick detour. I had expected to jaunt from my car, pick up Dad's bequest, and bolt before Anything noticed me.

Dad's garage door stood open when I pulled into his driveway. I spotted him working inside the cluttered space. *Perfect. Exactly what I need to make a quick getaway.*

"Wait here," I said to Susan. "This'll only take a minute." I exited my Camaro and moseyed up the steep driveway. Before I reached Dad, I heard a car door slam. Behind me, Susan sauntered toward me as if I'd summoned her.

Susan and Dad exchanged pleasantries.

"That's a pretty dress." Dad gave my friend a once-over.

Back from a month in Honduras, Susan looked like a bronze beach bunny. She adjusted her diagonally striped sundress and thanked him.

"We can't stay." I feigned regret. "She's been out of the country for a long time and needs to get home."

"Oh?" Dad searched Susan's eyes. "Where you been?"

Noooo! Don't engage him!

"Honduras," she replied.

"We've really got to go." I nudged her.

Susan gave me a wicked smile then sashayed back to my car with Dad's eyes glued to her backside.

About a month later, while I spoke with my father by phone, he asked, "Why was Susan in Honduras?"

"Huh?" I hadn't mentioned her name. Dad said he'd called to wish me a happy birthday. In late September, I'd long forgotten about Susan's trip.

Dad fake coughed. "You know, she said she'd been in Honduras. *Why* was she there? Did she go alone, or was she with someone?"

"Her boyfriend," I replied, drawing a deep breath.

"I bet she kept *him* busy."

"He was very busy. He's a scuba instructor," I said, my words clipped. "She spent all day on the beach by herself."

Dad steamrolled ahead like he hadn't heard me. "That dress she was wearing must have driven him *wild*."

My chest felt on fire. "There was nothing wrong with her dress. What are you *talking* about?"

Dad let loose his standard laugh. "It left nothing to the imagination."

I recalled Susan's outfit, a simple V-neck, spaghetti-strap dress with a handkerchief hemline that skimmed her knees. "I don't know what you're talking about."

"You *don't*?"

I unclenched my teeth. "No. I don't."

"You could see straight through it," Dad said.

"No. You couldn't." I wished I'd already hung up. "Her dress wasn't see-through."

"It *was* when she stood in the sunlight," he insisted. "I could see everything she had. I bet she dresses like that to attract men like me."

He'd pushed me too far. "Dad, listen to me very carefully. Susan doesn't even *notice* men like you."

A few months after the sundress conversation, Dad divorced Anything. He'd fallen for a woman my age, he admitted. But after he'd filed for divorce and professed his affections, the lady had rebuffed him. He'd immediately married another gal who'd left him soon afterward. For the first time in fifty years, my dad became a bachelor trolling for his next fix. Like most junkies, he couldn't be trusted—not even among family.

TWENTY

TWO MONTHS AFTER DAD'S THIRD wife divorced him, Grandpa suffered a heart attack. I wondered if disappointment might have hastened his demise. Dad had let him down again, lost another wife and home.

In a fog of grief, I studied my father as he conversed with hospital staff. The hallways outside the ICU had mostly cleared by midmorning. Only a few overnight visitors remained. "I'm sorry about your husband," I said to the blond lady seated next to me. She and I had shared the same waiting room and prayers for twenty-four hours. My grandpa and her spouse had died minutes apart.

"Thank you. It was God's will." The widow blotted her tears. She plodded toward the exit, her steps measured and heavy.

Dad joined me. Together, we exited the hospital. In the parking lot, he noticed the widow as she walked ahead of us. Nodding toward the fifty-something-year-old, he said, "It's sad. She's so young."

I agreed, but my mind was still back in the hospital with my grandfather's body. *Did that really just happen? Can he truly be dead? The only man who ever protected me is gone.*

Dad continued inspecting the woman's backside. "Good thing she's kept her figure."

I didn't respond.

January winds gusted. I pinched together my jacket collar and opened my car door, hoping to skirt a full-frontal embrace. I gave Dad a quick sideways hug. "You going to be okay?"

He puffed out his chest like a bullfrog. "I'm fine."

"All right." I shut my door and started my Chevy's engine. A rap on the window indicated he had more to say. I lowered the glass.

Dad bent forward and leaned in closer. "I forgot. I needed to ask you something."

"What's that?" His exits were never simple. First came the initial hint that he *might* be leaving, then came the I-forgot-I-needed-to-tell-you-something delay, and *then* he added the one-more-thing before departing. It was excruciating. I wanted to go home, be alone, and cry until I couldn't breathe.

"Actually, two things." Dad grinned sheepishly. "Can I bring you a box of stuff I need to store? And can I stay at your place next week, when I'm in town?" He spent most weekdays on the road, traveling for his employer. Ever since his recent divorce, he'd dragged his feet on finding an apartment.

"Sure," I said.

"All right. I'll bring the box with me when I come."

"What night?"

"Tuesday, and maybe again Wednesday."

"That's fine." A draft caught my hair and whipped it across my face. I waved goodbye and swiftly raised my window to avoid further delay.

I hadn't given that box a second thought until Dad arrived at my apartment on Tuesday, holding the two-foot cube in one hand and a small duffle bag in the other. "Here." He handed me the carton. "I'll let you know when I get someplace where I can put it."

It was difficult for me to see my fifty-four-year-old dad living like a drifter. He'd lost most of his belongings in three years and as many divorces. I accepted the box secured with transparent packing tape. It was small enough to fit in my guest bedroom closet.

"You'll have to sleep on this." I indicated a bamboo-framed, three-cushion couch. "Sorry. I don't have an extra bed."

"Not a problem." Dad set his duffle bag adjacent to the navy-and-white tropical-print sofa where Ronny slept on weekends. At twelve, my son resided with his father.

"There's only one bathroom," I said. "What time do you get ready for work?"

Dad unzipped his duffle bag. "Oh, not before eight." He rummaged for something.

"Government hours," I mused. "Must be nice. I'll be ready and out of here by then. You're welcome to stay up and watch TV as long as you like, but I'm turning in early." I rolled my shoulders forward to give him a good night hug. "Let me know if you need anything in the morning."

I closed and locked my bedroom door, but I couldn't sleep. I was twenty-nine, not thirteen, I mentally reminded, big enough to fight off unwanted advances. Grown and combat ready, I had nothing to fear. Yet the atmosphere felt foreboding.

The next morning, I exited my bathroom at seven a.m. dressed in a no-nonsense business suit, white button-up blouse, and pair of black leather pumps. For extra security, I had triple-checked the bathroom lock before showering. The thought of Dad being near while I was nude gave me the heebie-jeebies.

From my bedroom, I heard my father enter the bathroom and

switch on the water. Maybe I would slip out ahead of him. I'd shown him how to lock the door when he left. No need to worry about breakfast, he'd said. He would pick up something on his way to the office. Still, I felt cagey. I grabbed my earrings from my dresser and fastened them in place.

"Di-an-a?" Dad called from the bathroom.

No, no, no, no! What does he want? I had installed a fresh toilet paper roll and set out clean washcloths and towels. The toothpaste was on the sink counter.

"Yes?" I craned my neck past my bedroom doorframe.

"I need you to come here," Dad said.

"What can I get you?" *Why does he need me to meet him in the bathroom?*

"I don't need you to *get* me anything. I need you to come in here." He sounded irritated.

Intuition warned me Dad's plea was a setup. I ventured from my room to see what he wanted anyway, knowing I couldn't hide from him all morning. I had to go to work. And to leave home, I had to pass by the bathroom door.

Rounding a corner, I spied Dad standing on my scales—wearing nothing but a pair of fire-engine-red micro-briefs. His bulbous gut hung over the appendage he most treasured as he rocked back and forth, attempting to influence the numbers.

He gave me an innocent look. "Can you come read me what this scale says?"

An internal dialogue streamed while I fought for words. *What the hell? Where are your clothes? You're standing inside my apartment, for goodness sakes, not strutting the French Riviera!*

When I could force speech, I asked, "Why can't you read it yourself?"

"I don't have my glasses," he said as if that made perfect

sense. His eyewear couldn't have been far. My apartment was only seven hundred square feet. I considered finding his lenses, but that would prolong my misery. I didn't want to see his detestable, pasty, nearly naked body twice. Once was traumatic enough.

Without further debate, I darted into the bathroom, peered at the dial, and blurted, "One hundred and eighty-six." To read his weight, I'd had to draw a sight line between his barely packaged junk and the scales. Thankfully, I had not yet had breakfast. As soon as I'd announced his heft, I fled.

Driving to work, I struggled to see the traffic ahead of me. I felt dirty enough to scrub my eyeballs with a toilet wand. Dad had instigated that senseless encounter to shock me, I concluded. Probably, he was still laughing about how easily he'd conned me. *Why am I so gullible?*

I shook with rage. For every stupid trick he'd played on me, every ambush kiss he'd forced, every groping hug he'd stolen, every explicit joke he'd told, every line he'd crossed, he had escaped penalty. Each time he pushed his foot past a boundary and no one stomped his toes, he encroached farther. He had no discernable limits short of incarceration or death.

My silence ends here. I won't let him violate me like that again.

From my work desk, I dialed my father's office. When he answered, I said, "I'm just calling to tell you you'll need to find someplace else to stay tonight."

He said okay and didn't ask why. He damn well knew the reason.

I had found my voice. And its first word was "ENOUGH!"

TWENTY-ONE

1990

LIKE DAD, I SEEMED DESTINED to pick the wrong partners. My second marriage had dissolved as rapidly as my first. Jim was my third attempt to get it right. This time would be different, I believed, though Jim's history was no better than mine. Despite unfavorable odds, we planned to marry.

Our wedding was less than thirty days away. Already, we'd purchased a home and were moving our separate belongings there when Dad's long-forgotten box surfaced. The two-foot cube had been relocated and stored several times, unopened. A lifelong procrastinator, I was disinclined to sort and dispose of unnecessary items. Jim, however, refused to carry unidentified boxes to our home attic.

"We're going to work our way through this." He gestured to the towering cardboard pyramid ensconced in our bedroom. With a knife, he slit the yellowed packing tape from a carton and peered into it. "This one's not mine."

"I'll take a look in a sec." I rifled through an assortment of faded file folders.

Jim gawked at the exposed contents. "What *is* this?"

I glanced at the container. "Looks like stuff my dad asked me to store a long time ago."

He pulled free a photo from what looked like a batch of office supplies. "Oh my," Jim groaned. He handed me a picture of Chloe modeling a see-through, black-fringed hooker getup.

My head buzzed with angry thoughts. The cameraman behind that instant photo had to have been my father. He'd hidden the lurid picture in a box that I'd been safekeeping for *six* years. "That's one of my Dad's former stepdaughters," I half whispered.

Jim turned the photo facedown against the bedroom carpet. Seconds passed in deafening silence. "Let's burn it," he suggested.

"You bet your ass he's not getting it *back*!" I cried. "And he's not getting *this* back either." With my fingers, I fanned the ruled pages of a six-by-three-inch address book. No telling whose names and what sordid memories that booklet preserved.

It would be many more years before I learned of the swinger parties Dad had frequented. That little black book likely held the addresses and secret passwords to a hedonistic underground. I was too dismayed by Chloe's photo to explore further.

Scrutinizing that photo took me back to age fourteen, to the night when Dad had asked me to show him my breasts. Even when I hadn't willingly participated, he took advantage of me. I couldn't count the times he'd sneaked snapshots of me bent over. It didn't matter what I was wearing, jeans, a skirt, or a swimsuit, I had to remain on guard against the family paparazzi. Dad activated his camera when I least expected it.

But Chloe had *posed* for the photo in question. I could only imagine the line he'd given her beforehand. I knew how persuasive Dad could be, how innocuous he could make his grimy requests sound.

With a match, I set fire to Chloe's image and flushed the ashes down my toilet.

———✦✦✦———

I had disposed of Chloe's photo but not the memory. Though Jim and I didn't speak of it again, the picture haunted us. We wondered what to make of it—and what it might portend. Jim had two adolescent daughters to protect. We were hesitant to expose them to my dad.

"Can we have Thanksgiving at our house, with just our family?" Jim asked two months after we'd married. Busy with home renovations, between the construction cleanup and enrolling his girls in a new school district, I hadn't given any thought to the holidays.

"What do you mean by '*our* family?'" I asked.

Jim cocked his head. "Me, you, the kids. Just us. Without your dad."

Every Thanksgiving I'd ever celebrated had included my father and grandmother. To comply with Jim's request, I would have to break a long-held tradition. Some of those customs, like Dad's misbehaviors, I wouldn't miss. With two young stepdaughters, ages twelve and thirteen, my concerns about him had grown exponentially since finding Chloe's picture. When I imagined Dad leering at my stepdaughters, visions of squad cars and ambulances and guest appearances on the *Jerry Springer Show* surfaced.

"It's our first Thanksgiving as a family," Jim pressed, "the first one in our new house. Next year, we can do something different."

He wasn't being unreasonable. The history I had confessed to Jim would have given any man reservations about my dad.

"Okay. It's not going to be fun telling him he's not invited, but I'll do it," I said.

Thanksgiving was almost a month away. My kin had plenty

of time to secure other dinner plans. Yet I felt guilty for omitting them from my holiday table. I didn't wish to be selfish or stingy. Admittedly, the day would be more peaceful without my father's stupid jokes and juvenile conduct. I would miss my grandmother's loving presence, though. She deserved better.

Trapped between appeasing my husband or following my conscience, I cut off the one person I was most indebted to. Grandma had cooked a Turkey Day feast for her extended family every year until she turned eighty. For five decades, in her farmhouse kitchen, she had packed fifteen to twenty guests. Never did she excluded anyone. She had steeled her emotions and graciously accepted Anything and her children, when she would have preferred to ignore their existence. Dad and Grandma were a package deal, though. That was how it had always been. I couldn't invite one without the other.

With trepidation, I dialed my father's number. "It's not me. It's him," I said, offering my husband as a whipping boy. The changeup had been a joint decision that made sense for many reasons, the greatest of which was Dad's record. But I admitted no responsibility. Like a five-year-old, I cringed and waited for Dad's response.

"So, it's 'just us four and no more?'" he asked, his voice dripping with sarcasm.

Six, to be exact, but I didn't think it wise to correct him. He'd forgotten about my two sons. Ronny would be home from college for the holiday, and it was my year to have five-year-old Ryan, my son from my second marriage, for Thanksgiving. "I hoped you'd understand," I snipped.

"Oh, I *understand*. You've got your new family and don't need *us* anymore," Dad said. "That's not a very kind way to treat your *grandmother*."

"I knew you'd act like this." I blew air through pursed lips. "Why can't you be reasonable for once?"

Dad gave a sinister laugh. "I'll see you at Christmas, I guess. That is, if you don't cut us out then too."

———⧓———

Three days after Thanksgiving, Jim motored past a neighborhood shopping center and pointed to a Christmas tree lot. "When do you think we should get one?"

I studied the fenced assortment of conical fatalities. "Two weeks?"

Laura, Jim's youngest daughter, stared out the auto's rear window. "Can we get a *big* one? They've got *white* ones!"

"Those are snow flocked," I said, "and very expensive. Why do we need to buy a *live* tree? Artificial ones are so much easier and less messy."

No one volunteered an answer.

Jim steered into our subdivision, an early 1970s development undergoing a revival. He parked in the cul-de-sac and pointed to our contemporary home's vaulted roofline. "We need a big one. See how tall our living room ceiling is?"

"*Yes!*" Laura chirped.

The three of us spilled from the sedan. "Okay," I conceded. "Big. But does it have to be *real*?"

I might as well have asked if we truly needed presents. Jim and Laura stared at me, their faces blank.

Jim stiffened. "I don't like artificial ones. They never look real. And they don't have that Christmas smell."

We stepped inside the foyer. "I can burn a candle," I argued. "They sell that tree scent in a spray can. We can get that smell without destroying our carpets, you know."

"We need a *real* tree," Laura gushed. "Can we get one?" She widened her dark eyes at her father. With her long lashes and that entreating look, she could have milked him for a carriage ride through Central Park.

Jim searched my face. I telepathed him images of tree bark, pine needles, and sap staining wheat-colored carpet, then paused to consider my response. Maybe household cleanliness wasn't all that important. The carpets could be vacuumed, steam cleaned, or patched, depending on damage severity. A little rusty tree water had never killed anyone's pet. Not that I'd heard of, anyway. We owned two fire extinguishers.

"Oh, all right. But not until it gets closer to Christmas."

One week later, Jim dropped me off near our grocer's storefront. A wintery mist dotted my hair as I stepped from the car.

"I'll park and wait for you to come out. Pick you up here when you're finished," he said.

"It's cold. Watch for me, and don't leave me waiting," I warned through the open passenger door. He had the best end of the deal. I would bravely steer a shopping buggy through pre-holiday crowds while he held vigil from his heated leather seat.

"I'll be right here when you roll out," he promised.

We'd been married four months, not long enough for him to appreciate my concept of time—or for me to learn he had no internal clock. Easily distracted, he regularly drifted off in thought or afoot without warning. At times, keeping track of Jim proved harder than herding rabbits.

Exiting the grocery store's automatic doors, I scanned the parking lot for Jim's car. In the night chill, I watched my breath form clouds. Either he had overlooked me or was stuck behind the stream of autos parked illegally in the fire lane. I checked my watch. Six thirty-eight, half an hour since we'd parted.

One by one, the vehicles near the store entrance moved on. My ride appeared nowhere in sight. Excuses I'd made for Jim's absence were dispelled. No, he wasn't right behind that big monster truck in the fire lane, politely waiting his turn to pull forward. No, he hadn't parked anywhere that might have obscured his view of me. I walked multiple lanes to be sure.

Another five minutes passed. Shivering, I wriggled my toes to keep warm. What had begun as a mild annoyance swelled to an indefensible betrayal. *Where is he?* I was infuriated enough to slog the mile-and-a-half route home, but I'd purchased more groceries than I could reasonably carry. Reality set in. I was stranded.

My imagination whipped me into a frenzy. *Will the Tom Thumb manager notice me and ask if I need a ride?* As I clicked through possible scenarios, Jim motored into view. His car rolled to a stop next to me.

"Ohmigod!" Jim leapt from the vehicle. "I lost track of the time." He transferred grocery bags from my cart to the car trunk. "I'm sorry. Laura and I went to look at the Christmas trees."

I assumed a stately position in the passenger seat and refused eye contact.

Jim steered toward home, letting several seconds pass in tense silence.

"Christmas trees?" I asked. "You left me standing in the cold, wondering where you were, while you looked at *Christmas trees?*"

"We were just *looking*, not *buying*," Jim defended.

Inside me, bombs and missiles readied for launch. I prepared to verbally annihilate my husband, punish him for his momentary desertion, make him regret he'd ever *thought* about Christmas trees.

The observer inside my head asked, *What's the matter with you? Why are you inflating over such a minor incident? What do you hope to gain by acting spiteful to your husband?* But my emotions were too supercharged for me to power down.

Hours later, after my adrenaline had subsided and I exited DEFCON 2, I realized what had happened. Yes, I had felt betrayed. I'd been excluded from a holiday ritual, and maybe I had earned that. But the rage I'd unleashed on Jim had had nothing to do with Christmas trees.

Like an old movie clip, I watched images of a frightened little girl abandoned at a football stadium flicker into view. The child sat in the dark, winds licking at her face, unable to voice her pain and fear. She looked cold, helpless, lost, and lonely. Though the girl had been rescued, she had not forgotten the experience. Trauma doesn't dissipate the instant danger vanishes. Trauma hangs around, sometimes for decades, until it can be dealt with safely. Trauma waits to be triggered, then it strikes back. Often viciously.

———————

Before I could extend the holly branch to Dad, he invited my new family to have Christmas dinner with him and his wife-turned-ex-wife-turned-common-law-spouse, Betty. Their history was complicated.

Betty and Dad had divorced before my grandfather died. Never officially remarried, after a few months apart, they had reunited. But Betty had found no incentive to wed Dad a *second* time. Her choice to remain single had been a financial safeguard and nothing more. Neither she nor my father took issue with "living in sin," as Grandma called it.

Grandma was fond of Betty, and so was I. A professional woman six years younger than Dad, Betty was well-spoken, congenial, and unlike my father's prior wives, accessible. She had a thriving career. A Louisiana native, she had moved to Texas, as locals like to say, "as soon as she could get here."

For once, Dad had chosen an independent and successful spouse, and I had done the same. Christmas was the first opportunity since my wedding for Dad and Betty to greet my husband and stepchildren.

On Christmas Day, when we arrived at Dad's house, Betty was cooking jambalaya in the kitchen. "I'll bring in some gifts," I said to her, "then I'll come help you."

She waved me off with a serving spoon. "I'm almost done with everything. You go ahead and visit." I nodded and reversed course, tugging at my cranberry-colored suede skirt. Guarding my backside had become second nature. For extra insurance, I had worn opaque tights. A block-print sweater completed my getup.

In the hallway, I tried to edge past Dad.

He thrust out his right arm.

Here we go again with the holiday buffoonery.

He stood there, using his arm as a tollgate, preventing me from passing through the archway. Whatever game he was playing, he hadn't pulled his stunt on Jim. A few steps ahead of me, my spouse exited the front door.

Dad gave me an aggressive bear hug. Jerking my head to one side, I dodged his puckered lips. His kiss missed its mark and splatted against my right cheek. I wedged one forearm and elbow between his barrel chest and my sternum and wrestled free.

"What are you *doing*?" I screeched.

He pointed to the ceiling and sniggered.

Above me, mistletoe dangled from a tape strip. "Ewwwww! You're supposed to kiss your *lover* under that stuff, not your *daughter*!"

I must have been channeling my grandfather's spirit.

Dad shrugged. "*You* walked under it."

So had Jim, and so had my stepdaughters, but he hadn't taken advantage of *them*. Jim would have throttled Dad if he'd tried. I wiped my cheek with one hand and left him standing there, smirking.

It's Christmas. Don't make a scene.

In the driveway, while Jim unloaded gifts from our car, I grabbed his arm and relayed Dad's trick.

He gave me a bewildered look. "He better not try that again."

If I could have, I would have plucked the offending greenery from the ceiling. Being five-foot-three, I was much too short to accomplish the task. I studied my husband's six-foot stature. "Maybe you're tall enough to pull it down."

An hour later, while the rest of us dined, Jim slipped off without notice. In the hallway, he removed Dad's mistletoe and discarded it.

After the meal, the family gathered in the living room for the usual holiday gift exchange. While I was canted forward and sorting packages under the Christmas tree, I heard the dreaded *click*. Photographed in a compromised position—again.

I couldn't be sure what picture-worthy image Dad had seen. Though I was careful, my skirt might have ridden up. At a minimum, the leather had been pulled taut. Spinning a one-eighty, I locked eyes with the underhanded photographer.

Dad held his slender camera in a readied pose and laughed. "*That* ought to be a good one!"

What an idiot I must be to wear such a short skirt around Dad.

Jim stepped between me and my father and squared off with him. "John, that was uncalled for and inappropriate."

I hugged my ribs. My body vibrated. Finally, another soul was brave enough to confront my father, not simply to tsk-tsk him or act perturbed by his infringements. In front of the entire family, my husband had called Dad out for gross misconduct. On Christmas Day. In the man's very own living room. I knew then that I would love Jim forever.

My father's behaviors weren't about me or what I'd worn or how I'd moved. His actions had never been provoked. The embarrassment I felt that day and every day in the past belonged to him. I had no duty to accept blame when he rejected ownership. *What a breakthrough!*

All that time, I'd believed that anything Dad pitched to me was mine to catch. But I could let a ball hit the ground. I could allow someone else to field it. I could nonchalantly watch it roll out of bounds if I chose. Dad's game was strictly volunteer, and I could resign from his team anytime I wanted.

Dad turned his back to Jim. Unrepentant, he ambled over to an end table and set down his camera. "There's no film in it," he muttered. He gave my spouse a patronizing look.

I glowered back at him.

In hindsight, I regret not collecting my brood and leaving. Instead, I tried to salvage Christmas. I needed my dad in my life—even if that meant subjecting myself to his deplorable behaviors. Without him, I feared I would lose my connections to Betty and Grandma. I wasn't ready to give up my fantasy father either. I still held out hope that one day someone would utter the right words to cure Dad. The real dilemma, though, the one that existed below conscious awareness, was this: *If I separated from Dad, what would be left of me?*

TWENTY-TWO

1995

M Y RELATIVES WERE DIRECTLY RESPONSIBLE for my decision to pen humor stories. To relieve stress, I turned to comedy. Much safer than drugs or alcohol, I reasoned, and socially more responsible.

For five years, ever since I'd married Jim, I had been taking creative writing courses for fun. I'd become hooked on journaling in eighth grade, the same year I'd won a state essay competition. Writing stories was my favorite hobby, though often I wondered if I had a choice. An internal force compelled me to set words to paper, and I felt driven to comply. Recording my thoughts in print helped me feel sane and whole. Yet I wasn't sure I had any real talent for the craft.

One day, in a private session, a college instructor told me, "You need to get out of my class."

I tried to hide my hurt feelings but failed. His words pierced my thin skin. *I earned a bachelor's degree with highest honors. Now I'm being kicked out of a community college writing class?*

He pressed on. "What are you doing here anyway?"

For an assignment, I had submitted to him a few journal entries. I didn't think my writing was *that* bad. I decided the guy must be testing my mettle. I locked eyes with him in self-defense. I was forty, well past the age when a college instructor could intimidate me.

"Get out there and do what you already know how to do." The professor pointed to my composition book. "These pieces are publishable."

I didn't believe him. To prove him wrong, I submitted one of my short essays to the *Dallas Morning News* and received a whopping seventy-five dollars for the commentary. Several more guest columns led to national speaking gigs. Soon, bizarre fan mail arrived and, in many of those letters, readers pushed me to write humor. They had observed what I had not. Satire was my first language.

Poking fun at life's absurdities made me feel like I was in on the joke instead of *being* the joke. I found no better way to relieve passive-aggression—the outgrowth of suppressed rage—than making fun of people and conditions that irritated me.

"You'll never make it as a writer," Dad said when I told him of my decision to author a humor book. "You're not Jewish."

I held my phone receiver far from my face and tried to count to ten. At three, I gave up. "What does that have to do with writing?"

"They *own* the publishing industry. They're not about to let you in."

He might have uttered anything to murder my ambitions, but I intended to disprove his theory. I continued writing satire, and he kept plotting ways to discourage me.

------⧶------

Dad dropped by my house unannounced, a habit he'd recently acquired. Anything to disrupt my writing schedule. He said he wanted to show me his latest cruise photos. With muted interest, I flipped through images of unknown seascapes and women to find a few pictures of Betty and a lone snapshot of my grandmother. Seated in a semicircle dining booth, Grandma looked bewildered. I suspected I knew the story behind her expression.

Aghast, Grandma had told me Dad had paraded through the buffet line every afternoon in a micro-swimsuit and T-shirt. Far too vividly, I imagined the scene. "My lands. The first time he did it, I thought he'd forgotten his britches," she'd exclaimed.

Having shared proof of his vacation exploits, Dad collected his pictures. He asked nothing about my life or summer vacation plans. I'd become so accustomed to that, it barely registered. Seemingly as an afterthought, on his way out my front door, he mentioned he'd joined a square dance club.

"How is that different than any other kind of dancing?" I demanded.

"Oh, it's different," he rationalized. "You follow calls, kind of like the hokey-pokey."

I folded my arms and stared him down. I wasn't so much angry about his new social life as infuriated about the one I'd unjustly missed. "I'm not buying it."

Dad sniggered. "I guess maybe I was a little strict. But hey, it's not too late for *me* to dance."

Betty had steered Dad toward the do-si-do crowd. A dance that required multiple partners must have been an easy sell to my father. Something was in it for her, too, if only an escape

Cruise photo of John on Costume Night

from Dad's mindless chatter. To follow the calls and perform the correct moves, he had to *listen*. That wasn't Dad's strong suit. He filled most social silences with idle banter. For no reason, he might spout off Albuquerque's sea elevation, tell a longwinded joke, or recite a monologue about World War II, which had ended when he was twelve. I never knew where his mind had traveled while I'd been entertaining relevant thoughts. But he'd clue me in before too much quiet slipped by.

While Dad flirted with the petticoat crowd, I focused on writing. I was grateful he'd acquired an active social life. When bored, he phoned me to talk about politics or family dramas. Sporadically, he would call to ask, "Have you got your TV on?" I would tell him no. Then he would reply, "You need to turn it on, right now," his voice urgent. "Go to the *Travel Channel*."

Firmly, I would respond, "I'm writing right now."

"Yeah, well you need to see this," he would insist. "*I've* been there."

When he wasn't calling me or flitting around with his square dance club, Dad thought up new do-it-yourself projects. The more the better, I decided. Anything to keep him occupied. Otherwise, he was sure to phone and ask, "Have you got your TV on?"

I never knew when I might see or hear about one of his harebrained pursuits. In early September, peak camping season, he phoned and announced, "I built a camper top for my truck."

"Oh, yeah?" Modestly impressed, I stirred a pot of chili and balanced a portable receiver between my chin and shoulder. "I didn't think Betty was big on camping."

"She's not," he said. "It's to protect things I'm hauling."

"What are you *hauling*?" I giggled. He lived in the suburbs and owned no livestock.

Dad sidestepped my question. "I'm building a carport right now, out of fiberglass."

I recalled the celery-colored fence he'd built when I was a child. The milky, corrugated material had incited city officials to revise local fence standards. "That ought to look good," I said facetiously. "Is fiberglass an approved material for carports? Have you checked your city building codes?"

"Don't need to."

I couldn't see it, but I sensed Dad's bullfrog chest expanding. "Why not?"

"Because it's *my* house!"

He must have heard my eye roll. "I take it you didn't apply for a permit either."

"Sure didn't."

"The World According to John," as Betty liked to say. Laws and city ordinances and social norms didn't apply to him. He was the only recognized authority in his life.

———⊗———

"Your dad's here," Jim called out one Sunday. He stood peering through our dining room windows. "Wait 'til you see what he just parked in front of our house."

I greeted my father at the front door. Peeking past him, I spied an A-frame structure towering above his pickup truck.

"Come see my camper," Dad said, inviting me outdoors for a closer look.

Jim and I followed him to the curb. I hoped my neighbors wouldn't notice the atrocity he had stationed in our cul-de-sac. It was hard to miss a truck that looked like a mobile wigwam. I scrutinized the malignant growth on Dad's truck bed.

"Why did you make it so tall?" I asked.

Jim studied the interior, an empty hull. His deadpan expression disguised his befuddlement. When Dad wasn't looking, he gave me a what-the-hell look.

"You can stand up in the middle," Dad crowed. "Get in and see!"

"There's nothing inside, so you can't really camp in it," I pointed out.

Dad frowned. "Sure, you can." He gestured to a rolled canvas flap. "Got all the privacy you need when you let that down."

With a forefinger, I tapped my lips. "But no bed, stove, or toilet."

"I'll put a full-size mattress in it later," Dad said, as if a cushion was the only comfort required to spend a night outdoors. For starters, I would need windows, electric connections, and a mini-fridge, but I kept that thought to myself.

Dad may have believed Betty would warm to camping, which required a vivid imagination. Betty had no earth-momma, live-off-the-grid longings. Her employer, a high-power legal firm, sent her to five-star hotels on assignments, places Dad considered too highfalutin for himself. She wouldn't go anywhere that required pit toilets, bug spray, and dry shampoo.

After I'd seen my father's illustrious camper top, I understood why the carport was necessary. His oversized vehicle wouldn't fit inside a standard garage. To remedy that situation, he had erected a ten-foot, vertical steel structure with a turquoise fiberglass roof. A custom carport to house his one-of-a-kind camper. It was another of Dad's many confounding missions. I didn't perceive this one held any more significance than the rest.

TWENTY-THREE

THE SATURDAY AFTER DAD SHOWED me his camper, Betty phoned. "Have you heard from your dad?" She sounded unusually concerned. Often, Dad visited home improvement stores on Saturday mornings. He never left notes. I envisioned him inside Payless Cashways, examining hardware for his latest project, or at a bakery, hand-selecting glazed doughnuts from a glass display.

"No, I haven't," I replied. "Has he gone missing?"

"I've been calling him since yesterday," Betty said. "He's not answering his cell."

"Is he out of town?" I collected my bearings. Dad's government employer never assigned travel on weekends, and he didn't attend square dance conventions without Betty. "Where'd he go?"

"Supposedly to Florida." Betty sniffed. "He claimed he wanted to go camping."

The data didn't add up. "By himself?"

"That's what he *said*."

I noted the skepticism in her voice. Under normal conditions, Dad wouldn't have embarked on a long journey alone. He hadn't informed me of his trip for a reason. And that reason, I suspected—just as Betty did—had a vagina.

"My stepfather died," Betty said. "I need to get to Louisiana right away, to my mother's. And I wanted John to take me. I'm too upset to drive." She drew a deep breath. "But I can't get ahold of him. He hasn't answered his cell in two days. I was hoping maybe he'd checked in with you."

"I'll call him and call you back," I said. "He's up to something."

I dialed Dad's cell number, twice. No answer. A half-hour later, I dialed him again. Still no response.

Baffled, I considered what our next move should be. I could easily deliver Betty to Louisiana. *But what about Dad? Does she need to inform highway patrol of his disappearance?* Technically, my father didn't meet the criteria for a missing person. He had alerted Betty to his departure and vague travel plans. Giving him the benefit of the doubt, which required amnesia, I feared he might have been carjacked. Highly improbable, I decided. Nobody in his right mind would want that freak show truck of his.

Mentally, I clicked through a list of possible explanations. *Maybe he flipped over an embankment in that unstable truck. Or he's somewhere too remote to get a cell signal. His phone could have died.* Dad's calls weren't rolling to voicemail. Slowly I accepted the truth—he had battery power. He knew his wife and daughter had tried to contact him. The man didn't want to be found.

I dialed Betty. "He's not answering my calls either. What do you think we should do?"

"He'll show up eventually."

"What if something's happened to him?"

"I don't think he's in jeopardy." Betty sounded more aggravated than worried. She had more pressing issues to address.

I decided to drive her to Louisiana. On the way there and back, we would have time to compare notes about Dad's whereabouts. I needed more information than I was getting. Betty seemed to have clues she wasn't confessing. I didn't pump her for information right away. She remained subdued for most of the trip.

"Let's just wait him out," Betty said about Dad. So that was what we did.

Six days later, Dad returned my phone calls. By then, he had arrived home and confessed his hidden location to Betty. He'd been camped in a Florida state park with a female square dancer. I struggled to process that news, though I couldn't say it was entirely surprising. *What kind of woman falls for a sixty-year-old, two-timing hobbit driving a mobile yurt?*

Betty went radio silent on me. She and I had been close during the ten years she'd lived with Dad. I didn't know it yet, but Dad had delivered her an eviction notice. Shock reverberated through me when I found out. I wanted to shake my father until his teeth rattled, anything to make him snap out of it.

Dad had no guilt or remorse. By phone, he confessed he'd already proposed to his cowgirl concubine. No need to divorce Betty, he self-righteously proclaimed. "We aren't legally married." What he said after that I didn't hear because it wasn't worth listening to.

I wondered if he'd developed a brain tumor. That might have been preferable to whatever else was going on. Brain cancer victims had better survival rates than Dad's lifestyle portended.

"I hope to die from being shot by a jealous husband," he frequently joked.

I feared he might soon get his wish. His assailant, though, was more apt to be a spurned woman.

Dad had two major issues to contend with—a hostile ex and a notice from his local building and inspections department. While he was galivanting, he'd received a court summons for city code violations. Meanwhile, Betty threatened more serious litigation. Hers and Dad's assets were too entangled to separate with a simple eviction letter. Hoping to resolve both matters, Dad put his house on the market. However, he couldn't skirt his legal duty to demolish his carport.

Dad's neighbors must have relished watching him disassemble the fiberglass eyesore. Wine goblets may have toasted the Sold sign on his front lawn. I envisioned middle fingers saluting him when he and his traveling tepee left town.

SECTION III

CLOSE CALLS

TWENTY-FOUR

MY PARENTS WERE LOCKED IN a dead heat to see who could rack up the most marriages. Dad's first square dance dalliance hadn't ended in matrimony—or murder. His next affair, though, had put the seal on a fourth wedding license. His and Mom's score would soon be tied.

Mom had outlived two spouses, both of whom had been in poor health from the get-go. Within a year of her second husband's death, she had married the third. With husband number three now two years deceased, Mom was antsy. Single life didn't suit her. She needed to "belong to somebody," she said.

Having eliminated as suitable partners all the widowers at her church and local bingo parlor, Mom had turned to the personal ad section of *Weekly World News* to find a mate. More alarming than her matchmaking methods was her penchant for weird headlines, such as "Elvis's Tomb Is Empty" and "I Was Bigfoot's Love Slave." There, amidst reports of alien abductions and Loch Ness Monster sightings, Mom found Jessie, her fourth husband.

I didn't have the benefit of reading Jessie's solicitation for a bride, the one Mom had pounced on before anyone else could "beat her to the altar." She informed me by phone of her long-distance verbal engagement. Jessie would be arriving tomorrow to claim her, she said. He was already on his way from Florida to Texas when she called to tell me.

If my mother had said she was eloping with a psychologist, I would have been less surprised. "You've got to be kidding me," I said when she confessed her plans.

"I knew you'd have something to say about it," Mom snapped. She had no misgivings about marrying a stranger and thought I shouldn't either.

I'm not sure why I was so stupefied by her announcement. She'd always been impulsive.

"It's my life, and I'm going to live it the way I please." I didn't have to see her to know her foot was drawn, her toes suspended toward the ceiling. "We're in love. We're getting married. And you can't talk me out of it," she said.

She hadn't asked for my blessing or opinion. Suppressing my cynicism, I withheld further comment. If Jessie had the wherewithal to travel from Florida to Texas, he was financially better off and healthier than her prior two husbands.

Mom and Jessie had corresponded for a month, she said. Each had mailed the other a somewhat dated portrait before they'd agreed to get hitched.

"He looks like a tall drink of water," Mom gushed.

The next day, Jessie arrived on schedule. He'd driven cross-country in a Ford pickup, pulling an empty trailer to collect his fiancée. Mom called me before she departed for Florida. I heard her cup her phone mouthpiece and tell Jessie to introduce himself.

She was used to shoving receivers at unsuspecting bystanders like that. I might be talking to her, and without any pretext, she would blurt, "Here, speak to my friend Penny. She's standing right here." Before I could ask who was Penny and what Mom wanted me to talk to her about, a foreign voice would cut in. It was one of my mother's most maddening habits.

Demonstrating a talent for improv, Jessie said, "I just want you to know me and your mama are like peas and carrots." He might have had a mouthful of chewing tobacco.

How original, a quote from Forest Gump.

Mom's high stakes version of speed dating bewildered me. Already, she'd married three men who'd been mentally challenged or terminally ill—or both. All Dad had lacked was a professional diagnosis. Now this one was enunciating like he had a few stray lug nuts. I hadn't expected her to marry a professor, but each of Mom's husbands had been less educated than his predecessor. Jessie was an eighth-grade dropout. His monthly social security check didn't come close to covering his bills. He'd been getting by with help from his son, Mom admitted.

Mom, nevertheless, was willing to forfeit her survivor's pension to marry him. "We can't live in *sin*," she'd said when I'd suggested a private commitment with God instead of a legal union.

"Congratulations," I disingenuously said to Jessie. I could think of no appropriate response to a vegetable analogy. *Peas and carrots?* I'd never liked that combination. Truth be told, I didn't care for him either. Not yet, anyway.

Jessie was on his way to becoming my *sixth* stepparent. I had resigned from the Official Welcoming Committee. Our family tree had more branches than Starbucks, and I was dizzy from cycling through kin.

Married three times, I had no room to criticize my parents' matrimonial quotas. I'd made poor choices too. The difference was, I had learned from my mistakes whereas they seemingly never did. I still felt I parented them instead of the other way around.

More than anything, I wanted to unleash from their reckless behaviors and impulsive decisions. Yet my conscience argued against pushing too far away from my mom or dad. "Honor thy father and thy mother," the Bible said. Still, I couldn't justify any further investments in my parents' love lives—if love was involved. I suspected pathology.

In her midsixties, Mom retreated into a world of porcelain dolls, scratch-off lottery tickets, and infomercial purchases. She wrote poems and sent them to a scam agency that published her work in microscopic font alongside *thousands* of other rhymes and then sold her the anthology for fifty dollars. The company had taken her money so many times, they'd sent her a trophy as big as her head.

When she wasn't writing and submitting poems to con artists, Mom dialed toll-free numbers to purchase sparkly trinkets and exercise equipment her cardiologist discouraged. Gold-plated rings bejeweled with fake stones dilated her pupils. Home Shopping Network hosts were her best friends. I didn't understand her priorities, and she was equally confused by mine. We couldn't connect beyond a surface level.

Intimacy was not a state Mom desired. Reluctantly I accepted what I'd spent a lifetime denying. I would never have the relationship I craved with my mom or dad. With clarity, I recognized that didn't make me a bad person.

My parents weren't truth seekers on a path to enlightenment. It wasn't my job to educate or change them. My only duty was to acknowledge them for who they were and forgive them for their shortcomings. I was not obligated to praise, agree with, or suffer for their decisions. God had never commanded me to trust them either.

TWENTY-FIVE

D<small>AD'S FOURTH WIFE, EVELYN, INVITED</small> me and Jim to her home for Dad's seventy-third birthday celebration. We would be the only visitors. I didn't know what to expect because Evelyn wasn't big on entertaining. Or if she was, I hadn't made her guest list in a decade.

Evelyn was hard to read. When she spoke, I strained to hear her. Number Four, as I often thought of her, asked many questions about me and my brothers but disclosed next to nothing about herself. I suspected she was either Dad's lapdog or a wolf in domestic disguise. I couldn't decide which, though I bore no animosity toward her.

On the surface, Evelyn didn't appear to need my father's income or inheritance. She had her own home. He lived with her instead of the other way around. If and when their marriage dissolved, Dad would be the one on the wrong end of an eviction notice.

Mentally, I rehearsed for my visit to Dad's home turf. *Don't be offended by what he says. Don't swallow the lure when he plays his fishing games. And whatever you do, don't mention any topic he can wrangle into an off-colored joke.*

Being that it was Dad's birthday, calamity was all but guaranteed.

When Jim and I arrived at Evelyn's house, I handed my father some contact sheets of professional headshots. From the numbered proofs, I needed to choose an author photo for my first book. I had tacked sticky notes to a few potential choices, none of which stood out. "The paper on top shows the ones I'm considering," I said, hoping to divert Dad's attention from the duds.

From his overstuffed recliner, Dad wobbled to a stand. He steadied the prints under his reading lamp. Squinting, he studied the top sheet. "Boy," he said as if witnessing images of two-headed calves, "I definitely would *not* recommend using number one."

"I didn't choose that one," I hissed. "Give me those." Heat climbed to my neck and cheeks.

Dad handed over the proofs and averted his gaze. He plopped into his lounger as if rewinding his movements. Leaned forward, he petted his cat—a stray he'd taken in. He still knew how to insult me and appear oblivious.

Evelyn disappeared down a hallway. Jim and I were still exchanging mortified looks when she returned with a manila file folder. "These are our obituary photos," Evelyn said. She giggled nervously. Possibly, she hoped to distract me from Dad's earlier rude remark. "We had them made separately so they could be used for our funerals."

I smiled through clenched teeth, still seething at Dad. He continued stroking his cat and displayed no interest in Evelyn's show-and-tell. She opened the folder. The top picture was an eight-by-ten image of Dad in a tuxedo, flaunting that obnoxious grin he flashed every time anyone aimed a camera at him. His smugness vaulted from the print and all but dared me to smack him. I wanted to say, "Boy, I'm not sure I'd use *that* one," but I wasn't that discourteous.

"I thought he said he'd have to be dead before he'd wear a tux," I said.

Evelyn rushed to Dad's defense. "He has a problem with the studs—"

"Ahem. I wish you'd find another way to say that," Dad interrupted from across the room.

Before he could run south with Evelyn's remark, Jim intercepted it. "Oh, I know." Jim indicated the onyx-colored circles affixed to Dad's shirt buttons. "I mean, if he inhaled deeply, one of those things could fly across the room and *kill* somebody."

Diffused by my husband's remark, Dad switched subjects. He blathered about finding a first-place ribbon amidst my grandmother's belongings, a blue banner embossed with a mill company's moniker. How he had made the leap from portraits to mystery prizes, I couldn't fathom. I didn't waste brain wattage trying to figure it out. "I don't know *where* it came from." Dad sounded as if he'd uncovered an adopted sibling. "Nobody seems to recall the flour company, not even Susan Brunswick."

Ah, now I understood. He was name-dropping. This conversation, I gathered, was Dad's platform for announcing his esteemed associates. "Who's Susan Brunswick?" I pretended to care.

Dad looked at me as if I'd inquired who John F. Kennedy was. "Why, she's the *head* of the Emerson heritage club."

I stifled a supercilious laugh. "Maybe Grandma won it in some kind of cooking contest."

He inhaled deeply, inflating

Grandma, John, and Janis

his chest. "She sure *did* win a contest—" He waited for a stooge to respond.

None did.

"The prettiest baby contest." Dad gave Jim a smug look.

"That was for your sister, *Janis*. Right?" Jim wisecracked.

With my eyes, I sent him a high five.

Dad's sister and only sibling had been blessed with her mother's cornflower-blue eyes and ivory complexion. In her younger years, she'd resembled Elizabeth Taylor. Dad was less genetically fortunate. As a boy, his impish face, protruding ears, and round spectacles had made him look like a pint-size professor.

Dad's body deflated like a wounded balloon. "No. It was *me!*"

Jim shrugged. Evelyn chortled. On my way to the kitchen table, I sucker-laughed at Dad.

In August, seven months after Evelyn's birthday bash for Dad, my humor book *Driving on the Wrong Side of the Road* debuted. I anticipated a low turnout for my book launch because first-time authors seldom generate measurable excitement. One by one, guests trailed into a local Starbucks and filled the reserved section. About fifty loyal readers showed up.

Billed as a come-and-go affair, guests arrived early for free coffee, punch, and desserts. As I made small talk with friends and neighbors, my dad and Evelyn strolled in and claimed a distant four-top table.

Great. I wonder what he's up to. I hadn't specifically invited Dad because I feared he might make a scene. In passing, the date had been mentioned, and he'd shown no interest. I hadn't expected to see him there.

Uncharacteristically, Dad sat with his back to me. In my

nightmares, I envisioned him standing and recounting the potato chip story to my guests. Maybe he'd brought along some embarrassing childhood photos to share. I didn't put anything past him. Dressed in his standard uniform—chocolate-brown loafers, black socks, Bermuda shorts, a tropical-print shirt, and a straw hat—he was impossible to miss. Now and then, he would turn to catch my attention.

What does he want me to notice? There's something I'm overlooking. I spoke with my guests and kept signing books. But Dad's presence and demeanor unsettled me. Finally, he twisted his body far enough for me to observe his front half. Wedged in his hatband was a five-inch, vertical note card imprinted in bold font: "Page 165."

From my signing table, I fanned a book copy. An essay titled "Abnormal Dad's Day" began on page 165. *He must have perused the advanced copy I gave him.* I couldn't fathom why he would resent anything I'd written in that vignette.

Suddenly, Dad's reason for being there dawned on me. This wasn't my debut. It was *his.*

Dad and Evelyn did not approach me during the two-hour celebration that, to me, felt more like a public shaming. They didn't need to. My father had accomplished his goal without ever leaving his seat or opening his mouth. He knew how to wound my self-esteem. My life force evaporated in his presence. When he entered a room, he stole all the light and oxygen inside. I choked and withered like a sun-starved zinnia in his shadow.

But that day, he did not strangle me from existence. I didn't permit him to crash my book launch or diminish my accomplishment, though I felt certain that was his intent. My book signing concluded without me introducing him to anyone.

TWENTY-SIX

A YEAR AFTER MY FIRST BOOK release, the 2007 financial crisis struck America. Jim, a risk manager for a multinational lender, worked sixty- to eighty-hour weeks hoping to dodge the next layoff. Together we watched our retirement savings dwindle and benefits disappear. Almost overnight, our home value declined six figures. While we contended with serious losses, Dad complained about his CD interest rates—regularly phoning us to protest.

Usually, Dad called at dinnertime. Ours, not his. Jim and I consumed our meals against a backdrop of mind-numbing chatter, multitasking to preserve our precious few evening hours. I would balance a portable receiver next to my plate and mumble one-word responses. Sometimes I hit the mute button and conversed with Jim while Dad ranted.

One memorable night, Dad's conversation turned to the Bear Sterns bailout. Tongue-tied with revulsion, he said, "It's all those… those… damn *bankers'* fault." As Dad droned on about the economy and "the profiteers of peril," Jim pantomimed his sentiments. "If it wasn't for those greedy *bankers*," Dad continued, "none of this would have happened."

In my peripheral, I observed Jim stand, push back his dining chair, and climb onto the leather seat. I studied him, thinking perhaps he'd found a spiderweb on the ceiling or spotted a defective lightbulb. My father's monotonous diatribes compelled him to inspect light fixtures and smoke alarms. He might trim his fingernails or read condiment labels while Dad proselytized. Once, he'd grabbed a steak knife from the countertop and mimicked hara-kiri. I sensed another funny skit underway.

Jim pantomimed stringing a noose from the ceiling. He checked to be sure I was enjoying his phony execution. I was. Looping an imaginary rope over his head, he secured the pretend knot.

I muted the speakerphone and guffawed at his gallows humor. Always, I could depend on my soul twin to make me laugh when I most needed to.

Jim leapt from his chair to the tile floor, his legs stiff as a dead man's.

"They ought to take 'em all out and shoot 'em," Dad yammered.

Hunched over and grasping his neck, my spouse hopped on one foot. He no longer appeared to be joking. "Owwwwww, owww, owww!" he cried, his face twisted with pain. He hobbled to his recliner and collapsed like he'd been shot.

Jim's spinal fusion, one month later, gave his archrival more reasons to call. "How's Jim?" Dad would ask right off when I answered the phone. I hadn't divulged the truth about hubby's operation, and I never would. Dad would have relished it too much.

"He's doing okay," I would reply.

Before I could offer any specifics, Dad would fast-forward to his intended subject. It might be anything from Dr. Phil's guests that day to facts he'd learned from the History Channel to a crime he'd heard about from Nancy Grace, not directly but from her TV show. In retirement, he had little else to talk about. Often, he presented a litany of complaints about the weather, politics, or my brothers, whom he no longer called "The Boys." Fishing for updates, he would ask me, "Heard anything from South Texas?"

My brothers lived within the Gulf Coast region, not South Texas. We spoke infrequently and rarely saw each other. What little I knew about their lives had been gleaned from social media or filtered through Mom, which made my information suspect. Dad wanted me to be his go-between. When I declined, he recited to me the hazards of smoking, alcoholism, and underemployment—hoping I would relay his opinions.

Eventually, I quit answering Dad's calls and let them roll to my answering machine, a predecessor to digital voicemail. That afforded me no relief. Jim and I would suffer through four obnoxious phone rings before the recorded message clicked on. Twenty seconds of painful silence followed. Then, right before the machine cut off, Dad would blurt, "I need you to call me."

When I returned Dad's calls, his needs were never critical. He simply wanted to complain to someone, and I was the only one gracious or dumb enough to accommodate him. He would get all coiled up about an inconvenience or annoyance and expect me to listen until, like a windup toy, his gears quit turning.

For months, he argued that a cousin's gravestone violated cemetery standards. "It's turned the wrong way," he complained. "It's facing east, and it's supposed to face west." This type of affront could incite him to ring me four times in the same week with equal outrage.

I wondered how Evelyn escaped his constant rattle.

"Maybe if he'd talk to his *wife*, he wouldn't have to call *you* so much," Jim suggested.

Enjoying a glorious afternoon nap, I heard our home phone ring. "Ignore it," I told Jim before dozing off again.

"You know it's your dad," he snarled. "I swear I can tell by the sound of the ring."

Propped on our elbows, we listened as the answering machine engaged. I tugged Jim's neck, guiding him back to his pillow. "If it's important, he'll leave a message. And if it's *not*, he'll leave a message. Either way, I can call him back later."

The machine hissed for a full minute before the recording time ended. "Must have been somebody else." Those bright words had barely left my lips when my cell phone sounded. I counted four obnoxious rings before the call rolled to voicemail.

Jim threw back the sheets and stared at the ceiling. "Will the man *never* leave us alone?"

Lovingly, I stroked his arm. I couldn't believe it when Jim's cell phone rang. Four times.

"Dear God!" he raged.

This round-robin game of dialing the home phone, my cell, then Jim's cell, had become Dad's newest brand of punishment. He would ring *all* our phones precisely one minute apart and never leave a message. Every thirty minutes, he would repeat the process until someone answered. If Jim responded, Dad would instruct him to tell me to return his call.

"Is there anything I can help with, John?" my unbelievably tolerant spouse would ask.

Dad always told him no.

After about the sixth unanswered call, I would phone Dad. "What's the emergency?"

"There's no emergency," he would say, sounding surprised.

Suppressing a scream, I would remind him, "You've called me

every fifteen minutes for the past two hours." I was on the verge of losing my marbles and possibly my marriage.

The pent-up anger I carried caused me to withdraw from friends and family. Dad's demands had become so all-consuming that I had no energy to devote to others' needs—including my own. When I wasn't dealing with him, I was fuming about his incessant intrusions. *Don't I deserve a separate life? Why won't he leave me alone long enough for me to have one?*

I rose from bed, angrier than a provoked yellowjacket. "I might as well call him back before the phones start ringing again."

Jim stomped into the bathroom, mumbling something under his breath.

Evelyn answered on the fourth ring. "What's Dad calling me about this time?" I hoped she would catch my drift. *Get a handle on your husband!*

"I have no idea." She sounded groggy at two p.m. "He's not here. I'm not sure where he is." I waited while she checked the garage. "His car's gone," she said with detectible relief.

I hung up, as mad at her as I was at him. *She gets to nap while he disturbs me. Oh, I see how it works.*

"J-u-u-u-st *great*," I said to Jim. "He's not home."

Dad's most recent ploy involved showing up on our doorstep unexpectedly. As difficult as he made it, I still loved my father. But he needed to back off. I had a husband and extended family who deserved more from me than they were getting. Dad had a wife. I could not be a spouse to two men. It was hard enough to keep one happy.

"Let's go to the library," Jim said. "Turn your cell off. Ignore it when it vibrates. You can call him back at *your* convenience."

I gathered my book tote and purse. We left before Dad could repeat his drill.

We'd been away from home an hour when Jim steered onto our street and hit the brakes. "Your dad's car's sitting in front of our house." He groaned.

From a block away, we studied our stalker. "What's he doing?" I craned my neck to get a better look and observed Dad seated in his vehicle. His sedan's hood pointed away from ours. He couldn't see us without looking through his rearview mirror. "Oh Lord, he's waiting for us to return. I wonder how long he's been sitting there."

I checked my cell. It was still set on vibrate. "Yep, he's called twice since we left. The last call was at three-o-eight, a half-hour ago. No message, of course."

If I'd had a healthy relationship with my father, I might have rushed to greet him. But the more I catered to his whims, the more entitled he acted. He'd likely driven to our house to prove I couldn't shake him off by ignoring his calls. He would pester me every way he could until he got what he wanted.

Dad's car crept forward. We held a steady position until he'd turned a corner. He hadn't seen us.

"Phew!" Jim sighed. "That was close."

Thirty minutes later, our home phone sounded. The headset displayed Dad's phone number. On the fourth ring, right before the call rolled to voicemail, I answered. Out of spite, I'd made him wait. I wanted him to squirm, to sense his powerlessness, to fear being reduced to a digital recording.

"Where have you been?" Dad demanded.

"We went to the library," I said. "Is something wrong?"

"No, I just needed to tell you we're going out of town in a couple of weeks."

"Okay. But why's that urgent?"

"I thought I'd better tell you while I was thinking about it.

That's all," Dad said. "We're going to Colorado to see Evelyn's daughter for two weeks."

"Time to celebrate!" I said to Jim after I'd bid my father *adios, hasta la vista, bon voyage*, and *sayonara*. Maybe my nerves would settle while he was out of town. In my dreams, he and Evelyn would relocate to the Centennial State. For now, though, I had won a reprieve from his calls and visits. Time to break out the wine goblets and pour a toast.

TWENTY-SEVEN

I CALLED MY BROTHER KERRY TO compare notes about Dad. "He's showing up at my house unannounced if I don't answer my phone," I said.

Kerry laughed as though my grievance was nothing. "He's *always* come to my house without calling first. You should have seen what he did the last time he was here. I was mad enough to fight him."

I calculated the distance. "That's, like, a six-hour drive, isn't it?"

"Yes! And he refuses to call and see if I'm even going to be home when he gets here. Then he's mad if I don't answer the door immediately, even when I wasn't expecting him."

I sniggered at the thought of Dad and Kerry staring each other down. "You know that's crazy, right?"

"I think he's hoping he can catch me doing something."

"Like what?" I asked.

Kerry and his second wife, Barbara, lived in rural Texas. His lifestyle was anything but salacious. Retired, he sang and played guitars when he wasn't watching the Discovery Channel or mowing his two-acre lawn. Other than karaoke gigs on Saturday nights, Kerry hardly left home. "It's not like you're dropping acid with hookers," I teased. "What would he think you're doing?"

"Who knows? His mind's pretty weird," Kerry observed.

In a spirit of one-upmanship, I relayed to him Dad's most flagrant offense. "One Sunday, we heard the doorbell and didn't answer. We figured whoever it was would leave. But naturally, it was Dad, and he wasn't about to go anywhere until he was sure I wasn't home." I chortled. "He peeped through the garage windows and saw our cars, so he figured we were out back by the pool. We were in bed, though."

Kerry laughed. "I bet you didn't stay there."

"Oh no, of course not. I heard what sounded like someone in our backyard, so I peeked through the shutters. There was Dad, looking in all our windows like he was doing a welfare check." I snort-laughed. "He pounded on the back door until Jim let him in. I can't even take a nap anymore or leave my blinds open," I whined. "I never know when he might be out there staring in at me."

"Oh, that's nothing," Kerry replied. "When he came here, I was sitting in my room with my headphones on and singing. I didn't hear him knock at either door. And you know what? He got mad as hell 'cause he thought I was ignoring him." Kerry guffawed. "Barb was in the bathroom, so she couldn't answer. My truck was sitting out front. He *knew* I was here. He went around the house, knocking on all my windows until he banged on my office window so loud I almost had a heart attack!"

Kerry had always been jumpy and prone to panic attacks. I could imagine him rocketing from his office chair, startled from his moment in song.

"I went to the front to let him in, and he was *mad*," Kerry continued. "He said, 'Why aren't you answering your door?' And I said, 'Why don't you tell somebody when you're coming?'"

It appeared I wasn't getting preferential treatment, after all. Dad was imposing on Kerry, too, though far less frequently.

"Do you think he's losing it?" I asked. "Not that he's ever been right in the head."

"Nah. He's been this way as long as I can remember," Kerry said. "I'm just glad I don't live close to him, like you. He can't show up here anytime he wants."

"He can't show up here right now. He's in Colorado," I crowed. "And you know what? I bet he didn't arrive at Evelyn's daughter's house *unannounced*."

<hr/>

"I'm calling to tell you what's going on," Evelyn said, her speech clipped. "John's driven back to Texas, and I'm still in Colorado."

If Evelyn was phoning me for advice, she'd chosen the wrong lifeline—though I appreciated her alert. "Why'd he leave?" I braced to hear a lame excuse.

"He said he didn't want to miss Nancy's funeral. Chuck Jackson called and told him she died yesterday."

I searched my memory. Chuck Jackson was Dad's high school buddy, the one who'd introduced him to Mom. It took a second for me to recall the deceased. "Nancy? His fiancée from over fifty years ago?"

"Yes," Evelyn confirmed.

I wondered why Dad would drive twelve hours to attend an old—and I do mean *old*—girlfriend's funeral. Even for him, that seemed unreasonable. "Had he kept in touch with her?"

"He went to visit her in the hospital a few weeks before we left," Evelyn confided.

In my many recent exchanges with Dad, he hadn't mentioned that.

"He insisted on going." Evelyn's exasperation was evident in her voice. "I waited in the car." She paused. "The woman's been married for *sixty years* to the same man."

I squeaked out a perplexed, "Wow."

"I'll fly home when I'm ready," Evelyn said, ignoring the elephant begging her attention. "I just wanted to make you aware. I figured he hadn't told you."

He hadn't. Dad was a maestro at sharing mundane trivia and hiding pertinent facts. I hadn't heard a word about the legendary Nancy or her illness and most assuredly not her death. *Nancy.* I rolled the name around in my mind. *The gal with the big breasts? The woman whose memory he resurrected to taunt my mother?* He wasn't at risk of disappearing with *her.*

Dad didn't surface until a few days after Nancy's funeral when he phoned and asked me to meet him for lunch. I accepted his invitation with grave concern. Even for Dad, leaving Evelyn stranded so he could attend a previous girlfriend's funeral seemed off-kilter.

Dad scooted into the restaurant booth and sat opposite of me, his expression flat. He offered no immediate revelations after we exchanged greetings. We'd met at a diner near his house. He ordered the barbecue sandwich with fries and a Dr Pepper. No surprises there either.

After the waiter left our table, Dad leaned forward. "I've been listening to Neil Diamond in the car." His eyes welled, and I thought he might cry. "You need to hear this song I've been playing."

Neil Diamond's melancholy ballads were well-known to me. *"Stones"*? I wondered. *"Play Me"*?

"I've heard all his songs," I said. "Which one's your favorite?"

Dad gave me a reprimanding look. "You don't understand."

I didn't. I waited for him to elaborate. He couldn't possibly suggest a Neil Diamond tune had been his and Nancy's love song. Neil Diamond wasn't *that* old.

For several seconds, Dad fiddled with his shirt breast pocket. Pinching an object inside the fabric pouch, he said, "I need to show you something."

"All right." I willed my facial muscles to freeze. He was in a delicate condition, I could see, which made him all the more unpredictable.

With no further prelude, he offered me a folded card showcasing a woman's portrait. The black-and-white photo might have been a high school senior picture. There was nothing remarkable about the young lady's looks or figure, assuming the image belonged to Nancy. "Who's this?" I asked as if I couldn't have guessed.

Dad sucked in a series of short breaths. "The woman who should have been your mother."

Should have been my mother? He might as well have dumped a garbage pail on my head. His admission suggested he'd produced four accidental children and an equal number of second-rate wives. *Has he forgotten?* Nancy was the one who'd broken their engagement sixty-two years earlier. There'd never been any chance of reconciliation.

"You do realize she couldn't have been my mother," I countered. He deserved a dose of reality, and I had the medicine. "And if you'd married her, you'd be a widower now, and I wouldn't be sitting here."

Dad shrugged. "I didn't mean I wish I had different kids, but she was the only woman I ever loved." With a pitiful look, he studied the memorial card.

215

If Nancy was his one and only love, he'd comforted himself with a slew of substitutes. I couldn't be sure he'd ever been engaged to Nancy. Every story Dad told was suspect, including the one he conveyed now.

From Nancy's obituary, I gleaned more details. She'd been two years younger than Dad and a grade behind him. If his story was right, she'd broken up with him before she'd graduated high school. Nancy had married two years later, which matched the excuse Dad had given for why she'd refused his proposal.

Nancy's mother had expected her to work after graduation to help support her siblings. Dad claimed he hadn't learned that until years later. He said he would have waited for her if she'd confessed her obligation. I didn't believe that either. My father waited for no one.

Whatever the facts, Dad seemed to have forgotten them. His past and present were so entangled that he couldn't tease them apart. I no longer wondered if his brain was on the blink. I knew it was.

When two weeks passed and Evelyn hadn't returned from Colorado, I wondered if she ever would. Almost November, Denver's first snow had fallen. I presumed Evelyn might decide to stay at her daughter's house through the holidays. I wouldn't have blamed her. An extended visit might have been in Dad's best interest. Possibly, she was still cooling off.

Dad had been exceptionally quiet. Like a child, when he'd grown silent, he'd strayed off-limits. I both delighted in and worried about his sudden withdrawal. *Maybe he's incapacitated with depression.* Concerned, I phoned to check on him.

He answered on the second ring.

"Hey," I said, "what'cha been up to?"

"I met some very nice friends." Dad sounded as if he'd rallied from his grief. If he'd found somewhere to go besides my house and his local supermarket, I was eager to hear about it. He needed to stay entertained until Evelyn returned, assuming she eventually would.

"Oh, yeah? Where'd you meet these new people?" The news excited me. Maybe that was all Dad needed, *friends*.

"At the cemetery," he said.

Uh-oh. The wheels are off his wagon. "Only dead people hang out in cemeteries," I scoffed.

"No. You're wrong," he corrected. "I met a nice couple there on Sunday, sitting next to their daughter's grave."

"What were you doing at their daughter's grave?" He'd lured me into a game of twenty questions in which each answer would trigger a more baffling admission.

"I went to visit Nancy, and they were sitting a few graves away, having a Sunday picnic. They go every Sunday afternoon." Dad's sentences fired in rapid succession. "They said I could join them, so I did. I'm meeting them there again next Sunday."

I'd waded into deep waters and immediately regretted it. "Does Evelyn know you're doing this?"

"Why would she need to know?"

I held the receiver in one hand and pressed my other palm to my forehead. "Um, because she's your *wife*?"

"She's still in Colorado."

"Yeah, but I assume she's coming home at some point." *Why do I feel like I'm talking to an eight-year-old?*

"She sleeps real late," Dad said.

I quit asking questions. His responses were distressing me.

When I relayed the conversation to Jim, I asked, "Do you think he's gone completely nuts?"

Jim sat on the sofa, fiddling with his laptop. "No. That sounds totally normal for your dad." His gaze met mine. "What I don't understand is why you keep acting surprised by what he does. He's the same man he's always been."

Jim was right, of course. Dad had been nine kinds of weird for as long as I could remember. I'd simply never before witnessed this specific peculiarity.

A week after Evelyn returned home, she phoned me. "You're not going to believe where John took me on Sunday without telling me *where* we were going."

I played along. "Oh, I bet I would."

She didn't give me time to guess. "He wanted me to get out of the car and meet some strangers in a *cemetery*!"

TWENTY-EIGHT

WINTER SET IN HARD, AND spring came early. Dad sustained his Sunday vigils at Nancy's grave until July, when triple-digit heat finally drove him from the cemetery. Instead of graveyard picnics, he sought indoor events that offered chilled air and free food. His local senior center met both requirements, but Dad preferred a good memorial service to canasta and finger sandwiches.

Similar to the game "Six Degrees from Kevin Bacon," a link between my father and most any deceased person could be found if he searched hard enough. Under the guise of affiliation, he attended more funerals than a church organist.

"Why are you going to so many funerals?" I ask during one of our many phone conversations. "Your hairstylist's niece seems pretty far-reaching."

"It's like a high school reunion," Dad replied. "You never know who you might see there."

When he wasn't hobnobbing next to someone's casket, Dad sat outdoors under the large magnolia tree in his front yard. There, from his little red canvas folding chair, he would phone me in secrecy. Convinced that Evelyn was stealing money from his bank account, he begged my help. With urgency, he would call when she left home, commanding me to come quickly and chauffeur him to his bank and credit union. It was imperative, he said, that he verified his account balance while Evelyn was away. He didn't own a computer anymore. Statements were too dated to be trusted, he maintained. Only an up-to-the-minute printout from a teller sufficed him.

Unsure of Evelyn's guilt or innocence, I agreed to assist him. If I drove, I reasoned, at least I would know where he was—and I could see the facts for myself. In Dad's twenty-year marriage to Evelyn, I'd never ascertained who she was or why she put up with him.

When Dad checked his bank accounts, the debits and credits revealed no irregularities. Yet that didn't stop his suspicions. As the friction between him and Evelyn mounted, each used my phone as a crisis hotline. Complaints peppered me from both sides, often within the same day. One would wait until the other was absent to recite a laundry list of grievances that went something like this:

She sent him to the store for laundry detergent. He returned with bleach.

He couldn't get her to clean the house.

She couldn't make him change his clothes.

He threw away her favorite dish scrubber.

She wouldn't discard her empty soda cans.

He forgot to buy her roses for Valentine's Day.

No one reminded him what day was Valentine's Day.

She overslept.

He disappeared for hours without explanation.

On and on it went. I guessed they'd quit watching Dr. Phil.

A year after Dad stopped visiting Nancy's grave, I developed a heart flutter. Frankly, I don't know what took me so long. I was watching my grandson play lacrosse one afternoon in early spring when I first noticed what felt like a live bird striving to flee my chest. Immediately, I made an appointment with a cardiologist.

My chest flutter, as it turned out, was caused by a leaky heart valve. "Have you been under much stress lately?" my cardiologist asked.

I stifled a laugh. On a scale of one to ten, I seldom dropped below eight.

"You need to reduce the stress in your life right away," the doctor advised.

His recommendation seemed unrealistic. But I didn't want my father's mental health and marital troubles to *kill* me. I hoped to live at least twenty more years. At the rate my health was deteriorating, my father might outlive me.

I knew I had to establish better boundaries with Dad— and Evelyn. *How can I get him to respect limits when he's never acknowledged any?* Short of moving to Ecuador, I could think of nothing extreme enough to work. It was time to seek professional help.

SECTION IV

Hope, Denial, and Surrender

TWENTY-NINE

C HRIS DIDN'T LOOK LIKE ANY therapist I'd seen in movies. He was not a frail man in a three-button cardigan, seated behind a mahogany desk. His imposing stature and physique made him appear better suited for weight lifting than head shrinking. In a wingback chair, he sat across from me, his legs falling into a relaxed *manspread*.

"Tell me about your early childhood," he probed.

I had come to him seeking guidance for family problems. This was our second or maybe third session. I wondered if I could provide a thorough response to his open-ended question without going broke. *Early childhood? Where do I start?*

"My father and I were always close," I began. "But over time, he's demanded more and more from me. He wants…"

Chris let me drone on for several minutes before he raised a forefinger to cut me off. "You keep telling me about what your father wants. What do *you* want?"

Stumped, I searched for an answer. I needed time to think. This wasn't Trivial Pursuit. I couldn't blurt a snappy response to such a serious question. *Why is he pressing me like this?*

Chris's eyes soften. "That's what I thought." He peered unapologetically into what felt like my soul. "No one's ever asked you that question, have they?"

Not that I could recall.

My desires conflicted. What I wanted seemed impossible to achieve. I yearned for an independent life, a strong marriage, a loving extended family, and more writing time. Also, I wished to be a good wife, mother, grandmother, sister, and daughter. But how could I feel like an adequate daughter or a loving person if I didn't make sacrifices for my aging father?

"The problem is the phones—" I evaded Chris's question.

He interrupted me again. "Stop answering your phones. Turn them off. Unplug them. Let the calls roll to voicemail. If it's urgent, he'll call back. Otherwise, don't respond."

I'm paying him good money for this advice? "Won't work. I've already tried that. He just shows up on my doorstep."

Chris blinked and waited.

I had nothing more to say.

When that became obvious, Chris replied, "So, don't open the door." He might as well have added, "*Duh.*"

I shook my head. He didn't understand my opponent's expertise. I gave my therapist a patronizing look. "He won't go away that easily."

Chris studied me, probably calculating my emotional age. "Then call the police. Tell them there's an intruder in your yard. Trust me, he *will* go away if *you* stop responding."

Therapy was more painful than I'd imagined.

———

One morning, about six months after I'd begun counseling, my doorbell rang. Though it was not yet daylight, Jim had already left for work. Dressed in a sports bra and yoga pants, I was up and ready to exercise. The bell startled me.

I feared maybe a burglar had seen Jim's car exit the garage and was casing the house. Nervously I peeked out a window and observed Dad. Standing on my front porch in the early morning frost, he wore no coat or cap.

I creaked my front door partway open, careful to keep my body hidden, and craned my neck to greet him. "Dad? What are you doing here?"

Bypassing my question, he stepped closer.

I wedged one foot against the door. "You'll need to wait here a minute. I'm not dressed."

"Oh, you're not?" He looked surprised, as though I were the one out of sync with the clock.

I threw on a sweatshirt and let him inside. "Aren't you cold? Where's your coat?"

He glanced at one shirt sleeve and appeared stunned to see his outerwear missing. "No. I'm not cold," he said, excusing his forgotten jacket. "I need your help me with this... this... well, uh..." He tottered past me and into my kitchen. At my breakfast table, he took a seat.

Perplexed, I joined him. I pointed to the thick white wrapper jutting from his shirt pocket. "Is that money?"

"Yeah!" he said, appreciating the reminder. He removed the bank envelope from his pocket.

Dad couldn't remember his grandkids' names or how to spell them, he confessed. But he knew it was almost Christmas, and he was supposed to do something with money and cards. Some internal alarm had set him on a course from his house to mine, a twenty-five-minute drive in heavy morning traffic, to seek help. I'd ruled out any chance that Evelyn had prompted him. The two slept in separate bedrooms and observed different sleep cycles. I doubted Evelyn was awake at that hour.

Even outside my therapist's office, I could hear Chris's advice. It played like a recording on a continuous loop. "Tell him to ask his *wife* for help. You're his *daughter*, not his spouse."

My follow-through, for lack of a better word, sucked. What sounded reasonable and doable from Chris's cushioned sofa felt impossible to practice in my kitchen. Sure, Dad could have waited until Evelyn woke and solicited her help. He had found it more expedient to motor across town and seek me out. *How can I refuse?* Seeing him standing in the cold, improperly dressed, had tugged my heartstrings. Turning him away would have been senseless and cruel.

"The more you do, the more she'll let you do," Chris said of Evelyn, whom he'd never met. He didn't need to know her. In his profession, he'd met hundreds of Evelyns. "Call her when he shows up at your place so she'll know where he is, then send him home."

<hr />

"I couldn't do it," I confessed to Chris. "He's sick, and he's my dad. Good daughters don't bail on their fathers when they're ill."

"Okay," Chris said, his tone nonjudgmental. "But tell me one thing. When did he ever act like a father to you?"

My dad had taught me the alphabet and how to tie my shoes. He'd forced Mom to learn to drive on my behalf, I said. He'd taken me on extended vacations and shown me how to tackle difficult tasks and thwart school bullies.

"Uh-huh. And what happened later, when you were older?" Chris pressed. He already knew the answer. He simply wanted to hear my version, again, to listen to my rationalizations and denials so he could dismantle my false narrative. He had the unnerving ability to climb inside my head, divine my thoughts, and cry "Bullshit!" without ever opening his mouth. The guy could spot a lie from a hundred yards away, especially one I told to myself. At times, I both appreciated and detested his intuition and candor.

Recalling the jokes my father had played on me, the teasing, the pranks, I defended Dad. "He paid attention to me. It was just in strange ways, maybe the only ways he knew how."

Chris leaned forward, resting his forearms on his knees. His eyes held my gaze. "You do realize your father wasn't playing tricks on you, don't you? He was *grooming* you." He let that sink in for a second. "You were never your father's daughter. You were his substitute wife. And whether you know it or not, you're still playing that role."

Grooming? I thought I might have misunderstood him. *Isn't that what pedophiles do to seduce their victims?* Chris's indictments leveled me. Shocked and horrified, I wept for the rest of the session. The truth had not set me free. It had split my core, debunked lifelong beliefs that had, up until then, allowed me to deny my past. Myths I'd fabricated prevented me from accepting my betrayal. *How could anyone who loved me have been so cruel?* No obstructions were left to conceal the facts—or my pain. I wailed, grieving my shattered past, my lost childhood, and my unwitting participation in my misery. I had never wanted to be my father's emotional spouse. I had assumed that role the same way a tourist gets pick-pocketed in a foreign land.

"It's not your fault," Chris said gently.

Maybe not, but as an adult, I shared fractional ownership.

The father who was supposed to keep me safe had sexually abused me. I struggled to admit that dreadful reality. His behaviors hadn't been ambiguous. Nothing was accidental or misperceived. My dad had purposefully used me to gratify himself. And even with dementia, he was still manipulating me to meet his needs.

My world had spun topsy-turvy. Beneath my feet, the ground gave way, and into a dark abyss, I plummeted.

———— ⟶•⟵ ————

In therapy, I learned my alter ego was the cleaning lady. I felt invigorated when useful to others. Love, to me, was a commodity exchanged for goods and services, not a gift bestowed by birthright. Readily, I tidied up after those who had made messes of their lives or suffered crises of their own making. When I closed my eyes, I conjured images of Carol Burnett dressed in tatters, leaning wearily on a mop handle. The down-and-out janitor who stood onstage wistfully staring out into a dark theater made me wonder how my life might have unfolded under different circumstances.

How much more energy might I have put toward other pursuits if I hadn't wasted so much time being Dad's surrogate wife? All I had to show for my time and investment was a mountain of resentment—and a stack of therapy bills. My husband suffered from an anxiety disorder, I had developed two autoimmune illnesses and a heart issue, and my son Ron had nicknamed me Panic Room. My mental, physical, and spiritual health were in shambles.

"You're a classic enabler," Chris said. "It's not your fault. You have to learn to say no… then shut up. Don't explain yourself. *No* is a complete sentence."

I scoffed. He hadn't met my dad.

Writing in journals, I debriefed after my counseling sessions. My spiral notebooks couldn't make judgments or accusations, which made them the perfect depositories for my mounting anger. On ruled pages, I scrawled my most negative thoughts, raging at myself and those I perceived had hurt me. I grieved losses I had worked so persistently to deny. It was all part of the healing journey but not the final destination. Sometimes you have to slash through a jungle to reach the ocean.

THIRTY

WHILE I'D BEEN PREOCCUPIED WITH my father's decline, Mom fell ill in January 2012. Her condition worsened through March when her doctors diagnosed her with gallbladder failure. Further tests in April revealed pancreatic cancer.

Jim and I jetted to Florida, rented a car, and drove Mom and Jessie to Sandestin for Mom's liver scan. The outcome would establish her life expectancy and any recommended treatment. She needed compassionate support. Though Jessie possessed many good qualities, he had no aptitude for ushering Mom through complex emotions. I was better suited for the task, I reasoned. Yet I had no guarantees she would welcome my help or anyone else's.

From previous discussions with her doctor, Mom and I knew once cancer invaded her liver, her life expectancy would be three to six months. Jim, Jessie, and I sat in the hospital waiting room, as still and quiet as mannequins.

Mom exited radiology through stainless steel double doors, sniffling. She didn't need to say anything. I hugged her and wept. I didn't want to let her go.

Instantly, she stiffened. She gave me a defiant look. "You never know. I could live another five years. Patrick Swayze did."

I didn't tell her Patrick Swayze had died at fifty-seven, twenty months after his pancreatic cancer diagnosis. My seventy-nine-year-old mother didn't need to know that. Hope and prayers were all she had left. Any treatment she accepted would be strictly experimental, her doctor said.

At one p.m., we left the hospital for the hour-long drive back to Mom and Jessie's house. None of us had eaten since breakfast, so I suggested we grab lunch in Sandestin. Mom agreed. While I steered through midday traffic, Jim scanned for a suitable restaurant.

From experience, I knew not to suggest any eatery Mom might consider fancy. Menus exceeding two pages made her uncomfortable. Not knowing my way around the Florida Panhandle, however, put me at a disadvantage. Off the cuff, I couldn't think of a suitable diner.

"That looks promising." I pointed to a bistro with a tropical-themed exterior. "How about that one?"

Mom scrutinized the restaurant. "I guess that'll be all right. I don't want to spend too much money, though."

Never had I allowed her to pick up a tab. What she meant was she didn't want *Jim* to spend too much money. And she would be the sole arbiter of what equaled too much.

"Don't worry about the prices. We're paying," I reassured.

If my mother perceived a business guilty of price gouging, she would pitch a fit. I could still picture the scene she'd caused inside a Dallas hobby store two years earlier.

It was a few days before Christmas when Mom arrived at our house for a brief holiday visit. Together, we set out in search of gold glitter she said she needed for a craft project. Inside a major discount store, we found the elusive color she'd been hunting.

I retrieved the glitter bottle from a shelf and proceeded with Mom to the trailing checkout line. Near us, women stood with their arms and buggies full of gift-wrap, ribbons, artificial poinsettias, and colorful cookie tins.

Standing in queue, Mom glanced at the price tag affixed to the glitter bottle. At quadruple volume, she exclaimed, "Two dollars! I ain't paying no two dollars for that tiny bottle of glitter!"

The store's din quieted. I could have heard a frog fart. I imagined everyone staring at us. "That's right." I attempted to shush her. "You're not paying for it. I am." I peeled two bills from my wallet and handed them to the confused cashier.

"That's too much money," Mom protested. She argued with me all the way to the door and through the parking lot. Still griping, she slid into the passenger seat. "I wouldn't have paid that for *glitter*. It's *ninety-nine cents* at Walmart."

"You told me Walmart didn't have *gold* glitter."

"They didn't," she admitted. She had dropped the argument there.

I didn't want to repeat that experience today. If the diner I'd selected didn't suit her, she might object with an outburst. Already, her nerves were frazzled, and so were mine. It was a somber day. She deserved a nice meal in a relaxed setting, and I intended to give her exactly that.

Together, we entered the restaurant.

Uh-oh. White tablecloths. Not good.

Mom pressed her lips together.

Yellow Alert.

The hostess gestured and said we could sit anywhere we liked. I let Mom choose a table. The four of us scrutinized menus affixed to wood planks.

She's going to despise this gargantuan board. "I'm having a tuna sandwich," I said, hoping to distract Mom from the calamari. She would ask me what that was if she noticed the appetizer. If she found out it was squid, she was sure to be aghast. I could imagine her refusing to dine anywhere that served *baitfish.*

Mom scanned her menu. "That sounds good. Where'd you find that?"

Orange alert! Dear God, please don't let her see the price *of that sandwich.*

Her jaw clenched.

Red alert!

She set the menu on the table, regarding it like a soiled diaper.

FIRE IN THE HOLE!

"I'm not paying *ten* dollars for a sandwich," Mom snapped.

"It comes with fries," I said in my most chipper voice. "And in case I didn't mention it, we're buying."

She scooted her chair back and crossed her arms and legs. In full lockdown mode, she fashioned her suspended foot into a stop sign.

"She ain't going to eat nothing here," Jessie said, conceding defeat.

I nodded and collected my purse. On any normal day, Mom would have resisted an expensive lunch, but this was no average afternoon. She had just learned she has less than six months to live. I wanted to comfort not aggravate her.

"Let's go," I said to the group.

The four of us clamored into our rented sedan. For several minutes, we rode in silence.

"Let's try that one." Mom called my attention to a familiar chain cafe.

I veered into the parking lot, barely tapping my brakes.

As we funneled into the entrance, Mom took the lead. I couldn't catch up to her. At the counter, she ordered a tuna sandwich, chips, iced tea, and a chocolate chip cookie, totaling eleven dollars and change.

⟶◈◈◈⟵

Throughout the rest of May and into June, I called Mom daily. She refused experimental cancer treatment but consented to hospice. I was grateful for that. Her decision allowed me to regularly speak with a knowledgeable caregiver about her condition. I couldn't glean much from Mom.

She would cry when we spoke and apologize for being emotional. "I'm sorry. My nerves are just shot."

"It's okay. You don't have to apologize," I consoled. "That's perfectly normal." I did my best to sound calm, to conceal my constricting throat and addled emotions. I felt like crying with her, but always I waited until after the call ended to fall apart.

When I phoned, I made sure to ask Mom if she would like to talk about anything specific. I hoped to invite intimate discourse since we'd never had any.

"No," Mom would snip. "I just have to get better. That's all."

Failing my mission, I would let the conversation drift where it may, tell her "I love you," and say goodbye. Each time we spoke, I wondered if it might be our last conversation.

Perhaps I should have exerted more effort to understand my mom. I knew her solely at a surface level—and I believed she planned to keep it that way. The person I better sympathized with was Jessie.

Mom complained that Jessie, who wore hearing aids and had a pacemaker, didn't investigate fast enough when she signaled him. In her haughtiest voice, she said, "I told him I'm calling him once, and only *once*. He keeps that darn TV turned up too loud."

Arguing with Jessie, I suspected, was Mom's substitute for

railing at cancer. But Jessie was fighting his own invisible battle. Television was his refuge from reality. I couldn't be critical of him. I was no better. I traveled back to Florida to spend Mother's Day with Mom, but I left forty-eight hours later. Jessie's house had no spare rooms or beds, so I stayed at the nearest hotel—twenty miles away. I'd been unable to handle that arrangement for very long.

Phone calls only partially relieved my guilt for avoiding the frontlines. My mother's churlish remarks, though, occasionally eased my remorse.

"I wish you wouldn't call me every day," she scolded me. "Nothing's going to change overnight."

THIRTY-ONE

CANCER COULDN'T PREVENT MOM FROM doing what she wanted. And what she wanted was to see Texas and her extended family one more time. In mid-June, a month after her liver scan, Jessie delivered her to Houston, where she visited my brothers and their families. Two days later, she and Jessie traveled to Dallas to see me and my brood.

Though I'd asked her to spend the night at our house, Mom insisted on a hotel. I had only one guest room. And she didn't want to sleep in the same bed as Jessie because he snored. For her two-night stay, she selected a hotel room facing a busy interstate freeway in Renner. I intercepted the pair there.

"Take me to see our old house," Mom said right off. "Jessie needs to rest anyway. You and I can go." She wanted to view the home where she and Dad had lived for seven years, the residence from which I had walked to school.

Happy to have some one-on-one time with my mom, I did as she asked. Motoring past where Jerry's Dairy Way had been demolished to make room for a private school, I said, "I wonder if that brick patio Dad built is still there."

Stoic, Mom stared through the window glass and offered no thoughts. I imagined her sifting through fifty-year-old memories, recalling a time when the future seemed endless.

Mom would view her prior home as it appeared after forty-seven years of serial ownership. Age likely had taken a toll on that structure as much as it had on her. But the residence's condition didn't matter. That homestead was a memorial to my mother's past, tangible proof that her previous life had existed. The house had survived. Maybe that was the only evidence she sought. I veered to the curbside and parked.

"The brick's still gray," I marveled. "I thought they might have painted it. That's the *in* thing now, painting brick."

Mom stared intently at the house exterior. "I wonder who lives there."

In her eyes, I thought I saw more introspective questions. *Is she wondering what she'd do differently if she had the chance to start over?*

Quickly her mood shifted as if a timer had dinged. "Take me to see the house in the country," she said. "I want to see it again too."

Earlier that year, I had driven past the residence Dad built when I was twelve. A real estate agent had given me a tour while the home was listed for sale. The floorplan hadn't resembled the one I recalled. My visit had been a downer.

Heading east toward the farm, I warned Mom of what she was about to see. "It doesn't look much like the place you remember," I said, hoping to lessen her disappointment. "There's a barn up close to the house now."

"You've *got* to be kidding. I don't believe it." She crossed her arms over her seatbelt strap. "Why would anyone build a *barn* next to a *house*? We already had a barn in the pasture."

"Oh, yeah, *that* barn's not there anymore. I'm afraid you're in for a surprise."

I turned onto what once was a white rock, farm-to-market road but had become a paved city street. Drawing near our former homestead, I noted the bridge across the bar ditch had disappeared along with the drainage gulley. A new subdivision enclosed the acreage on three sides, which made it impossible to see the house until we were directly in front of it. Despite all the changes, the bone-colored brick house had prevailed like a raised middle finger to progress.

"There it is." I gestured toward the house and slowed my car to a crawl.

"Stop," Mom said. "I want to look at it for a minute." From her purse, she wrangled a small digital camera. She lowered the passenger window and studied her subject. "When did all this happen?" Mom indicated the new homes that had consumed the countryside. Mini-mansions with three- and four-car garages dwarfed the adjacent two-thousand-square-foot, 1960s farmhouse my father had built.

"I don't know. I discovered it a few months ago." I couldn't bring myself to tell her the home she and Dad had sold for $35,000 had recently listed for $600,000.

Mom's expression hardened. For a second, I thought she might cry. I understood. I could barely look at our old farmstead without sobbing. If she'd shed a tear, I would have dissolved into a liquid mess. Tired of choking back my emotions, I was ready to share my grief. *Maybe this will be our breakthrough moment.*

Mom lifted her camera and snapped a picture. "Okay, I've seen it now. You can take me back to the hotel."

At Comfort Suites, I retrieved Jessie, and the three of us met Jim and my children and grandchildren for dinner. It was a bittersweet gathering, the first time in several years that all nine of us had shared a meal. I'd selected the most down-home, family-style restaurant I could find—Babe's Chicken in Garfield.

Gazing at the extended table heaped with fried chicken, biscuits, and vegetable casseroles brought to mind the Last Supper. Our reunion felt surreal. The extended family would not again have an opportunity to dine together. I wanted every clock in the room to stop and Father Time to grant me special privileges, but I knew that was folly. Lined up for a group picture, I forced a smile.

The next morning, I met Mom and Jessie for breakfast and, afterward, brought them to my house. We sat outdoors, drinking iced tea by the pool and watching birds and squirrels. I snapped a few pictures to commemorate Mom's visit before her energy faded. At her request, around four p.m., I drove her and Jessie back to Comfort Suites. They would head home to Florida the next morning. I promised to be there to see them off.

When I returned to the hotel, at seven thirty a.m. the next day, Mom said she'd been awake since four thirty. She was antsy to depart, but Jessie insisted they wait until traffic thinned. In another hour, the freeways would be less crowded.

Mom waited inside her room, impatiently fiddling with her purse straps. When she was ready to depart, she expected to leave that instant—no matter what. I sat next to her on a double bed while Jessie loaded the rental car. Already, her thoughts seemed five hundred miles away. I swallowed hard. I would never again see my mother in Texas, and we both knew it. It might even be my last chance to speak with her in person.

Mom gazed through the hotel room windows at a new dawn, her hands resting in her lap. She grasped an unused handkerchief as if it were a life rope. I wanted to take her palms in mine, but I couldn't summon the courage. *What if she recoils?* Selfishly, I waited for her to make the first move. Like two granite statues, we sat frozen in history.

I listened as my mother's Timex watch announced the seconds. *Tick, tick, tick.* "Do you ever have any regrets?" I don't know what I expected her to say.

"No. None at all." She gave me a sideways look before bowing her head and studying her hands.

What could be better than facing the end with no regrets? I had a boatload of disappointments, enough for both of us. Yet I couldn't verbalize them. Articulating my feelings to Mom was begging for frostbite. I regretted she had cancer and that we had never connected like I thought a mother and daughter should. I was sorry I'd never confessed to her the truth about Dad. I had resented her for not being the mother I'd needed when I most needed a mom. For that, I felt punishing shame. Holding a grudge against Mom for being inattentive made no sense. I didn't expect dandelions to smell like roses. She was a wounded person who'd given me all she had to offer.

I grieved the times my mother and I had regarded each other as competition. She should have been my cheerleader, and I should have been her best fan. I regretted ever arguing with her over two-dollar glitter. How insignificant that seemed now.

Glumly, I escorted Mom to her car. With one arm, she clutched her purse to her body and wept as we walked. I clung to her vacant elbow.

Of course, she had regrets. Her disappointments were buried too deep to exhume.

Jessie stowed Mom's suitcase in the car trunk while she and I shared a sideways hug. It was the best we could manage with her massive purse wedged between us.

Chris had cautioned me I would receive no meaningful last words from my mother. I hadn't believed him. *Doesn't everyone make amends on their deathbed?*

"Not necessarily," Chris had said. "As a rule, people don't change personalities because they're dying."

I studied the blue pinstripes on his shirt. Between shallow breaths, I recounted Mom's Texas departure. "She wouldn't even look at me. I was waving to her, but she couldn't see me. She had one hand covering her eyes." Tearfully, I simulated her gesture.

Through an imaginary lens, I could see myself standing on the hotel sidewalk, desperately trying to establish eye contact, waving to my mother again and again as Jessie backed from the parking lot. In the early morning light, I bent my head to peer under the sun visor Mom had lowered. Still flapping one hand vigorously, my gaze followed the rental car as it proceeded onto the access road. A quick U-turn and the vehicle headed south and out of sight. I didn't know how long I stood there staring after her.

Distraught, my chest heaved as I stammered out the story.

"It's okay," Chris soothed. "She was only doing what she's always done."

I sat up straighter. *Did he not register what I just said? My mother refused to look at me during what might have been my last chance to see her alive.*

"Hiding herself from you," Chris clarified. "Blocking you from seeing her." He hid his eyes behind one hand to demonstrate. "You can't see me now. I won't show myself to you."

Ah, yes, he had understood.

Though he shouldn't have undertaken such an extensive drive, Dad transported Alan and Kerry and Kerry's wife, Barbara, to

Florida for Mom's funeral. It was a route he'd embarked on many times. He knew it well. Besides, I justified, Evelyn was in tow to help with the driving.

My mother had died three weeks after her trip to Texas, fifty-seven days after her liver scan. I'd been with her before she passed, though she'd been unconscious the entire time. Despite her refusal to believe it, anything *could* change overnight, and it had. We'd shared a normal phone exchange on Independence Day. By the next morning, her brain had shut down.

I was grateful my brothers could attend our mother's funeral. Kerry was scared of airplanes and had never flown. He seldom drove more than a few miles from his home before panic set in, and his wife didn't drive at all. If Dad hadn't transported him and Alan to Florida, they would have missed Mom's service. As it was, our youngest brother, Joel, couldn't attend.

When Dad wasn't around to hear him, Kerry said, "You should have seen how he drove. Oh my gawd! He even parked the car *sideways* in two parking spaces at a grocery store!"

Barbara giggled and made a funny face, agreeing with her husband.

It was the night before Mom's service. We were congregated inside what might have been the hotel's presidential suite. The gal at the front desk had generously provided me and Jim a three-room suite with a full kitchen and dining room at no extra charge. She'd remembered me from my prior stay and was appreciative I'd reserved rooms for my brothers.

Kerry and Barbara and Alan had two rooms across the hall, but we had more space to spread out in the larger suite. Using reward points, Dad and Evelyn had booked their stay at a different hotel. Already, they'd turned in for the night. Now it was just the five of us catching up and sharing a two-foot submarine sandwich.

"Why is he driving and not Evelyn?" I teased apart my bun to be sure it didn't contain mustard.

Alan shrugged. "I think she did some."

Barbara set her beer on the coffee table. "Not much."

"He shouldn't be driving *any*," Kerry said. "I'm scared we might not get home alive!"

I couldn't get all that worked up about Dad's driving. My thoughts were centered on all of us surviving Mom's service. I had arranged the funeral in a daze and didn't know what to expect. *Will the flowers arrive on time? Will Dad show up wearing a button with #1 printed on it? "Look at meee! I was her* first *husband."*

I drew a sigh of relief when, around ten forty-five the next morning, Dad arrived for the service properly attired—no attention-stealing signs or buttons. He and Evelyn sat on a pew at the back of the sanctuary—and stayed there. Neither one joined the line of friends and family snaking past my mother's open casket.

Beyond that, I remember almost nothing about the funeral except my anxiety.

For starters, a mortician had taken it upon himself to give Mom an enviable breast enhancement. Still recovering from that visual shock, I witnessed Jessie crumple into a heap inside the church vestibule. His son helped him to his feet. Like an avalanche set in motion by a single stone, the service careened downhill from there.

The officiating priest conducted Mom's funeral like a Saturday mass. All of my mother's family, including Jessie, were Baptist. Right off, the priest referenced his faithful church member's attendance "despite her spouse's unwillingness to join her." I felt like throttling him.

Jessie had insisted on a Monday service following Mom's demise on Friday. "I just want to get it over with," he'd said. He hadn't thought it through. Travel distances and rushed arrangements had prevented many relatives from attending.

I'd had little time to assemble photos or speak with the priest about my mother's life. The officiating cleric had improvised by sharing what he knew of her, which appeared to be her attendance record. Possibly, he was irked I hadn't called him to my mother's deathbed. Sprinting between Mom's hospice room and the nurse's station to beg for more morphine, I hadn't thought to contact clergy. All my attention had been focused on ending my mother's pain.

I wished I had prepared a eulogy for Mom, but I was too exhausted to speak. My head throbbed from lack of sleep and medication—the two worst enemies for Addison's disease sufferers. Earlier, I had tried to guess the correct cortisol dose for my circumstances. *What's the right amount for a full-blown, crash-and-burn breakdown?*

I wasn't sure what I could have told anyone about Mom. A gap existed in my knowledge. Most of what I knew about my mother's recent history pertained to grievances. She detested chilidogs, spicy foods, noisy aircraft, George Bush—both of them—and anyone she perceived had taken advantage of her or tried to "tell her what to do." Her happiest moments she kept to herself.

For nine years, my mother had volunteered two days a week as a hospital aide, crafting patients' door decorations and routing wheelchairs. The work must have been rewarding, but she hadn't told me much about it. I listened closely as several of her fellow volunteers offered tributes.

"Mary Ann was a giving, nurturing person who dedicated her time to helping the sick," one woman recalled.

"She gave of herself, even when her own health was failing," said another hospital aide.

Misty-eyed, I listened in awe. I would have given anything to have known the woman whose virtues they extolled.

The morning after Mom's funeral, Dad pulled his Hyundai sedan to a stop under the hotel awning. He'd arrived to retrieve my brothers and sister-in-law for the journey home. He popped his trunk release, forcing the rear compartment to yawn wide. Into the overfilled cavity, Kerry and Alan deposited small duffle bags. I stood behind his vehicle, observing my father's packing strategy—or lack thereof. Maybe all men packed like that. Already, I had resituated several items in our rental car. I suppressed an urge to rearrange Dad's ice chests, luggage, water bottles, soda cans, snacks, shoes, and clothes encased in see-through bags. It looked as if he'd loaded his car in the dark—amid evacuation orders.

From the porte cochere, I breathed in exhaust fumes mixed with salty air. My brothers hugged me goodbye before sinking into Dad's car for their ride home. Jim leaned on the passenger door, conversing with Evelyn. She had claimed what Dad referred to as the "ninety-percent seat." I don't remember exactly why he called it that. Something to do with auto fatalities.

From my stance, I couldn't see Kerry's face, but I imagined his eyes bulging with dread. Between him and Alan, he was the more likely to hyperventilate. Kerry had never been at ease on highways, no matter who was behind the wheel or what seat he occupied. Maybe Dad's ninety-percent comment had left Kerry permanently scarred.

The trunk lid shielded me and my father from view of other family members. I stared mindlessly into the car's rear cavity, hoping Dad's driving surpassed his organizational skills. I remembered what Kerry had said about getting home alive. It was somewhat comforting to know four passengers could scream "Watch out!" if necessary. The group had arrived safely in Florida. I imagined they would return to Texas equally intact.

All at once, Dad sprang toward me. With startling strength, he looped his arms around me. "I love you, darling," he crooned like a smitten lover.

My skin stung with embarrassment. He hadn't pulled one of his ambush moves on me in years, and he'd never called me "darling." *What brought this on?*

Maybe Mom's funeral had triggered a brain glitch. Whatever the cause, I didn't want to rile him, not before he embarked on a cross-country journey. I told Dad I loved him too. He had, after all, driven my brothers to my mother's funeral. It had been a generous act. I was appreciative. Impatiently, I waited for him to release his possessive grip.

Instead of letting go, Dad leaned into me and knocked me off-balance. I scrambled to regain my footing as he passionately locked lips with me. I'm unsure how many seconds his embrace lasted, but it felt interminable. With one arm, I wrestled from his viselike grip and pushed free.

Immediately, I felt stupid for dismissing my therapist's warnings. When I'd told Chris my father no longer sexualized me, he'd said, "That'll be the last part of his mind to go." His prediction had been accurate.

Before I could speak, Jim appeared at my side.
Did he see it?

My spouse gave his father-in-law a congenial smile, answering my silent question. I stood there, my mouth agape, unable to squeak out a sound. Dad cut his eyes at me and sniggered.

Nonchalantly, Dad closed his auto trunk and climbed into the driver's seat. With one arm extended past his open window, he waved goodbye to me and Jim.

"Ready to hit the road?" Jim asked.

I nodded, unable to orient myself. *Where am I? What year is it? Who was that man who forced his affections on me?*

SECTION V

FINAL RESCUE

THIRTY-TWO

2015

INSIDE A NEUROLOGIST'S OFFICE, DAD perched on an exam table. "There's nothing wrong with me," he insisted.

Evelyn and I sat in stackable chairs on either side of him. The three of us awaited the doctor whose job it was to evaluate my father's faulty self-appraisal. In particular, his ability to drive safely lay in question.

Dad accused Evelyn of overreacting to a few minor mishaps. As far as he was concerned, it didn't matter what the neurologist said. "That doctor can go to hell," he announced proactively.

In recent months, while motoring alone, Dad had collided with several inanimate objects—some of which had never been identified. On one occasion, he'd traveled an arc around the Dallas-Fort Worth metroplex and gotten lost during a joy ride. He'd gone missing for twelve hours before a stranger had intervened.

A danger to himself and others, Dad was no longer competent to operate anything with an engine. He had no sense of time or direction and no fear of getting lost. As much as I hated to think of him as housebound, I didn't want to see his mug on a Silver Alert either.

The exam room door swung open, and in marched the neurologist. Introducing himself, the doctor asked Dad what he could do for him. Evelyn had phoned ahead, so there shouldn't have been any guesswork involved. The physician, I presumed, wanted to build rapport with his patient.

Dad shrugged. His legs hung limply from the exam table. He would divulge nothing but his superb physical and psychological condition. From the doctor, he wanted only a professional agreement and a dressing down of his wife and daughter. The two delusional women who'd delivered him there were unfit to assess his faculties. Their inferiority and hysterics should be obvious. And should the neurologist dare to ask, his driving skills were nothing short of impeccable, thank you very much. Dad communicated all of that to his physician with one obstinate look.

The doctor asked him several direct questions. "Can you tell me what day it is?"

Yes, he could.

"Do you know what year it is?"

Yes, he knew.

Then, without fanfare, the neurologist inquired, "Are you having any difficulties driving?"

Dad straightened his posture. "Nope. Not a one."

A three-way argument ensued in which Dad's spatial recognition and reflexes were hotly contested.

The doctor remained unconfrontational. "How about we let an expert tell us if you should still be driving? If you're not having any problems, would you be willing to take a test?" he asked Dad.

The blush color partially drained from my father's face. He appeared to consider the challenge.

"If you're not having any issues, then the test results will prove you should keep your license," the neurologist said convincingly.

Dad nodded. Scanning him for signs of resistance, my eyes came to a full stop at his feet. Alarmed, I glanced at the doctor.

The physician shot me an I'm-way-ahead-of-you look. "I noticed it first thing," he said.

Dad's shoes were on the wrong feet.

———— ◦✐◦ ————

One week later, Dad flunked his neurological exam.

For the next two months, he raged at Evelyn and me about the evaluating doctor's incompetence. It was all our fault. Why had we participated in the scheme? Why had we convinced him to trust that man? By God, he wasn't giving up his driver's license even though the state had revoked it, he said.

Concerned about his disposition, I phoned Evelyn to see if he had calmed yet.

"He's out in the garage, building some kind of camper top for his truck," she said, referring to Dad's ancient Nissan Frontier.

"What do you mean? How's he capable of doing that?"

"Oh, he bought metal tubing and is building the frame for it right now. He found some kind of blue tarp he thinks he can snap around it," Evelyn said.

I gasped. Sensing déjà vu, I recalled the truck camper Dad had built when he left Betty. *Different truck. Different wife. Same motives.* "You *do* realize he's building an escape vehicle. Right?"

A day later, I witnessed Dad's ill-conceived invention. It looked more like a liability than a camper top. The cobalt-blue shell made of rain-resistant fabric seemed better suited for covering firewood than a truck bed. At high speeds, the tarp would surely detach and land on an unsuspecting driver's windshield.

I discussed with Dad the dangers of his completed project.

253

Begrudgingly, he canceled whatever had been his intention for the camper. He didn't need a vehicle to escape his confinement, he decided. His legs would suffice.

For the next few months, Dad's part-time caregiver, who'd been hired to assist him at home, couldn't keep up with him. When she stripped his bed to wash his sheets or let him out of her sight for any reason, he would make a jailbreak. Once, he exited through the garage and hoofed it across six lanes of traffic before she'd caught up to him.

Each time my phone rang, my stomach lurched. *What's Dad done this time?* Whether or not I permitted him to consume my life, he did. It wasn't his fault his brain malfunctioned. He hadn't asked for Alzheimer's. When I lost patience with him, I reminded myself of that. He'd become a toddler in an elderly man's body. I couldn't hold him responsible for his misdeeds. His illness excused him for raising havoc anywhere, at any hour. And that was pretty much what he did.

"You can't bargain with chaos," my therapist told me. "All you can do is exit the drama."

But I couldn't let go of my relationship with my dad. My conscience wouldn't permit it. He was a part of me. Every harm he suffered, I imagined equal injury. Boundaries I'd previously set for him—few of which he'd ever respected—seemed irrelevant. He was sick. Catering to his needs felt as much an act of self-preservation as my duty.

Other than my husband and therapist, no one fully appreciated my predicament. "You should get guardianship and move your dad in with you," well-meaning friends advised. They couldn't understand why I didn't *want* responsibility for my father. I had spent my whole life buckling under his load. I couldn't explain to anyone who'd been raised in a healthy family why my ailing father, who had an able-bodied and younger wife, shouldn't live with me. It was easier to give up socializing.

Dad thanked me for my attentiveness. "You're my best girl," he would say.

That was the problem. I wasn't his girlfriend. He merely thought of me as one. All his life he had thrived on emotional triangles, relishing his part as the leading man between two romantic rivals. I had been his alternate spouse, the third party necessary to complete his preferred dynamic.

As the master of ceremonies, Dad had hosted a competition in which only one contestant could win the grand prize—his affection. Even with a diseased mind, he could still deliver a rote performance. As much as I desired to exit my role, I was too addicted to showbiz to quit.

THIRTY-THREE

IN PREPARATION FOR RETIREMENT, JIM and I purchased a downsized home thirty miles farther from Dad. I'd given my father a tour of our future residence, once, during construction. But I wagered he couldn't find his way back.

With each rung down the mental health ladder Dad stepped, he grew more hostile, impatient, and demanding. Though I'd anticipated he'd eventually forget my phone number, he had me on speed dial. All he had to do to reach me was punch the One key. And he wore it out.

I needed to decompress someplace where I could step outdoors into peace and quiet—or scream without summoning police. Our new home, bordering a wildlife preserve and small lake, offered both advantages.

On a Saturday morning in mid-March, Jim and I arrived at the new house to intercept a refrigerator delivery. We'd closed on the mortgage three days earlier. With our official move date still two weeks away, we lollygagged, mentally arranging furniture in empty rooms. On the back patio, we set up two folding chairs. Together, Jim and I savored the quiet.

I stared across the adjacent lake at the horizon. "I can't believe this is really ours." I had to pinch myself to believe that pastoral setting would soon be my daily view.

Jim's eyes told me he was equally awed.

In the distance, ducks formed V shapes on the surface waters while snowy egrets fished the shoreline. Bois d'arc, pecan, and oak tree canopies glimmered in renewed shades of emerald and chartreuse. A blue heron glided past us.

"We're going to love watching sunsets here." Jim indicated the skyline.

I stood and pointed with my cell phone. "The porch steps will be there, leading to the pool deck." I spun on my toes. "I can't wait to see how the pool turns out."

"They said they could start in a few weeks," Jim said. "Probably have the hole dug before we leave on vacation."

My cell phone rang in my hand. I noted the number. "Of course," I quipped, "who else would it be?"

"Let me guess," Jim drawled. "Your dad?"

I hesitated then answered.

Instead of dad's voice, Evelyn's filtered through the receiver. "John insisted I drive him to see your new house," she blurted. "And I don't have directions. Can you tell me how to get there?"

How does she even know we're here? I told her we weren't moving for several weeks. "Oh, please wait," I begged Evelyn. "We're not set up for company yet. I'm only planning to be here until the refrigerator arrives."

"He wouldn't take no for an answer," she insisted. "We're already on our way. Where do I turn off the highway?"

If I wanted a more tranquil life, it seemed I should have moved overseas.

One week later, Jim and I were in transit between households when Evelyn again rang my cell. "Can you please talk your father into going to the ER?" she asked when I answered. "He's acting very confused."

"Has he eaten anything today?" I inquired, noting the time. It was after four p.m.

"He says he doesn't want anything. He's had a Dr Pepper."

I was used to receiving that kind of response from Evelyn. Before Dad had dementia, he'd survived primarily on bananas, candy bars, sodas, and brown 'n serve rolls. Evelyn seldom challenged him about his eating habits, and he didn't oppose hers. Apparently, it was a deal they'd struck early in their marriage. When Dad said he wasn't hungry, she didn't badger him. When he said he wasn't thirsty, she took him at his word. But it had become a dangerous practice. Dementia sufferers often lose their sense of thirst and hunger, leading to dehydration and malnourishment.

It would have been easy to leap into rescue mode and reprove Evelyn. As compelling as it was to question her judgment, I knew doing so would only worsen matters.

"She's his wife," Chris repeatedly reminded me. "You have your own marriage and husband to protect. No one else can do that but you."

"But she's incapable of handling him," I argued.

Chris nodded. "She might be. But remember, both your parents chose to marry dependent people. The consequences for that are not yours to suffer."

Talking to him was like consulting Yoda. *Rescue wrong person, you do.*

Always, it had seemed like I was betraying someone. I believed the best person to disappoint was myself. That way, at least I controlled the outcome.

In the silent space between Evelyn's request and my reply, I evaluated what to say. *If she can't convince Dad to get in her car and ride five minutes to the hospital, what makes her think I can? How do I know if he needs emergency care? Maybe he just needs to eat.* I needed one of those recorded messages like my doctor had. "If this is a medical emergency, please hang up and dial nine-one-one."

Evelyn had thrown the ball to me, and like an excited puppy, I retrieved it. "Put him on the phone."

While Dad was hospitalized overnight for evaluation, I had time to reflect on my evolving predicament. As irrational as it might seem, I loved my father and wanted only the best care for him and the most compassionate conclusion to his life. Alzheimer's guaranteed he would not meet the ending he'd wished for. At age eighty-three, he had no jealous husbands left to shoot him but mine. ☺

Evelyn served as my dad's proxy for instigating life disruptions. Beaten down by relentless demands, I retreated inward. I didn't want to talk to anyone. Mobile phones, I decided, had breached the last frontier of civil respect. And yet I had a Pavlovian response each time Dad's phone number appeared on my cell screen. *Ohmigod! What if he's dying?*

For six years, I'd striven to gain some distance from my father. Not because of his illness, but because his and Evelyn's distress calls were destroying my health. The more I retreated, the more diligently they advanced. Steadily, I lost ground. I had to stop retrenching and defend myself. My purpose wasn't to be everyone else's problem-solver. Dad's Alzheimer's couldn't be reversed. Neither could his demise be forestalled.

"*You* still have a chance to live a good life," Chris had said.

DIANA ESTILL

An austere message, one I needed to hear. Still, I berated myself for abandoning a submerging ship. *Aren't I supposed to be my father's lifesaver?* No shoreline appeared within sight. I felt Dad and I might both drown with him clinging to my back.

Inside Dad's hospital room the next morning, I watched his movements. Asleep, he twitched like a hooked trout. Alternately, his feet pumped the sheets. His eyelids fluttered. In his dreams, he might have been running from a bear. From his right arm, an IV line protruded, taped more securely than I was used to seeing. Air whooshed from the pneumatic compression cuffs on his ankles.

Evelyn exited the room. While she was gone, a nurse approached to collect Dad's vitals.

He woke and spotted me. "Oh, I didn't know you were here," he chirped.

I smiled and nodded, distracted by the nurse and all the electronics.

"Do you know who this is?" the attendant asked Dad. She pointed to me.

Dad glanced from me to her. "Sure."

"Who is it?" The nurse smiled.

"That's my *mother*."

She gave me a sidelong look. "That's your mother? What's her name?"

Dad studied me for a beat. "Deborah."

I drew an elongated breath. "No, Dad. I'm your daughter, *Diana*."

He shut his eyes and fell back asleep.

"It's the Ativan," the nurse said. She'd caught me staring at Dad's twitches. "It agitates them when they get too much. They gave him some in the ER. But it appears he'd already been given a high dose before he got there." She arched her eyebrows at me.

Dad rustled awake. He stared at his surroundings as if seeing them for the first time.

I patted his arm and told him to relax. "Are you hungry? I can get you some pudding if you would like."

He wrestled one hand from his bed linens. Affectionately, he stroked my arm. "You're a good kitty."

THIRTY-FOUR

THREE PARAMEDICS REMOVED DAD FROM an ambulance. Slowly, they wheeled him toward me on a gurney. His head tilted forward, eyes darted back and forth.

"Hey, Dad! You're here!" I called out to him as if he'd arrived at Disney World instead of a memory care home. *What a dumb thing to say*, I immediately thought. *He has no idea where* here *is*.

Evelyn and I followed behind the gurney driver to Dad's appointed room. With a key, she unlocked the door and stepped back. Inside, I could see my grandmother's old sofa. The maroon-and-forest-green fabric appeared to have aged better than its current owner. It still looked new. The books I'd read suggested familiar items would help Dad transition to his new digs.

The rest of Dad's room furnishings were a patchwork of colors and styles that made my eyes hurt. His full-size bed—smaller than the queen-size one he'd had at home—displayed the indigo-and-white comforter I'd given him last Father's Day. In one corner sat a decrepit *greige*-tint club chair that had been relocated from Evelyn's living room. A new cocoa-brown fake-leather recliner was stationed next to an eighties-era end table and lamp. The array was unsettling enough to trigger a seizure.

Released from his medical transport, Dad shuffled around the room, inspecting the layout. He bent his head to see past the orange-plaid curtains framing the windows next to his bed. The murky glass between him and the enclosed patio looked like it hadn't been cleaned since the Clinton years.

"What's out there?" Dad pressed a quivering finger against the splotchy panes.

"It's a courtyard. I'll take you out to see it in a few minutes," I promised.

An empty gurney and two lingering ambulance staff blocked the room's single door. Apprehensive, I entertained Dad with idle chatter until they left. I couldn't be sure how much he comprehended. *Does he know this isn't a rehab unit? Does he understand this is now his home, that he can no longer live as a free man or with his wife?*

When the three of us were alone, Evelyn set her purse down next to the sofa and sank into the cushions. "Have a seat in your new recliner," she said to Dad.

He blinked and stared at the foreign chair as if it were a dog he'd almost tripped over. Leaning in for closer inspection, he fingered the recliner's stiff vinyl arms. Slowly, he rotated his body and plunked into the seat. He gave me a flummoxed look.

I held my breath. So far, Dad seemed approving of his new residence. Once he adjusted, I would worry less about him. He was safe now, in a home where he would be supervised around the clock and fed nutritious meals. He wouldn't wander off because it was a maximum-security unit. It was a prison, actually, only with better-appointed rooms and fewer visitors.

Finally, I could be my father's daughter—not his wife or girlfriend or mother. No longer would I hold myself responsible for monitoring his diet. I could come and go and visit him at my convenience. I could set down my self-imposed burden of management. But I was too distressed about Dad's confinement to fully appreciate all that.

Dad bolted from his recliner and tugged excitedly at his pants. Urgently, he paced.

"The bathroom is right over there." I pointed to the open restroom door.

The lights had been switched on in advance. Jim had installed outlet covers that illuminated at night. The family had tried to think of everything to ensure Dad's safety, but I knew there would be glitches. I prayed any oversights would be minor.

Dad stood over Evelyn's purse with his back turned to me.

From the look on Evelyn's face, she sensed he was about to whiz in her satchel. "No-o-o-o!" she hollered at Dad. "Not *there*!" She leapt, grabbed him by one hand, and guided him to the restroom.

Meanwhile, I scrambled to find the nearest caregiver. Whatever had come over Dad exceeded my pay grade.

"You just have to redirect him," a staff member explained upon arrival.

"You don't understand," I said. "I'm not going to be in this room with him all day. And I don't wish to view my father's... you know..."

Good grief, aren't residents entitled to restroom assistance when needed? Once the rent check cleared, it seemed the kumbaya reception ended.

The caregiver flashed me an annoyed look. She might as well have said, "Exactly what I needed today, another clueless princess."

I hadn't meant to be condescending, but I must have been. I couldn't have explained my revulsion to my father's genitals to someone who dealt with old men's privates every day. "Will you be on duty tonight?" I asked the attendant.

She checked her watch. "I'm leaving in a half-hour."

Possibly, she'd just decided.

"It's okay," Evelyn reassured me. "I'll sleep here on the couch tonight."

Evelyn had slept near Dad for twenty-two years, but that hadn't kept him out of trouble. I tried not to think about what might happen after I left—not that my presence improved anything. Maybe some fresh air would help.

"Dad, would you like to walk to the courtyard?" I tugged his arm.

He nodded, but I wasn't sure he understood what I'd asked.

I led him from his room to the enclosed gardens, where padded chairs encouraged guests to loiter. Dad chose to sit on a brick retaining wall instead. *Just like the one he had at home*, I noted. Before he'd become disoriented, his favorite pastime was sitting on his retaining wall and plucking weeds from his flowerbeds.

Dad fingered a bromeliad leaf and grunted. *Excellent. He still connects with nature.* I smiled at the thought of us sharing sunny afternoons here, surrounded by live greenery. We had the whole courtyard to ourselves. It didn't appear we would ever have to clamor for seating.

Fifteen minutes passed. My face felt dewy. The sunlight was more intense than I had expected. "Do you want to go back inside in the air conditioning?" I asked, jolting Dad from his trancelike state.

His brain and body occupied different dimensions, it seemed. I observed a faint flicker.

"Okay," he said.

I extended a hand to help him rise. He flanked me, his head and torso bent forward like a wilted dandelion. Gradually, he found low gear. Ever so gently, he reached one arm behind me and, with three quick taps, patted my buttocks.

Does he know what he's doing? Does he even realize what part of me he touched? His gesture hadn't felt predatorial. Grabbing his mitt, I redirected his contact and escorted him back to his room.

The next day, when I visited my father, he looked like he'd gone a few rounds with a heavyweight boxer. His swollen left eye formed the bullseye of a bloody contusion. A series of three cuts lacerated the skin near one lower eyelid. He sat in his recliner, sporting a cherry-red sweatshirt that accentuated his injury. With both eyes closed, he appeared asleep. White stubble covered his chin and neck. His wounds were severe enough to prevent his aide from shaving him, I assumed. My heart hurt.

"*Omigod*! What happened?" I asked Evelyn.

"He tried to get up and come over to me during the night. I didn't hear him get out of bed. I was sleeping so soundly. I guess he tripped on the recliner and fell into the end table."

His lids still closed, Dad sputtered a weary, "Ye-ah."

I studied the points on the octagonal table, the distance between the furnishings, and the now readily apparent hazards. I should have known Evelyn would sleep through a fall. If explosive chemicals had ignited the warehouses next door, I doubted she would have roused. She probably wouldn't have heard a fire truck if it had parked next to her bed—or in this case, her sofa. Maybe Dad wouldn't have wandered during the night, trying to get her attention, if she hadn't been there. We both had to surrender the belief that we could help him.

"She needs to go home," a staff member advised, pulling me aside. "She's not supposed to stay overnight. The night shift won't check on him as long as she's asleep in there."

Dad's facial wounds would heal quickly. Though I guessed his feelings would not. In those fleeting seconds of cogency, ones he experienced from time to time, he must have grieved his bleak future. During those mental flashes, he likely thought I had abandoned him. I turned my face so Dad couldn't see my tears.

I didn't know if my father would survive a month, a year, or a decade in his current condition. The only certainty was Jim's retirement in three weeks. That date shared calendar space with a European tour we'd booked a year earlier to celebrate the milestone. The moment felt bittersweet. Our golden years were beginning as Dad's were drawing to a close.

THIRTY-FIVE

A BACKHOE TORE THROUGH WHAT HAD once been my freshly sodded lawn. PVC pipes rose like angry zombies from the disturbed soil. Blue and red and white wires bled from the narrow cylinders. Our yard had become a hazard zone. I didn't dare step from the patio.

I'd been through that drill before. Only after I'd survived the ugly stage would any improvement be evident. In the interim, it wasn't unusual to second-guess my original vision and succumb to crippling doubts.

Doubts were all I had, it seemed. My guilt fired accusing questions at me. *Do we truly need a pool at this stage in life? Will Dad live to see our finished addition? Will he ever again visit my home? Should we be leaving in a week for Europe with construction underway in our backyard? Should we be going anywhere at all?*

The decision about the pool had already been evaluated. Dad might or might not survive long enough to see where Jim and I had sunk our retirement funds. It made no difference. I hoped he would again visit our home. But maybe any departure from memory care would only confuse him. He was decidedly ill, according to medical professionals, but death didn't appear imminent.

Jim deserved a retirement celebration. When I'd proposed canceling our vacation, he had staunchly protested. "For all you know, your dad might outlive *us*."

He was right. It could be years before my father's health failed further. We would advance with our plans, as agreed.

While I stood on my patio, mentally rehearsing the pros and cons of my decisions, my cell phone rang. It was my eldest son, Ron.

"Are they there yet?" he asked.

I affirmed the yard was being destroyed as we spoke.

"I'll be right over," he said. "I want to watch."

I chuckled. *One person's pain is another's entertainment.*

Ron arrived right away. The drive between our houses took less than ten minutes. From my patio, he surveyed the gaping hole into which I'd pitched his inheritance. "How deep are they going?"

I stared at the backhoe that looked to be clawing its way to China. "Five feet?"

A dump truck rolled over what was left of the lawn. I studied the two-foot-wide tire tracks and four-inch ruts. *Go ahead. That's fine. Just leave me living here in ruins for the next three months.*

The two-week vacation Jim and I had planned couldn't come soon enough. Maybe when we returned, there would be some signs of progress. Presently, it looked as if a forty-foot meteor had struck our backyard.

The cell phone I habitually carried outdoors rang once more in my palm. I checked the screen and noted the number. Dad's memory care. "Oh, Lord. I better take this call."

The dump truck had driven off with a load of dirt, and the backhoe had halted for a few minutes, so I answered the phone outdoors. I feared Dad had fallen again. I prayed he hadn't broken a hip.

The woman on the line spewed sentences at me like machine-gun fire. "This is Debbie, from The Abbey, and there's been an accident. Your father stabbed another resident, and we need you to come get him right away."

Whoa, whoa, whoa! Stabbed? Did she say stabbed? My father was in a memory care home, not San Quentin. He had no access to knives to my knowledge. "Excuse me. Hold on," I replied. "Are you sure you've dialed the right person? I don't think my dad's capable of stabbing anyone."

"Yes, you're the right person. You're Diana, John's daughter, right?"

"I am."

"Okay," she said. "He stabbed another resident with his fork during lunch. Her injuries aren't critical, but we can't keep residents here who're threats to others. You need to come get him *immediately*."

Maybe it was her demanding tone or untimely directive. Maybe it was self-preservation finally kicking in. My mouth suddenly seemed controlled by my therapist's brain. "Have you tried calling his *wife*?" I asked, my voice laden with attitude.

"No. We called you because… well—"

She'd hit my nuclear defense switch. "Now just wait a minute. Let me be clear. Evelyn is his *wife*. I'm his *daughter*. She lives less than five minutes from there. I'm more than a half hour away. She has the power to make his healthcare decisions. I don't. And," I added with a crescendo, "he's under *hospice* care. Any changes to his treatment will have to be authorized by them."

"But… but…"

"Listen, I've told you what you need to do and who to call.

I'm not driving there, and I'm not about to put a violent man in my vehicle and carry him anywhere. I can assure you, neither will Evelyn. I can't even believe you're recommending that. If you need him moved, you'll have to arrange an ambulance. They're equipped and trained to handle something like this. I'm not."

Before The Abbey's enforcement officer said goodbye, she apologized for panicking and dialing the wrong person.

"Thank you for informing me of the situation." I tamed my tongue. "Hopefully, Evelyn will answer when you call her." I drew a deep breath and pushed the End button.

Ron smirked. "I take it that wasn't what you were expecting."

Nothing ever was.

THIRTY-SIX

FROM THE PARKING LOT, THE psychiatric hospital looked like a generic office building. Concrete exterior, tinted windows, metal facade, and no signage. I double-checked my GPS to confirm I'd arrived at the right address. Never had I expected to enter a mental ward, at least not intentionally. The thought of it gave me the shakes.

I strode into the lobby as if I did so every day. My inexperience, though, must have been obvious. From behind a glass partition, an employee barked, "You'll need to return your purse, cell phone, and eyeglasses to your vehicle."

I shot the frosty receptionist a quizzical look. *Glasses?*

"It's possible someone could use the side pieces as a weapon and stab you in the jugular," she drawled.

My anxiety needle swung far right, from I-need-a-glass-of-wine to somebody-give-me-a-Xanax. To my extensive list of reasons to avoid mental hospitals, I added gruesome fatality risks. As instructed, I exited and returned empty-handed and vision impaired.

Seated in a plastic chair at a four-top table, I fidgeted and waited in the visitation room. The gal at the front desk had indicated someone would escort my father to me. She offered no further guidance on what to expect—other than potential homicide. *What more,* I wondered, *would anyone need to know?*

Collected around other tables, a dozen visitors conversed with plain-clothed patients. Absent hospital gowns, the mentally unstable appeared indistinguishable from guests with normal thoughts—sort of like in Walmart. No one looked walleyed, spastic, or catatonic. My cinematic-inspired assumptions about sanitariums, thus far, had proven false.

Relieved, I slouched in my chair and breathed normally. *Why do you let your imagination get the better of you?*

Without warning, a primal cry blared like a siren. Beyond my view, a distraught patient bleated, "Help! Help! Help!" The mournful pleas amplified as the source advanced from a distant hallway. The detainee shuffled into sight. Ushered like a convict with an attendant at each side, Dad emerged.

If not for his illness, he would have been behind bars, but Alzheimer's had given him a permanent get-out-of-jail pass. Nonetheless, memory care facilities had limits. Even there, consequences existed for attempted murder.

To earn his detention, I learned, Dad had attacked a wheelchair-bound woman as if she were a mass shooter. Inside their shared dining hall, he'd wrestled the octogenarian and her baby doll to the floor. Before anyone could stop him, he'd stabbed a fork into the terrified woman's chest. Possibly, the doll had triggered him. He'd never been keen on infants.

Dad hobbled toward me.

From four yards away, a lady who'd been monitoring his yelps leapt from her seat and approached me. "I'm so sorry, hon. Is that your father?"

I nodded, blinking back my grief.

"My grandma had Alzheimer's, and she was just like him," the stranger prattled. "I'm sixty-two, and I'm scared I might already be losing *my* mind." She leaned in close, one hand on a table corner.

I offered a grim smile, masking equal concerns.

From seemingly nowhere, a man in scrubs darted between us. With authority, he ushered the patient back to her chair. The woman's act had fooled me. I needed to remain vigilant. The confined weren't entirely checked out. Some of them could be slick.

Dad took a seat next to me without making eye contact. Scowling, he squeezed his attendant's wrist until her hand dappled crimson.

"Turn me loose," she pleaded.

He strengthened his grip, seemingly determined to drag his chaperone with him to wherever he had mentally traveled. The nurse winced.

Fearing Dad's strong hold might elicit orderlies to respond with a straitjacket, I caressed his clenched fist. "Please let go of the nurse's hand." My voice signaled a composure I didn't possess. Any second, I suspected he might release his hostage in a rage-filled exchange for my throat.

Dad freed his victim and slumped in his chair. I studied the green- and plum-colored bruises on his meaty knuckles. He must have swung at something or someone and made contact. He looked too fragile to be my dad, his face a road map of defeat.

Visions of my father assaulting a disabled matron interrupted my sympathetic thoughts. *This is my* father. *He wasn't supposed to turn homicidal at age eighty-four! He was supposed to denounce violence, atone for his sins, and die peacefully in his own bed.*

How can I reconcile my past with him when all his yesterdays have disappeared? I couldn't even be angry at him anymore.

Resentments I'd once harbored had been tempered by my father's stark fate.

Before dementia had robbed him of reason—stolen what negligible discernment he'd ever possessed—he'd made his wishes known to me. "I never want my body to outlive my brain," he'd said. And yet, there he was. His greatest fear had manifested. Like a conjoined twin, I shared his grief and anguish.

It was hard to believe I'd once itched to beat my father at anything. I recalled the many staring contests he'd instigated when I was a child. It felt like only yesterday that, at age twelve, I had slid into Mom's vacant dining chair and taken him on.

Dad sat opposite me—a five-foot gap between us. He rested an elbow on the maple surface. "You ready?"

I nodded.

"Okay. Go."

In a battle for supremacy, we locked eyes. Whoever blinked first lost. The winner would reign as champion until the next game, for which Dad decided the timing.

I zapped him with a billion volts of electricity, fired at full ocular strength.

He returned my lightning strike with greater intensity.

Zdt, zdt, zdt, zdt, zdt! I blasted him with laser beams.

Blinding rays ricocheted back at me.

My searing gaze torched him. *You'll never own me! Ha, ha, ha, ha, ha!*

I already do, his dagger eyes countered.

I had always been the first to blink.

"Are you in any pain?" I asked him, ignoring the perturbed nurse.

"No."

"Has anyone hurt you?"

He retained his poker face and waited a beat. "No."

Does he remember? "Have *you* hurt anybody?"

As if he might find the answer on the ceiling, he stared at the rafters. "No… and yes."

Perhaps I should have provided a time context. He'd harmed more individuals than I could name. "Can I get you anything?"

"Yes." His eyes met mine.

I brightened. "What would you like?"

"A bullet."

On my second visit to see Dad in the psych ward, he appeared less agitated. The drugs had kicked in, I guessed. I sat with him and his attendant at a table.

With a grin, his chaperone asked, "Did your father work in construction?" She spoke as if he weren't there or might be deaf.

I checked Dad for a response. He stared at a vacant wall, maybe listening, maybe not. I couldn't be sure.

"No, not really," I said. "He built a few houses, but it wasn't his profession." It would have taken more time to explain that statement than I cared to expend. "Why do you ask?"

The nurse flitted one hand in the air. "He's been fixated on the baseboards in his room." She suppressed a giggle. "Actually, he removed them all."

I studied Dad's face.

He stared stoically at the space between me and his attendant. "What do you mean?"

"He peeled all the baseboards off in his room using his fingernails," the tattletale expounded. "They're made of laminate." She laughed openly. "We thought maybe he'd worked in some type of construction. Dementia patients often revert back to their career behaviors."

I shook my head in disbelief. *How long did he sit on the floor, prying his unclipped fingernails behind glued floor trim, before someone noticed him?* I didn't have time to ask before the next disclosure arrived.

"He also broke his glasses when he threw them across the room," the informant added. "I gave them to his wife. She said she'd get them repaired."

I frowned and said nothing, grasping the connection between geriatric rage and eyewear. Corrective lenses don't restore dementia sufferers' sight. Their pupils don't dilate normally, and over time, they lose depth perception and peripheral vision. Trapped in a world they can't recall or make sense of, surrounded by people they can't identify, discounted by those who speak about them as if they aren't there, they likely consider eyeglasses a reminder of what can't be remedied. I would have thrown mine too.

Why wouldn't Dad be infuriated? His illness had stolen his home, his dignity, his vision, and his voice. At least this time he'd confined his attacks to eyewear and floor trim. I considered that progress.

"Y'all can go outside in the atrium if you like," the nurse offered. She gestured to a glass-enclosed area fifty feet from us. I surveyed the adjacent courtyard. *Is that every architect's solution to senior anxiety?* No flowers. No chairs. Only a metal bench surrounded by nondescript shrubbery. Sunlight dappled the bare concrete patio.

"Would you like to go out there?" I asked Dad, indicating the atrium.

He nodded.

Maybe he wasn't as mentally absent as I'd feared. *Is that positive or negative?* Knowing he was confined in a mental hospital would hasten his decline, I presumed. *Is a shortened life span any less desirable than years of prolonged grief?* In that moment, luck and tragedy appeared indistinguishable.

Dad and I ambled toward the glass-door exit surrounded on either side by spotless, floor-to-ceiling windows. I let go of his hand to open the door for him. Instead of tracking with me, he listed sideways and smacked, full-body, into a stationary glass panel.

THIRTY-SEVEN

I DID MY BEST NOT TO worry about Dad while Jim and I visited Paris. My cell phone worked in France, yet it never rang. Touring the Louvre Museum, Eiffel Tower, and Notre Dame Cathedral, I couldn't stop rubbernecking at my surroundings. While my father endured seclusion from the outside world, I gawked at sights I'd read and dreamt about since childhood.

From Paris, Jim and I flew to Rome where we kissed and took selfie pictures next to the Trevi Fountain. Arm in arm, we strolled through the Pantheon and Colosseum. Easily, I could have spent a month in Italy, dining on fresh ricotta and pasta drizzled with savory olive oils. But after two days of balmy weather and intense sightseeing, we boarded our cruise for Barcelona.

I so much reveled in my vacation that I seldom checked my email or texts. The few times I did,

Jim and Diana in Paris (2017)

I found no emergency messages. Unbeknownst to me then, while I drifted between the isle of Palma de Mallorca and the coast of Spain, Dad's mind found a safe port in rough waters. Either he'd convinced psychiatrists that he was no longer a threat to society or he was too destructive to detain further. His doctors released him to a new Alzheimer's unit after his former one declined his return.

Green Meadows, Dad's new home, was a miniature version of his prior residence. To all but the most observant, the five-bedroom house resembled others on Purple Martin Street. At full capacity, the memory care unit served ten residents and employed two daytime staff and two nighttime attendants.

On my first morning back in Texas, I rang the bell for entry.

A woman named Dee invited me in. Her jovial smile, colorful scrubs, and elegant braids conveyed more cheerfulness than her job likely warranted. "You don't even have to tell me who you are. You look just like him."

Dee led me through a wide vestibule. As we passed a wall mirror, she mentioned Dad had stood there earlier and spoken to his reflection. "They all do that," she said airily. "He's in here now." I followed Dee into the living room, where Dad paced in socked feet.

Festooned by two rows of oversized vinyl recliners, the room smelled of Pine-Sol and laundry detergent. A TV tuned at high volume echoed in the background. Under normal conditions, the deafening telecast would have sent Dad in search of relief. But being trapped with a woman named Leona, who chattered to a toy giraffe, and two sleeping matrons sliding Dali fashion from their recliners didn't strike me as normal. Like a caged rat, my father darted between walls and chairs in search of an exit.

My hopeful mood plummeted. I hated his dehumanizing disease and the limited means to manage it.

Along one wall, smudged windows accented a decommissioned fireplace. Overhead, ceiling fixtures counterbalanced the absence of natural light. Like droopy eyelids, half-closed mini-blinds obscured backyard views. Outdoors was The Forbidden Zone. Locked at all times, exterior doors were accessible by coded entry. No one offered to share with me the secret four-number sequence.

Dad was no less confined here than he'd been at The Abbey. But now he had all the accoutrements of home, except his wife—and maybe forks. Meals here, I would soon learn, were served with a singular spoon.

I introduced myself to Amelia, the house manager, before addressing my father. Squatting low to sit on the fireplace hearth, I cued Dad to have a seat in the adjacent recliner. Dodging the vacant chair as if it might swallow him, he plonked his body on the fireplace hearth next to mine. In a sotto voce, he mumbled incoherent sentences.

Dee asked me about Dad's missing belt. "I had to tie shoelaces together to hold up his pants!" she exclaimed, failing to hide her frustration. "His wife didn't bring him a belt or any shoes. He needs *shoes*. He's going to fall in them socks."

Evelyn's alleged oversight caught me off guard. "I'll see if I can locate them. By the way, where are his glasses?"

Amelia, who'd said little up to that point, sprung her eyes wide. "*Glasses?* Nobody told *us* he wore glasses!"

"He's legally blind in his left eye and can't see much without them. Maybe they're still being repaired," I offered. "He broke them a few weeks ago."

Amelia gave Dee a confirming look. "*That's* why he swung at me when I came up on his left side."

I gasped. "He swung at you? Did he hurt you?"

Amelia laughed. "Oh, honey, no. I'm too quick for that."

Amelia didn't look the least bit athletic. She did, however, possess ninja skills. Still, I thought it best not to mention the recent stabbing incident.

"By the way, how's your mother?" Amelia asked me.

"My mother? Oh, she's been dead for several years."

Amelia apologized. She'd mistaken Evelyn for my mom. To Dee, she offered a reproving nod. Possibly, they'd had a running bet. Evelyn's age exceeded mine by eleven years. She wasn't old enough to be my mother.

"I thought maybe you'd know if she was all right," Amelia explained. "She hasn't been here in almost a week. She called and said she'd been real sick."

Is there no end to these insinuations? I supposed this was my punishment for taking a two-week vacation, for not being there on move-in day, for having the audacity to enjoy the first days of my husband's retirement, a retirement that had taken him forty years to earn. My shame turned to resentment and cycled back to guilt.

Dad's world had unraveled while I'd been gone, as it always seemed to. And Evelyn's illnesses had suspicious timing. "I talked to her on my way home from the airport. She never mentioned being sick." I tried recalling our exact conversation.

Amelia cut her eyes at Dee. While I conversed with Dad, she studied me with intermittent glances.

I asked Dad if he was happy with his new home.

"Yeah," he said. "But you better hurry and get out of here. They'll lock you up if you don't." He pointed to the front door. "You better get going while you still can."

His cogency took me by surprise. He hadn't uttered anything

that coherent in more than a month. Maybe the drugs he'd been given in the psychiatric hospital had worn off and he could think more clearly. *Maybe he's recovering! Maybe he doesn't need to be here at all and can return home soon*, I fantasized.

Amelia folded laundry and studied a soap opera, pretending to ignore me. I imagined her inner monologue: *Yeah, she's here and acting all concerned. Let's see how long it takes her to turn up a belt and shoes. Probably won't see her face again for a month. Don't nobody care about this poor little man.*

Thirty minutes later, Dad transferred himself to the vacant recliner he'd been avoiding. Within a minute, he'd drifted off, mouth agape. I rubbed his sock-covered toes. His feet were the only part of him, other than his head, not enveloped by a comforter. Though it was ninety-eight degrees outdoors, the room felt arctic.

I kissed his bald head. "Goodbye, Dad. Behave yourself. See you soon."

Amelia escorted me out. "You going to find out about them shoes and glasses?"

"I'll try," I said apologetically.

She gave me a look.

Driving home, I fought to see the roadway.

Dad's missing shoes never arrived. Evelyn accused the behavioral hospital of losing them. From online, I ordered him a new pair with Velcro fastenings. But I wasn't sure he needed them. He wasn't going anywhere. And his steps were uncertain enough without adding two-inch rubber bumpers to both feet.

When I arrived at one p.m. to deliver his new cushioned sneakers, Dad was snoozing in his chair, lids fluttering, mouth open.

"You should have seen him this morning." Amelia rolled her eyes. "He snuck up behind me while I was feeding Olivia and attacked me!" She offered a bare arm as proof. Pink etchings marred her dark skin. "Took three people to get him off me."

I stared at the slumbering gnome. *How is he capable of such brutality? And where did the extra two people come from to rescue her?* Maybe hospice aides, I guessed. Help arrived in early mornings to assist residents with showering and dressing. Physical therapists followed the aides. Weekdays buzzed with activity until around ten a.m.

"Are you going to report him?" I assumed Amelia was obligated to document physical aggression. *How many times can he get expelled from memory care before he's institutionalized?*

"Nah, I'm used to it." Amelia chuckled good-naturedly. "He just surprised me is all. I'll be watching him more closely from now on, though. He's *strong*!"

About an hour after Amelia disclosed Dad's assault, his eyes fluttered open. His cloudy irises suggested he'd received extra medication that morning. He'd earned it too. Without warning, he threw back the blanket he'd been napping under and rose, unassisted, to greet me.

"Hi, Dad. How are you feeling today?"

He looked at me as if I were an apparition. Turning away, he lumbered into the kitchen—the scene of his latest offense. I followed him, prepared to dodge a punch if he threw one.

Amelia wasn't in the kitchen. She'd left to attend to Leona, who roomed on the home's opposite side.

Through the kitchen windowpanes, I spied Dee. She sat outdoors, taking a smoke break. It wasn't easy tending to folks who would rather strangle you than surrender their pee-soaked

CLARITY

diapers. I didn't want to disturb her. I could manage Dad for a few minutes.

He strode next to a dining chair and pulled at his pants' waistband. "No, Dad. Not here. Do you need to go to the restroom?" *Cue the scary music!* I touched his elbow. "Follow me," I instructed.

He moved away from his mistaken toilet and pattered behind me.

A chime rang, signaling Dee had returned indoors. She rounded a corner and spied us.

"Can you help him?" I pleaded.

She glided past me and positioned herself in front of Dad. He'd stopped short of the restroom door like a shying mule. Intently, he eyed the hallway sofa, his mother's old couch. Familiar items were *not* always beneficial. Facing the cushions, he fiddled with his privates.

"Come on, John," Dee coached from the restroom doorway. "You're almost there!"

"No!" he shouted at a volume I would have guessed impossible.

Dee sighed and reversed direction. "Come on, Papa," she said with a lilt. She clutched his arm. "Come on, now. Follow me."

I watched in amazement as Dad scooted his feet and held on to Dee. The two disappeared into the restroom.

"He needed his diaper changed, was all," Dee said when she returned. "He's good now."

Amelia called Dee from somewhere out of sight, and Dee yelled back, "I'm coming!"

Dad lumbered back toward the kitchen, spinning in the wrong direction at the last second.

I shadowed him like I was on security detail. "Where're you

285

going? Your chair's this way." Careful to avoid startling him, I tried to steer him by one shoulder.

"Right here," Dad said, resisting my guidance.

He had entered the laundry room and refused to exit. Nearby, a woman moaned plaintively. The sounds filtered from an adjacent hallway I noticed for the first time.

From a garage conversion suite came the pleas of a bedbound resident. Like violin music to Frankenstein's ears, the matron's cries lured Dad. As if entranced, he shuffled toward the woman's bedroom. His steps quickened as I followed him.

The suite Dad entered housed a paralyzed woman who yipped like a coyote. The lady, whose name I later learned was Nettie, lay trembling in a three-quarter bed, her hazel eyes wide with relief or maybe fear at the sight of me and Dad. She grunted at our presence.

"Come on. You can't be in here," I warned Dad. "Let's go to *your* room."

He yanked his elbow from my grasp. "No!" Spinning a half-turn, he flopped on top of Nettie.

The frightened woman yelped.

"No. Stop that!" I cried. I grabbed Dad's hands and tugged him forcefully.

He leaned his full weight onto Nettie, almost toppling me onto the heap.

"Stop! Stop! You're going to hurt her!" I screamed.

Dad narrowed his eyes at me. "I'm staying right here."

Despite her compressed diaphragm, Nettie howled louder.

Hearing all the commotion, Dee rushed into the room.

Relieved, I turned Dad's hands loose. "I can't budge him," I said, defeated.

Dee grabbed him by his elbows. "Come on, John," she said,

all the niceties missing from her voice. She meant business, and he knew it. What happened next was a blur.

A flurry of arms and legs whirled. Dad kicked and swung at Dee, knocking her backward into Nettie's bedside table. Nettie shrieked. The table flipped, and Dee fell backward onto her rump. A Tiffany-style lamp crashed to the floor and sparked.

On impulse, I unplugged the electrical hazard. All the while, my confused father persisted sandwiching Nettie to her mattress. She'd quit making any sounds at all. I feared he might have smothered her.

Dee struggled to stand but couldn't.

In the pandemonium, I didn't know what to do next. *Should I find Amelia? Check Dee for injuries? Tackle Dad? Call nine-one-one?*

While I stood paralyzed by indecision, Amelia came as close to sprinting as I imagined possible. Her feet sliding in rapid succession, she skied into the room. Using her heft, she scooped Dee from the floor and hoisted Dad off Nettie, who had by then resuscitated.

Ousted from his entrenched position, Dad flipped to compliance mode. As meek as a newborn ewe, he let Dee escort him from Nettie's room. Within a minute, she had him seated in his lounger and snug under a plush throw.

I sat on the fireplace hearth, next to Dad's chair, one hand bracing my head. My pulse throbbed in my temples. I glimpsed my father's angry but surrendered gaze. "Dad, why are you mad?"

"I can't do anything about it," he said.

"What do you mean?"

"I can't do anything about it," he repeated. "You just don't know."

I reached across the two-foot space between us and placed one hand on his. "No, I don't. Help me understand. Do you know you could have hurt that woman?"

"I… ginet… am… so…" His language center had shut down again. One minute, his words made sense, the next, he spoke gibberish. He looked at me as if only an idiot would ask that question.

"What I know is, if you don't control your anger, you're going to end up back in that psychiatric hospital. Do you want to go back there?" I extended my arms, palms up. "I thought you liked it here."

He looked tearful. "I'm sorry." A beat passed before he spoke again. "I'm sorry. I can't do anything about it."

That was the first time I'd ever heard my father apologize for anything.

THIRTY-EIGHT

A FEW MONTHS AFTER DAD MOVED to Green Meadows, he tripped smack-dab in the middle of the tiled entranceway and landed on his skull. Like a broken clock restored by a hard knock, his fall reinstated his brain's language center. From his wheelchair stationed next to the dining table, he spoke with me about his spill.

"I don't know what happened." His modulation suggested the accident had shocked him as much it alarmed his caregivers. "I tripped over my feet, making a turn."

"It was them *shoes*," Dee chimed. "He's not used to wearing them. We put them on him 'cause he'd run out of gripper socks." She shook her head. "He only has one pair."

That was how I learned that most of the socks Evelyn had supplied for Dad were the regular kind, ones she'd transferred from his home chest of drawers to Green Meadows. If there'd been a memory care supply list, I hadn't received a copy. I doubted Evelyn had either. It was mid-August. In *Texas*. Fuzzy gripper-sole socks weren't back-to-school merchandise. *What's he going to need next? A down-filled parka?* It had been difficult enough to find his all-season attire, sweatpants and shirts, in May.

"I'll see what I can find," I assured Dee.

Presumably, she'd lost Evelyn's phone number. Or maybe she told us both what Dad needed, hoping one would follow through.

Dad rubbed at the tape sutures pinned to his noggin.

"You probably shouldn't touch that," I said.

He picked at the adhesive anyway.

I thought maybe the headphones I'd brought with me would distract him. From my purse, I removed the earmuff-size headset. "Would you like to listen to some of your favorite music?"

Dad nodded. Yet when I slipped the headphones over his ears, he winced.

"Is that too loud?"

"It sure is!" He shoved the leather discs backward onto his neck.

I unhooked the sound collar. Checking the volume, I listened as Neal Diamond's "Play Me" streamed at a moderate level. Dad's hearing had grown more acute, possibly because of his illness. He couldn't read a menu, but he could detect a mosquito in the next room. He registered sounds that individuals half his age couldn't hear.

I dialed back the decibels and resituated the headphones. Patting his foot to the music, Dad stared intently at a vacant wall and listened. If his facial muscles hadn't already atrophied, he might have smiled.

After I returned home, I said to Jim, "It's amazing. Dad's speaking to me in whole sentences again. He knows who I am, and he makes sense when he talks."

Jim peered at me from behind the refrigerator door. "Must have been that fall."

I shoved past him to grab a soda. "I don't care what did it. He's back, and now I have the father I've always wanted."

Studying me in silent amusement, Jim filled his water mug.

"I mean, he's *kind* to me now." I sat at the kitchen table with my back to my spouse, chattering away. "Completely safe. And he knows who I am... even says '*thank you*.'" I caught hubby's look. "What? You don't believe me?"

"He was all those things *today*." Jim took a swig from his stainless steel tumbler. "You can't tell me you've always wanted a *toddler* for a father. Oh, wait." He smirked. "He's *always* been a toddler. His brain just finally caught up with his emotions."

"It's better now than it's ever been with him," I insisted. I stared at my half-empty plate, refusing to believe Dad's sudden recovery could be a fluke.

Jim hugged my shoulders. "I know he's your father. I'm sorry. I mean, I'm not sorry he's your *father*. Or maybe I am." He let out a laugh. "Look, it's just that he's controlled so much of your life already. Don't let him keep doing it. We're not going to live forever either."

"You can't be serious." I gave him a puzzled look. "We're both healthy, and he has Alzheimer's."

"All I'm saying is, don't let your guard down. This could all be a trick." Jim set his tumbler on the table.

"What? You don't believe he really has Alzheimer's?"

Jim's eyes softened. He struck a more serious tone. "I don't think he's really the guy you think he is, not even now. You're seeing what you want to see and not what's really there."

I stormed to the sink, switched on the faucet, and rinsed my dinner plate. Brusquely, I scrubbed at a stubborn grease spot. *What does it matter how I choose to see my father? Am I not entitled to interpret my relationship with him any way I see fit?* My therapist and husband kept challenging my perceptions. *Why won't anyone allow me the luxury of a happy thought?*

Jim eased behind me and kissed my neck. "Forgive me. I'm just trying to protect you from getting hurt."

⟶ ⬦ ⟵

Two days later, when I next visited Dad, I found him slumped forward in his wheelchair. His head drooped low. With three fingers, I lifted his chin. Gone again. His pupils pointed in different directions, neither one focused on me. I tried to feed him a tuna sandwich and fruit salad with a spoon, but the grapes kept rolling from his lips onto his plate.

"You should have seen him this morning. He woke up talking trash to me and Dee." Amelia surveyed me from across the dining table where she ladled pureed mystery mash into Nettie's eager mouth. "When she tried to get him up, he told Dee he'd punch her if she didn't leave him alone. And when the aide came to bathe him, he started doing this." Amelia popped a knuckled fist into one palm. "Woo! I'm telling you, he got up ready to *fight* today."

I studied Dad's posture with fascination. I would have thought it impossible that the feeble old man next to me could have been that cantankerous four hours earlier. He'd lost eighty pounds and almost all of his mobility, though his brain refused to register his frailty.

"Did he hit anybody?" I asked, concerned.

Dee piped up. "He's not fast enough to get me." As though abruptly reminded, she said, "He threw his glasses again and bent them." She looked up at me from under raised eyebrows. "I put them in his room on his bedside table."

I caught her drift. That was my cue to send his eyewear out for repair—or to dog Evelyn about it since I didn't know which optometrist held Dad's prescription.

As much as I disliked seeing Dad look catatonic, he'd earned his zombie meds that day. I couldn't be upset about his condition after all I'd heard. My assumptions about his improvement were wrong, as Jim had suggested. Dad had good and bad days. The person inside his skin perpetually mutated. Like a rat, Alzheimer's disease gnawed holes when no one was watching. The vermin didn't show up every night. I couldn't witness the destruction. I could only observe the evidence after the fact.

I rolled Dad in his wheelchair to the living room, his lifeless feet mopping the floor as I steered him backward. The chair's footrests had been removed, potentially to save caregivers' shins. For the life of me, I couldn't figure out how to reattach them. Busy assisting Leona, Amelia ignored me.

After she ended Leona's fit over her missing service giraffe, Amelia hoisted Dad from his Ford Fiesta of wheelchairs and helped him into his assigned recliner. Exhausted, she dropped her ample backside into Dad's transport. It was a shame Dad hadn't qualified for the extra-wide Cadillac version. Amelia's head lolled to one side. Her arms hung slack over the distressed tires. "Woo! My back hurts! I can't do this no more."

I hoped she wouldn't have to.

⟶ ⬦ ⟵

Dad had resided at Green Meadows for a year. In those twelve months, he'd outlived four residents. One died peacefully in his sleep. Two were hospitalized and never returned. The most recent death had occurred from nutritional wasting, a common symptom of end-stage Alzheimer's.

I had prayed my father would be one of the luckier ones granted a shortcut to the hereafter, but his journey traced the long route. Gradually, his body dissolved into a gelatinous glob. Too limp to be physically lifted, he earned permission to fly. Dad's new hydraulic lift glided him effortlessly through stagnant air by remote control.

"Look at him!" Amelia exclaimed, maneuvering Dad like a professional crane operator. "He don't even mind it."

Inside his sparsely furnished room, I stood next to my father's suspended form. Against one wall, his bed sat flush under a window that offered views of a mature crepe myrtle. His brown recliner, which he had seldom sat in, consumed the wall space next to his closet. A three-drawer particle board chest flanked the restroom doorway. No photographs decorated the walls. *Why remind a dying man of people he can't recognize or recall?* Dad had never posed for a family portrait with Mom and me and my brothers. I had no reason to believe he cared about sentimental pictures now. His room's spare backdrop offered no vestiges of the past, only grim reminders of the future.

Like a caged bird, Dad floated next to my shoulders, his bald head cradled in a gray stocking cap designed for cancer patients. The soft beanie hid the indentations in his temples, visual evidence of his shrinking gray matter. Looking at him made me want to rend my clothing and tear at my hair.

Dad's cucumber-colored T-shirt rolled up his back as his body compressed into a C shape. He couldn't have moved inside that mesh sling if he'd been healthy enough to try. Caught like a seined fish, he hovered above his mattress. Amelia lowered him onto the bed. In his vacant eyes, I saw resignation. He would expire in captivity. Victory would not be his.

It seemed like a lifetime ago that I'd tried to defeat this man at anything, hoped to outmaneuver him, defy him, and escape his suffocating control. Now, he governed nothing—not even his own body. With the push of a button, anyone could direct him anywhere, against his will. He couldn't vocalize his protests, couldn't exert superior strength. Come to think of it, I hadn't heard him utter a sound, not even a grunt, in over a month. Maybe his silence *was* his protest.

Amelia adjusted the aqua-blue inflated boots on Dad's feet to protect his pressure sores. She lifted his blanket to his chin and patted his chest. "I'll be back to check on you."

I sat on the outer edge of Dad's bed, one palm on his shrouded torso. Already, his eyes had closed, but I knew he wasn't yet asleep.

"I forgive you, Dad," I said. "I forgive you for everything. You don't have to hang around here for me. You can leave whenever you want. It's okay. I love you."

His eyelids fluttered like a newborn's.

THIRTY-NINE

"**Y**OU'RE NOT GOING TO BELIEVE this," Dee said. "I had to call you and tell you!"

I had answered my phone while driving home for a quick rest. No longer capable of eating or drinking, Dad had entered his final turn. I'd been commuting for the past five days, spending as much time as possible with him. Death could come at any moment, and I didn't want him to pass away alone. *God, please don't take my father while I'm away*, I begged. *I just need to catch a little sleep.*

I imagined Dee telling me the worst news. Maybe Dad had taken his last breath right after I'd left his bedside. Time and again, I'd heard stories of loved ones who'd waited to expire when no one was with them. I listened to Dee's voice amplified through my car speakers.

"I walked in to check on him," she said, "and he cried out, 'Momma, Momma, Momma, *Diana*!' louder than I've ever heard him yell."

Is he remembering how he treated his mother when she was dying? I recalled Dad standing next to Grandma's bed, counting the seconds between her waning breaths. Leaning above her head and staring at her mouth, he had coldly studied his watch. "That's twenty seconds," he said to no one in particular. "Two, three, four…"

I wept and clung to my grandmother's hand as I had done for the past six hours. I would not let the woman I'd thought of as my mother leave this world without my comfort.

"I'll come right back," I said to Dee, searching for somewhere to make a U-turn.

"No, no," she replied. "He's fine right now. He's gone back to sleep. You get some rest."

At eight the next morning, Jim and I set out for Green Meadows. As he drove, Jim asked, "Do you think he's holding out for your birthday?" He shook his head. "It'd be just like him to pick that day to die."

Unless Dad passed away by midnight, he would have to survive another twenty-four hours to circumvent the outcome Jim suspicioned. "He can't do that to me," I sputtered, knowing he could and very well might.

When we arrived, Dad looked no different than he had the day before.

"It could be any time," a hospice chaplain said. "I'm here for the family. I'm not leaving. Don't worry."

I set a folding chair next to Dad's bed and touched his chest lightly. "I'm here, Dad. And Jim is too. You can go anytime you're ready." I flung my body across his torso and sobbed. "I'm going to miss you so much."

Dad's gargling slowed, but his eyes didn't open.

For hours, my mind felt detached from my body. I sat with Jim and Evelyn and the chaplain and waited. Dad's death rattle stopped. His breaths grew so faint I couldn't hear them over the room's clamor. Evelyn had claimed the chair nearest Dad. She sat with her back turned to him, conversing with the chaplain. I stared past her, willing her to shut up. I couldn't take another second of her droning. *My father is dying right next to you, and you're sitting here smiling and making small talk.* I wanted to tell her to be more attentive or get the hell out of the way. Examining that thought, I knew where it had originated.

As Evelyn and the chaplain prattled on, the air in the room precipitously shifted. I glanced at Dad. He lay perfectly still. For several seconds, I watched his chest. It did not move.

"Stop it. Be quiet," I said to the two chatterboxes. I rushed to my father's bedside. With one hand, I felt for his heartbeat.

Nothing.

Dad had died when no one was paying attention to him.

I admonished myself for not being there the day before when he'd cried out for me. My name was the last word he'd uttered.

My father's final beckoning haunts me now. I cannot think of his death without wondering about his last appeal. Was he frightened and begging for his mother's and daughter's protection? Did he feel abandoned? In his altered state of mind, had he confused me for his mother—again?

I choose to believe my father was given a life review before he died. His final petitions were ones of repentance. He called out to his mother and daughter because he regretted how much he had hurt them. I have no proof of this, of course. It's my narrative to write. As a wise person once told me, "You can't control life's circumstances, but you get to determine the meanings."

———◦✄◦———

"I don't know what to do about his underwear," Evelyn confessed. She and I stood inside her house in my father's former bedroom. I had delivered a new suit, shirt, tie, and belt for her to carry to the funeral home. It hadn't occurred to me that underwear was necessary for Dad's burial.

"They said I needed to bring a pair. I'm not sure what to take to them." Evelyn's eyes flashed. She grinned conspiratorially. "You know he always wore the little bikini kind."

Well, no, not always, I wanted to say but didn't. I was too bereft for that discussion. She'd clobbered me with one of my least favorite memories of Dad. With visual precision, I recalled the image of him standing on my bathroom scales in a pair of red nylon micro-briefs.

"I guess I could take them a pair from here." Evelyn pointed to Dad's dresser drawers. Whatever she'd referenced had to be prehistoric. My father hadn't shopped for clothing in a decade, and he'd lost a hundred pounds in the past three years.

"No one will ever know," I stammered, willing her to say no more.

For the record, I never asked Evelyn if she followed through on her underwear idea. If I'd had any gumption for that type of research, I might have queried Dad's undertaker. With confidence, I can say the mortician would have remembered those briefs. It's safe to assume a skimpy pair of underwear accompanied my father to his grave. Garnet-colored ones, if I were to guess, and that's exactly what he would have wanted.

FORTY

O N OCCASION, I STILL IMAGINE myself and Mom and
Dad and my brothers in a park overflowing with pink
azalea bushes, cheerful daffodils, and spikey lavender
blossoms. Sunlight dapples the patchy ground behind us. Rust-
colored squirrels follow an obstacle course of trunks and branches.
Under the tree canopies, a picnic table adorned with a festive
tablecloth and three-tiered cake awaits our party.

My father's and brothers' shirts complement my mint-colored
blouse and Mom's seafoam-green dress. We line up. Using hand
gestures, a photographer motions the six of us to squeeze closer
together. We form a tight huddle. Behind me, Dad hooks one arm
around Mom's waist. Relaxed, she leans her body into his. The
two exchange an affectionate look. If not for their four children,
they could be mistaken for newlyweds.

On my right shoulder, Dad rests a steady but gentle hand.
Mom clasps my left arm tenderly. I am sixteen. An aura of familial
accord encircles me. My palms rest on Kerry's shoulders. He and
Alan and Joel sit in front of me. They jostle each other and giggle.

"Y'all be good and smile now," I tell them. "Then we can have some Father's Day cake."

They snap to attention, their backs straight, chins lifted. The camera clicks.

"That's a good one," the photographer enthuses.

It's a beautiful dream.

Author's Note

THE VOID MY FATHER LEFT in my life was a black hole from which, if I ventured too close, I thought I might never return. When Dad died, it seemed unimaginable that I could still be alive. I underwent a period of confusion and distress I can only compare to survivor's guilt. Subconsciously, I had expected to expire with him. That might not make sense to those who've never experienced a trauma bond. The relationship between an abusive parent and child victim can become so blurred that the child perceives no separate identity. I was unaware of that before therapy and research.

My dad's well-being had been my central focus for most of my life. Though I yearned for separation, I could not conceive of it. Then one day, like a mega lottery win, it happened. Overnight, the personal time I'd dedicated to my dad was restored to me in lump sum. I wandered about aimlessly, as lost as a buggy horse without its carriage and driver.

What was my purpose if it wasn't to make life better for my dad? My husband and adult children had adjusted their expectations to fit my former schedule. Now that I was available all the time, no one seemed to need me, and that equated to being unlovable. My self-worth was incorporated in my usefulness to others. Wrongly, I had believed the path to a place called Love charted a road named Codependency.

Nobody had forced me to devote my time and energy to my father's comforts. I had done so willingly and with love. Yet I couldn't claim wholly altruistic motives. I wouldn't have known how to prioritize my needs above my dying father's if I'd wanted to. That wasn't in my emotional makeup. And seven years of psychotherapy hadn't altered my predilections much. Every step I'd taken in recovery required a mental battle. I was hardwired for guilt, shame, and manipulation. I always would be.

Daily conscious efforts, vigilant self-awareness, and active religious faith are my tools for managing life. I've found no other paths to wholeness.

As I sit here today, in my head, I hear my therapist whisper, "You're still trying to keep the dance going. Only now, you're doing that by writing about him." I lack sufficient objectivity to refute that allegation. Trauma bonds aren't easily severed.

My relationship with my father was as damaged as its two participants. I would be lying if I said I suffered no long-term effects from my upbringing. To this day, I cannot sleep with my bedroom door open. I startle at indeterminate sounds and detest psychological games. Anyone who tries to scare me risks serious injury. I've no desire for anything that stimulates adrenaline. I dislike roller coasters, haunted houses, and sports that merit protective gear. If an apocalypse should ever occur, though, I'll be fully prepared because I'm always planning for catastrophes.

I trust almost no one.

Though I could go on, I won't. My list of quirks is extensive and boring.

I will close with this thought. Although some might consider my dad a monster, I viewed him as a broken man incapable of introspection or empathy. Alzheimer's disease accentuated his preexisting deficits. While the pain and injuries he inflicted on others should not be discounted or forgotten, by my assessment, my father was mentally disturbed for most of his life. Not in a functionally limited, has-no-idea-what-he's-doing, and needs-to-be-on-disability way. But in a personality-disordered fashion that justified ducking him at cocktail parties, weddings, funerals, and especially beaches.

The decision to reveal unflattering information about myself and my family was made with great forethought and trepidation. As the late psychologist M. Scott Peck wrote, "To come to terms with evil in one's parentage is perhaps the most difficult and painful psychological task a human being can be called on to face."

It was not my intent to retaliate for my father's misdeeds. I wished only to reveal the dangers inherent in upholding appearances. Family secrets can extend a perpetrator's reach. What doesn't get reported gets repeated.

In his book *The Next Person You Meet in Heaven*, author Mitch Albom wrote, "Secrets. We think by keeping them, we're controlling things, but all the while, they're controlling us."

I will not live another day in captivity to secrets.

In the final analysis, or as close to one as I can approximate, the ego-sustaining fuel my dad amassed from untold victims didn't liberate him from himself. His fiery temper and outsized needs exposed his arrested maturity. No one possessed the power to free him from his inner torment. One day, the volcano simmering inside him simply sputtered and flamed out.

DID YOU ENJOY THIS BOOK?

If you liked this book, please share your thoughts in an Amazon review. Independent authors like me greatly appreciate reader feedback.

Connect with me.

I would love to hear from you! Visit me on **Facebook** or my website, **DianaEstillAuthor.com**

Join my private email group.

To receive your **bonus epilogue for *Clarity*** and previews of new books, please join my private email group. Follow the link provided at DianaEstillAuthor.com.

ACKNOWLEDGEMENTS

All credit goes to God for sustaining me through difficult times. He is my daily refuge.

I owe a special thank-you to my brothers, Alan, Kerry, and Joel, for helping me remember family details. Sadly, Kerry didn't survive to see this book's completion. He lost his battle against cancer in 2020.

I remain grateful to my mom and dad for giving me life—and writing material.

"Betty," my sweet ex-stepmom and forever friend, has supported me throughout my writing journey. She will always be my kin. Betty, Paige, and Suzanne slogged through early book drafts and helped me refine these pages.

Red Adept Editing staff polished my grammar. A special nod to Angie Lovell for her recommendations.

Streetlight Graphics designed this beautiful book cover.

Chris Lorenc, my former therapist, ushered me to clearer horizons. Without his help, I couldn't have told this story.

My deepest appreciation goes to my husband, Jim, who deserves a medal for his abiding love—and for not shooting my dad. ☺

OTHER BOOKS BY DIANA ESTILL

When Horses Had Wings, a novel
Idiots and Children
This Can't be Normal
Stiletto's No More
Deedee Divine's Totally Skewed Guide to Life
Driving on the Wrong Side of the Road

Made in United States
North Haven, CT
11 May 2022

19107286R00183